D1806750

MEDALS AND
DECORATIONS OF
HITLER'S GERMANY

MEDALS AND DECORATIONS OF HITLER'S GERMANY

Robin Lumsden

Airlife
England

Copyright © 2001 Robin Lumsden

First published in the UK in 2001
by Airlife Publishing Ltd

British Library Cataloguing-in-Publication Data
A catalogue record for this book
is available from the British Library

ISBN 1 84037 178 1

Typeset by Servis Filmsetting Ltd, Manchester, England
Printed in China

Airlife Publishing Ltd
101 Longden Road, Shrewsbury, SY3 9EB, England
E-mail: airlife@airlifebooks.com
Website: www.airlifebooks.com

Contents

Preface

Adolf Hitler held power in Germany for only twelve years, but during that relatively short period his regime produced the country's first and only complete range of truly national orders and decorations. These were destined to have a significant effect on the design of military and civil awards in other parts of the world, including the United States of America and the Soviet Union, which unashamedly based some of their Second World War combat badges on those of the Third Reich.

This is the first book to cover the subject of Nazi awards comprehensively and chronologically in a single volume. The last similar work, Dr Heinrich Doehle's ground-breaking *Die Auszeichnungen des Grossdeutschen Reichs* (Berlin, 1943) excluded the 1944–5 period, when a vast number of new honours were created to bolster the flagging morale of fighting troops and the besieged civilian population.

The old adage 'A picture speaks a thousand words', however clichéd, still holds true. A good photograph renders unnecessary the excruciating detail of verbal description which can so easily soak up valuable space in a volume such as this.

Where possible, therefore, original examples of the decorations concerned are illustrated. Genuine pieces were not always available for photography, so surviving plates from Dr Doehle's official wartime archive and representative line drawings have been employed to fill the gaps in this respect. The use of pictures of known or suspected reproductions was consciously avoided, as the waters have already been muddied far too much by the frequent depiction of postwar fakes in modern reference books.

The orders and decorations covered in the following chapters include the highest honours which the militaristic and very uniform-dominated Third Reich could bestow. They were intended to promote and mirror the grandeur that was Hitler's Germany in its heyday, before the horrors of the holocaust. Consequently, it is perhaps not surprising that their superb quality, striking appearance and sheer variety have never since been surpassed in the field of medals and awards.

Robin Lumsden
Cairneyhill

Picture/Illustration Credits

Source   Picture/Illustration No.

Author: Covers; 2, 3, 4, 6, 7, 8, 9, 10, 12, 13, 16, 17, 20, 22, 23, 26, 28, 30, 31, 32, 33, 35, 37, 40, 41, 44, 45, 46, 47, 48, 49, 51, 53, 57, 59, 60, 61, 62, 65, 69, 70, 73, 74, 76, 89, 90, 91, 92, 93, 94, 98, 99, 101, 102, 103, 104, 105, 107, 110, 111, 117, 119, 126, 130, 132, 137, 142, 150, 153, 154, 156, 159, 162, 165, 169, 170, 172, 173, 174, 175, 176, 178, 180, 181, 182, 183, 184, 185, 186, 187, 188, 189, 195, 196, 197

R. Bender: 19, 43, 64, 66, 71, 81, 86, 97, 106, 109, 118, 127, 129, 131, 141, 144, 147, 168, 171, 190, 192, 193

V. Bowen: 77

R. Cowdery: 115

B. Davis: 11

H. Doehle Archive: 14, 27, 29, 52, 56, 68, 72, 75, 96, 108, 112, 120, 122, 123, 124, 128, 136, 138, 139, 143, 145, 146, 148, 155, 158, 163, 164, 166

A. Forman: 24, 54, 55, 114, 152, 157, 198, 199

J. Halcomb: 100, 194

T. Hartmann: 38, 39

F. Hermann: 18, 21

Imperial War Museum: 25

T. Johnson: 5, 34, 121, 149, 177

R. Kahl: 36, 42, 50, 63, 78, 82, 84, 85, 87, 88, 113, 116, 125, 133, 134, 135, 140, 151, 160, 161, 167

K. Klietmann: 79, 80, 83

US Military Academy: 15, 179

D. Niemann: 58, 95

J. Nimmergut: 191

Wallis & Wallis: 1, 67

Introduction: 1914–33

Before and during the First World War, imperial Germany boasted a vast array of orders, medals and decorations, the majority of which were distributed on an individual state or kingdom basis rather than a national one. No fewer than one-third of the entire world's awards at this time were German. From Anhalt and Baden to Waldeck and Württemberg, kings, dukes, princes and even city councils bestowed honours on their soldiers and civilians. Most were divided into several classes, with oakleaves, swords or crowns, and could be worn on combatant or non-combatant ribbons. A few, notably the Bavarian Military Max-Joseph Order, which carried a 25 Reichsmarks per month pension for life and was conferred only 192 times between 1914 and 1918, were very highly prized. Many others, however, like the Hanseatic Crosses of Bremen, Hamburg and Lübeck, with over 100,000 awards, were of little real value.

As German Emperor, Wilhelm II, King of Prussia, was *Oberster Kriegsherr*, or 'Supreme Warlord', of all the armed forces of the German states, and he alone could create military awards on a national basis. Examples included the Army Pilot Badge instituted on 27 January 1913, the Observer Badge of 1914, the 1915 Naval Pilot Badge and the U-Boat War Badge and Wound Badges of 1918, which were presented to all suitably qualified personnel regardless of their primary state allegiance. Another result of Wilhelm's overall authority was that his hitherto purely Prussian decorations began to be routinely issued to soldiers of other German states. The Order *Pour le Mérite*, for instance, soon came to be regarded as the highest bravery award for all German officers, with 687 recipients during the First World War. It is interesting to note that this decoration owed its title to the fact that French was the official 'court language' of many eighteenth-century royal houses, including that of Frederick the Great. The award was known colloquially by the British as the 'Blue Max', a term never used by the Germans and one which may have resulted from contemporary Allied confusion between the blue-

1. The Prussian Order Pour le Mérite *came in various grades, including a highly prized Oakleaf Cluster presented only 122 times between 1914 and 1918 and restricted to senior officers in recognition of battles won. Criterion for award of the anniversary crown device shown on the cross at the top of this illustration, however, was nothing more than surviving fifty years beyond the date of original bestowal.*

2. *Above: Imperial German decorations.*
From left to right:
The 1914 Iron Cross 2nd Class by 'CD', with rim in '800' silver, on court mounted ribbon;
The 1914 Iron Cross 1st Class, convex type, in '800' silver;
The Hamburg Hanseatic Cross, created on 14 September 1915 by the Hamburg City Senate and awarded until 23 November 1923, by which time 20,018 had been distributed;
The Brunswick War Merit Cross 1st Class, instituted on 20 March 1918 by Duke Ernst-August von Braunschweig. Clearly modelled on the Iron Cross, it emphasised the traditionally close ties between Brunswick and Prussia.

3. *Below: The Army Wound Badge was instituted by Kaiser Wilhelm II on 3 March 1918 to be conferred in Black, Silver and Gold grades depending upon the number and severity of wounds sustained in action. Belated awards of this decoration continued to be made throughout the 1920s and early 1930s, and a range of variants was produced by different manufacturers for private purchase by recipients. Those shown are, from left to right:*
Wound Badge in Gold with silhouetted details;
Wound Badge in '800' silver;
Standard Wound Badge in Black;
Variant Wound Badge in Black, of the type worn by Adolf Hitler during 1930-4.

enamelled *Pour le Mérite* and the unrelated Max-Joseph Order.

The most important effect of these unifying developments was that the Iron Cross, Prussia's general bravery and merit award for all ranks since 1813, started appearing on uniforms throughout the entire Reich and took on a special status as the first truly national German decoration. By the end of the First World War 163,000 awards of the Iron Cross 1st Class and over 5 million of the 2nd Class had been made, with no fewer than one in every three soldiers receiving the latter grade. This liberal distribution can be accounted for by the fact that, prior to the institution of the Wound Badge on 3 March 1918, the Iron Cross 2nd Class came to be conferred almost automatically on all troops seriously maimed in battle, in recognition of their suffering and self-sacrifice.

The list below shows the range of medals and decorations which could be won by German soldiers in the First World War. Many orders were subdivided into several different classes. Where those listed were conferred nationally, their direct equivalents in later Nazi awards are also shown for purposes of comparison.

Duchy of Anhalt
Order of Albert the Bear
Friedrich Cross
Marien Cross

Grand Duchy of Baden
Order of the Zähringen Lion
Order of Berthold I
Karl-Friedrich Military Merit Order
War Merit Cross
War Auxiliary Volunteer Cross
Medal of Merit

Kingdom of Bavaria
Military Max-Joseph Order (equated to the Nazi
    Knight's Cross of the Iron Cross with Oakleaves and
    Swords)
Order of Military Merit
King Ludwig Cross
Military Bravery Medal
Military Merit Cross
Military Merit Medal

Military Medical Order
Cross of Merit for Voluntary Medical Personnel
Pilot Badge
Observer Badge
Air Gunner Badge
Aircrew Commemorative Badge

Duchy of Brunswick
Order of Heinrich the Lion
Military Merit Cross
War Merit Cross
War Merit Cross for Women

German Reich
Army and Navy Pilot Badges (equated to Nazi
    Luftwaffe Pilot Badge)
Army and Navy Observer Badges (equated to Nazi
    Luftwaffe Observer Badge)
Army and Navy Aircrew Commemorative Badges
    (equated to Nazi *Luftwaffe* Retired Aircrew
    Badge)
Air Gunner Badge (equated to Nazi *Luftwaffe* Air
    Gunner Badge)
Honour Goblet for Victors in the Air War (equated to
    Nazi *Luftwaffe* Honour Goblet)
U-Boat War Badge (equated to Nazi U-Boat War Badge)
Army and Navy Wound Badges (equated to Nazi
    Wound Badge)
National Motor and Air Travel Decoration

Free Hanseatic Cities
Bremen Hanseatic Cross
Hamburg Hanseatic Cross
Lübeck Hanseatic Cross

Grand Duchy of Hesse
Order of Merit of Philipp the Brave
War Decoration
General Service Decoration
Military Medical Cross
War Welfare Decoration

Principality of Lippe-Detmold
House Order of Lippe-Detmold
War Decoration for Heroic Actions
War Merit Cross
War Merit Medal
Military Merit Medal

Grand Duchy of Mecklenburg-Schwerin
House Order of the Crown
Cross of Military Merit
Friedrich Franz Cross

Grand Duchy of Mecklenburg-Strelitz
War Merit Cross
Adolf Friedrich Cross

Grand Duchy of Oldenburg
House and Merit Order of Duke Peter Friedrich
    Ludwig
Friedrich August Cross
War Merit Medal
Red Cross Medal

Kingdom of Prussia
Order of the Black Eagle
Order of the Red Eagle
Order *Pour le Mérite* (equated to the Nazi Knight's
    Cross of the Iron Cross with Oakleaves)
House Order of Hohenzollern (for officers only: its
    various grades equated to the Nazi Knight's Cross of
    the Iron Cross and German Cross)
Order of the Prussian Crown
Order of the Crown
Order of Louise
Military Merit Cross in Gold (for NCOs only: equated
    to the Nazi Knight's Cross of the Iron Cross and
    German Cross)
Iron Cross (equated to the Nazi Iron Cross 2nd, 1st
    and Grand Cross classes)
Military Decoration
War Merit Medal
Cross of Merit for War Assistance (equated to the Nazi
    War Merit Cross)
Red Cross Medal (equated to the Nazi Social Welfare
    Medal)

Principality of Reuss
War Bravery Medal
Cross of Honour
War Merit Cross

Duchy of Saxe-Altenburg
Bravery Medal
Medal of Merit
Duke Ernst Medal

Duchy of Saxe-Coburg-Gotha
Carl Eduard War Cross
Duke Carl Eduard Silver Medal
Medal of Merit
Honour Cross for Home Service
War Commemorative Cross 1914–18

Duchy of Saxe-Meiningen
War Merit Cross
War Merit Medal
Medal of Merit

Grand Duchy of Saxe-Weimar-Eisenach
House Order of the White Falcon
Wilhelm-Ernst War Cross
Cross of Merit
General Decoration
War Merit Decoration for Women
Cross of Merit for Home Service 1914–18

Kingdom of Saxony
Order of Albert the Valiant
Military Order of St Henry
Order of Merit
Cross of Merit
Albert Cross
War Merit Cross
Friedrich-August Medal
Carol Medal
Cross of Honour
Cross of Honour for War Medical Auxiliaries

Principality of Schaumburg-Lippe
House Order of Schaumburg-Lippe
Military Merit Medal
Faithful Service Cross

Principality of Schwarzburg-Rudolstadt
Schwarzburg Decoration
Anna Louise Decoration for Merit
Silver Medal for War Merit
Medal of Merit
Commendation Medal

Principality of Waldeck-Pyrmont
Cross of Merit
Friedrich and Matilda Medal

Kingdom of Württemberg

Order of the Württemberg Crown
Friedrich Order
Order of Military Merit
Military Merit Cross
Medal of Merit
Wilhelm Cross
Charlotte Cross

When the imperial government collapsed in November 1918, revolution broke out across Germany. Demobilised right-wing troops hastily formed themselves into *Freikorps*, or Volunteer Corps, to defend Germany's eastern borders, smash riots, keep order in the streets and prevent the country from becoming a Bolshevik regime. These units were unofficial and were obliged to create their own service awards such as the Silesian Eagle, the Baltic Cross and the Iron Division Medal. Moreover, the President of the new Weimar Republic soon abolished all of the established imperial military orders and decorations and decided not to authorise a general service medal for active participation in the First World War, although a handful

4. Freikorps *awards.*
From left to right:
The Iron Division Medal, featuring the death's head emblem common to several Freikorps *formations, awarded as a commemorative piece to 15,000 men under the command of General Rüdiger von der Goltz and Major Joseph Bischoff who carried out raids in the Courland region of Latvia during the first half of 1919;*
The Kurland Medal or Medaille des Soldaten-Siedlungs-Verband Kurland, *for members of other German* Freikorps *units serving in Courland;*

The Silesian Eagle 1st Class, designed by Prof. Dr Theodor von Gosen and instituted on 16 June 1919 by Generalleutnant *von Friedeburg, commander of the* VI Armee-Korps *in Breslau. It was presented for six months' service defending German interests in Silesia during three Polish uprisings there. Oakleaves and Swords for enhanced service were added in June 1921; The Silesian Eagle 2nd Class, for three months' service; The Baltic Cross, created by the Baltic National Committee on 1 July 1919 and given for three months' service in that region. The cross took the form of the badge of the Order of Teutonic Knights, and 21,839 were awarded.*

of former airship and tank crews received commemorative badges in 1920 and 1921 respectively, at the behest of Defence Minister Dr Gessler. Understandably, the ordinary veteran of the trenches felt unrecognised and betrayed. During the 1920s, dozens of local and national ex-servicemen's organisations sprang up, and some of them duly contracted private firms to produce unofficial and often grandiose war-service decorations for their growing membership. A prime example was the German 1914–18 War Veterans' Association, based in Leipzig, which oversaw the creation of the Federal Decoration, the German Field Decoration, the Somme Cross and so on. The group known as the German Legion of Honour produced the German World War Commemorative Medal, while the Kyffhäuser Association distributed the Kyffhäuser War Commemorative Medal. As time went on, such bodies became overtly political in their support of right-wing parties like the National Socialists (*NSDAP*) and opposition to the republic. The *Wehrwolf* League, for instance, operated under

5. SA-Oberführer *Wilhelm Kleinmann, whose sleeve stripes denote* SA *membership dating back to 1931, wears the Baltic Cross and the Silesian Eagle below his 1914 Iron Cross 1st Class. The other badge commemorated the* NSDAP *rally held at Nuremberg in September 1933, and was not classed as an award. Note also the narrow ribbons of the EK2 and Cross of Honour 1914–18 worn from the buttonhole of the left breast pocket, an unofficial but fairly common practice during the 1930s.*

6. *The Tank Badge, instituted on 13 July 1921 for wear by former imperial* Panzer *crews. This award had to be applied for, and only 100 or so applications were received and approved. Those concerned were presented with authorisation certificates but were obliged to buy the badge themselves. No official regulations governing manufacture were ever published, and so several makers' variants in silver and plated brass emerged during the 1920s and early 1930s. Early examples featured a Prussian-pattern death's head and small leaves to the wreath, while the definitive version illustrated had a more substantial representation of the Brunswick-style skull and larger leaves. SS-Oberst-Gruppenführer* Sepp Dietrich *is known to have worn the Prussian variant until mid-1934, and the Brunswick type thereafter.*

the *Freikorps* banner of the death's head and stirred up resistance to the French occupation of the Ruhr. Founded in November 1923 in the wake of the Munich Putsch, *Wehrwolf* eventually spread throughout Germany with a membership of over 200,000.

Most former soldiers were members of several veterans' organisations simultaneously and so were eligible for a number of their awards, and it was not uncommon to see ex-servicemen during the 1920s and early 1930s sporting chests full of impressive-looking medals and badges earned simply by virtue of having served at the front during the First World War, or in a *Freikorps* unit during the 1919–21 period. A considerable number of small badge-manufacturing companies kept themselves busy producing examples not only of these awards but also of replacement imperial decorations in varying qualities for private sale, with no official sanction whatsoever.

The list below indicates the variety of un-official awards, some with very grand titles, which were created by ex-servicemen's organisa-tions and *Freikorps* commanders after the First World War.

1914–18 War Veterans' Decorations

Anhalt Field Decoration

Argonne Cross

Artillery Cross 1st and 2nd Classes

Baden Field Decoration

Bavarian War Commemorative Cross

Brunswick Field Decoration

Champagne Cross

Colonial War Veterans' Medal

Danzig Shield

Eastern Front Cross

Federal Decoration 1st and 2nd Classes

Flanders Naval Corps Commemorative Cross

Frankfurt Medal

George Cross

George Medal

German Field Decoration

German Front Soldier's Badge

German World War Commemorative Medal

Golden War Cross of Honour with Swords

Hanover War Commemorative Medal

Keller Cross

Kyffhäuser War Commemorative Medal (with ninety-seven possible bars)

Knight's Cross of the German Legion of Honour

7.   *Unofficial 1914-18 war veterans' decorations. From left to right:*
The oval Kyffhäuser Association War Commemorative Medal with Swords, mounted alongside an Iron Cross 2nd Class;

The Commemorative Medal of the German Legion of Honour, with ribbon emblem denoting front-line service;
The star-shaped Field Decoration, or Feld-Ehrenzeichen, *of the German 1914-18 War Veterans' Association.*

Langemarck Cross
Mackensen Cavalry Cross 1st and 2nd Classes
Maltese Cross
Munich Front Cross
Prisoner-of-War Commemorative Cross
Prussian Knight's Cross of Honour 1st Class
Prussian War Cross of Honour
Saxon Knight's Cross of Honour 1st and 2nd Classes
Saxon World War Medal of Honour
Somme Cross
Verdun Cross
War Cross of Honour with and without Swords
War Volunteers' Commemorative Cross
World War Commemorative Cross of the League of
    German Railwaymen
Württemberg War Commemorative Badge
Miscellaneous Regimental Medals and Campaign Bars

Freikorps Awards

Altenburg Loyalty Badge
Annaberg Cross
Awaloff Death's Head Cross
Baltic Cross
Bergerhoff Commemorative Badge
Beuthen Cross of Honour
Black Guard Cross of Loyalty
Bremen Commemorative Medal
Bug Star
Danzig Decoration
Diebitsch Cross
Ehrhardt Brigade Decoration
German Knight's Cross
German Legion Commemorative Badge
German Self-Defence Division Medal
Grodno Decoration
Guard Cavalry Decoration
Hindenburg Merit Badge
Iron Division Medal
Iron Flotilla Medal
Iron Roland
Kreuzburg Cross
Kühme Badge
Kurland Medal
Lautenbacher Merit Badge
Löwenfeld Cross
Lublinitz Cross
Lützow Cross

May Decoration
Munich Medal
Northern Military Hospital Battalion Decoration
Oberland Commemorative Decoration
Pitschener Cross
Rossbach Cross
Silesian Cross
Silesian Eagle
Silesian Medal
Silesian Shield
Sudetenland Volunteer Regiment Decoration
Teutonic Shield
von Aulock Commemorative Badge
von Epp Staff Company Commemorative Medal
von Heydebreck Merit Badge
von Oven Decoration
von Pfeffer Merit Decoration
Weickhmann Order
Wolf Battalion Merit Badge

While they were no doubt worn with pride, all of the above medals and awards were, in fact, worthless trinkets.

When Adolf Hitler became Reich Chancellor on 30 January 1933, he therefore took over the running of a country with no comprehensive centralised series of decorations to reward its citizens. This gave him *carte blanche* to create entirely new honours in a manner befitting his anticipated 'Thousand Year Reich'. As a former front-line soldier, one of his first moves in this direction was to arrange for the institution by President von Hindenburg of the Cross of Honour 1914–18, a national award to recognise service in the First World War. Patterned after the War Commemorative Medal of 1870–1, and utilising the same ribbon, the Cross of Honour was presented in bronze with swords for combatants, bronze without swords for non-combatants and black for widows and parents of those killed in action. The award had to be applied for, and by mid-1937 the following numbers had been issued:

Combatants	6,202,883
Non-combatants	1,120,449
Widows	345,132
Parents	373,950

8. The Cross of Honour, 1914-18.
From left to right:
Cross for Combatants, by 'GG';
Cross for Non-Combatants, by '4 RV';
Cross for Widows and Parents of the Fallen, by 'HKM'.
Holders of these decorations had the option of
purchasing display cases for them embossed with a
facsimile of von Hindenburg's signature and the
motto Treue um Treue *('Loyalty to the loyal'). Such*
cases could be bought direct from the makers or from
Nazi party uniform outlets, and were available in
leather-covered wood at a unit cost of 1 Reichsmark or
in paper-covered cardboard at 0.75 Reichsmarks each.

The Cross of Honour 1914–18 replaced the plethora of unofficial veterans' medals which could no longer be worn. All *Freikorps* awards except the Silesian Eagle and the Baltic Cross were also quickly banned by Hitler, and a new decoration, the short-lived Schlageter Memorial Badge, was introduced to replace them. It was superseded in 1936 by a *Freikorps* Commemorative Certificate issued by the *Kyffhäuserbund*.

During the years 1933–45 more than 450 military, political and civil decorations were created, in various grades and classes, as a means of showing that the Nazi regime recognised achievement in all fields of endeavour. Many of these awards were firmly based on their imperial and Weimar predecessors, and included everything from orders for arts, science and diplomacy to badges for sporting prowess and long service on the railways. For the first time in German history a series of truly national decorations emerged, open to all ranks in the military and to all levels of society. Inevitably, the majority of these awards featured the swastika, undisputed emblem of the new Reich.

1. Military Decorations

Adolf Hitler understood very well the philosophy of decorations, as embodied in Napoleon's famous statement: 'Give me enough ribbons to place on the tunics of my soldiers and I can conquer the world!' The permanent display of war badges, campaign shields, cuff titles and other awards, a practice which reached its height during the 1942–5 period, gave the veteran *Wehrmacht* soldier his own distinctive appearance, calculated to play an important part in the morale-boosting psychology of Nazi Germany. Photographs of highly decorated officers and men were regularly spread across the front pages of

newspapers throughout occupied Europe, and their stories were recalled in radio broadcasts and on the cinema screen. There is little doubt that the incentive of the Iron Cross alone was instrumental in spurring many troops on to perform almost superhuman deeds during the last few hopeless months of the war.

Senior Military Awards

THE IRON CROSS

On 1 September 1939, the anniversary of the Battle of Sedan during the Franco-Prussian War of 1870–1, Hitler invaded Poland and, anticipating a major conflict as a result, reinstituted the Iron Cross. More commonly termed the '*EK*' ('*Eisernes Kreuz*'), it now officially became a German rather than a purely Prussian decoration and, initially at least, was referred to as an order. During the next six years, the Iron Cross was awarded to Germans and their allies not only for personal bravery but also for outstanding military achievements and effective war planning. Senior officers occasionally received higher grades of the cross in recognition of the success of the units under their command. The *EK* was open to all ranks of all branches of the *Wehrmacht*, and members of non-combatant uniformed civil organisations like the Police, Fire Brigade and Railway Service were also eligible. Even Jews or part-Jews in military service could receive the award prior to 8 October 1944. All this must be borne in mind when considering the large numbers of Iron Crosses distributed. Contrary to wartime Allied propaganda, the *EK* was not 'dished out with the rations'. It was much prized, and rightly so.

The *EK* of 1939 initially comprised four grades or classes, but these had increased to eight by 1945. It

9. *A selection of Third Reich military decorations showing the deliberately overt manner in which they would have been worn. Such displays were beloved of the Nazi propaganda machine.*

10. The Iron Cross.
From left to right, top to bottom:
Standard 44 mm Iron Cross 2nd Class, by Eugen Gauss;
Ritterkreuzgrösse, or Knight's Cross size, 47 mm Iron Cross 2nd Class, a rare variant produced for a short period during 1939–40, here suspended diagonally from a 25 mm ribbon as worn from the second buttonhole;
Standard Iron Cross 1st Class, by Steinhauer & Lück;
Reverse of convex Iron Cross 1st Class by Schauerte & Höhfeld, showing screw-back device;
Reverse of convex pin-back Iron Cross 1st Class, by Boerger & Co.

11. Below: From 1 June 1940, members of the uniformed services who were seriously wounded as a result of enemy action automatically received the Iron Cross 2nd Class. These railwaymen, who lost their legs in Allied bombing raids on Germany, were so decorated in 1943.

was necessary that a recipient hold the lesser grades before a higher class could be awarded. All grades awarded were worn simultaneously.

During the Second World War, Iron Crosses were made by well over thirty different manufacturers, but all of these firms used master dies produced by just one company, Steinhauer & Lück of Lüdenscheid, whose senior engraver, Emil Escher, designed the 1939 Iron Cross. This ensured that all genuine pieces, irrespective of maker, conformed to a single ideal with identical detailing. By 1 April 1942, *Wehrmacht* demands for Iron Crosses had exceeded stocks available and this resulted in a new fully automated manufacturing process, devised to speed up production. Even so, a high-quality finish was maintained.

The lowest grade was the Iron Cross 2nd Class, or *EK2*. It measured about 44 mm in diameter and was suspended from a ribbon bearing the colours of the Third Reich – black, white and red. The cross was made in three parts: a core, an obverse rim and a reverse rim. In construction, both rims were soldered together, sandwiching the core between them. The core obverse displayed a mobile swastika (i.e. rotated to stand on one leg, giving the impression of an advancing movement) on its centre and the date '1939' on its lower arm. The reverse was plain save for the original institution date '1813' on the lower arm. The core was normally solid cast iron, long symbolic of the hardness of the *Eiserne Zeit*, or 'iron time' of war, stove-enamelled to give a matt black finish. A small number of crosses were produced with blackened brass or bronze cores and these were favoured by naval personnel, whose iron-cored crosses tended to rust after months at sea. The rim of the *EK2* was polished and lacquered nickel silver, with a frosted beading. Most suspension rings were stamped with a manufacturer's code number. Like all Nazi awards, the *EK2* was issued unnamed.

The Iron Cross 2nd Class was bestowed in recognition of courage or exemplary conduct. When presented, it was hung from the second buttonhole of the tunic, a traditional German fashion reserved for war decorations. Thereafter, the recipient usually wore the ribbon alone, either from the buttonhole or on a ribbon bar above the left breast pocket. The cross itself was worn only during parades or at other ceremonial occasions. Authority to award the *EK2* was delegated down to divisional commander level. An estimated 5 million awards were made during the Second World War, and many officers considered it a personal disgrace to return home from active service without one. *Luftwaffe Oberst* Hajo Herrmann, who went on to win far more prestigious decorations, related in his autobiography that the day he received the simple Iron Cross 2nd Class always remained the proudest day of his life. The youngest recipient was 12-year-old Hitler Youth Alfred Zeck of Goldenau, who rescued twelve wounded German soldiers pinned down by enemy fire in his home town in March 1945. Twenty-seven females, mainly front-line nurses, received the cross, and boxes full of *EK2*s were retained at all field hospitals for distribution to the most severely wounded.

The Iron Cross 1st Class, or *EK1*, was the next highest grade. It had the same dimensions and obverse design as the *EK2* but had a plain reverse, as it was worn on the left breast pocket at all times, in the form of a badge. The *EK1* was normally attached to the pocket by means of a wide, tapering pin bar on the reverse, although the recipient could, if he desired, purchase an official copy with a screw-back device. Screw-back crosses were less likely to become detached in action and were sometimes bent to a slightly convex shape to improve fit. A small hook on the reverse upper arm prevented the screw-back cross from swivelling around on the tunic pocket. Many officers bought half a dozen duplicate crosses and affixed them permanently to all their combat and dress tunics. The primary reason for this was to avoid the damage which would have been caused to the tunics by the constant attaching and removal of a single pin-back or screw-back award. Construction of the *EK1* was much like that of the *EK2*, except that some *EK1*s featured hollow alloy cores, making them lighter to wear on shirts and denim tunics. The use of convex crosses was officially forbidden in February 1940, and again in March 1941, but they continued to be worn until the end of the war. The maker's code number tended to be stamped into the pin or on the back of the lower arm.

Authority to bestow the *EK1* was delegated down to divisional commander level, and around 730,000 awards were made between 1939 and 1945. Unlike the *EK2*, the 1st Class could not be conferred in recognition of serious wounds. Bravery or repeated meritorious combat service had to be demonstrated to qualify for the cross. A few examples follow to give an idea of the wide criteria involved. U-boat commanders were usually nominated for the *EK1* on sinking 50,000 tons of enemy shipping, while *Luftwaffe* pilots might expect to receive it on downing five enemy aircraft or completing eighty operational sorties. The Army or *Waffen-SS* soldier could be recommended for the *EK1* on performing three or four noteworthy acts over and above that which gained him the *EK2*, or for one act of exceptional courage or daring. On a very few occasions, the *EK1* and *EK2* were conferred simultaneously, as in the case of *SS-Oberführer* Dr Eduard Deisenhofer, who received both classes on 26 June 1940. Two females were awarded the *EK1*, namely Austrian Red Cross Sister Else Grossmann and the test pilot *Flugkapitän* Hanna Reitsch.

Immediately above the *EK1* was the prestigious Knight's Cross of the Iron Cross, or *Ritterkreuz des Eisernen Kreuzes*, usually known as the *RK*. It was

12. *The Knight's Cross of the Iron Cross was the most highly valued combat decoration of the Third Reich. It was the only cure for the colloquial 'neck ache' said to be suffered by ambitious* Wehrmacht *officers who were desperate to win it.*

13. Hauptmann *Zäller and* Leutnant *Schätzle, newly decorated with the Knight's Cross, surrounded by their jubilant grenadiers in Russia, 1944.*

created on 1 September 1939 as an entirely new grade of the Iron Cross and was intended to fill the gap which had been left by the abolition after 1918 of the Military Max-Joseph Order, the military division of the Order *Pour le Mérite*, the House Order of Hohenzollern and similar imperial decorations. The Knight's Cross was therefore the highest gallantry award which Germany could bestow at the outbreak of the Second World War, and, on average, only one soldier per regiment might expect to win it. All sentries with rifles were obliged to present arms to anyone holding the *Ritterkreuz*, regardless of his rank. The *RK* retained the same basic design as the *EK2* but was larger, measuring 48 mm across. It was worn around the neck on all occasions. The frame was made from real silver, normally 80 per cent pure to allow sufficient hardness to withstand daily wear and tear, and the rim and suspension loop were usually stamped with the corresponding continental hallmark '800'. Authority to confer the *Ritterkreuz* was vested in Hitler alone, although in cases of emergency, for example where the German troops concerned were besieged, he could delegate it to corps commander level. About 7,300 awards of the Knight's Cross were made between 1939 and 1945. While a high degree of bravery or achievement was always a prerequisite, criteria for award varied considerably throughout the *Wehrmacht* and were adjusted upwards as the war progressed. *Luftwaffe Leutnant* Egon Mayer, for example, won the *RK* in 1941 for his twentieth aerial victory, while *Oberleutnant* Otto Kittel had to shoot down 123 enemy planes before he received the cross in 1943. *Fregattenkapitän* Heinrich Lehmann-Willenbrock, the commander of U-96, upon whose exploits the feature film *Das Boot* was based, was decorated with the *Ritterkreuz* for sinking sixteen ships in three months. On land, Erwin Rommel earned the Knight's Cross during the Battle of France in 1940, when his 7th *Panzer* Division (the 'Ghost' Division) captured 10,000 prisoners in two days, for little loss. *Gefreiter* Werner Wrangel, a gunner with *Panzerjäger* Battalion 183, was presented with the *EK2*, *EK1* and *Ritterkreuz* simultaneously on 8 February 1943 for outstanding valour in repulsing a Russian attack virtually single-handedly, thereby saving the lives of literally hundreds of his comrades. *SS-Obersturmführer* Michael Wittmann of 1st *SS-Panzer* Regiment received the *RK* on 13 January 1944 for having destroyed a total of sixty-six Soviet tanks. On that same day, as if to celebrate, he shot up another nineteen T34s and three heavy assault guns! All *SS* holders of the Knight's Cross automatically qualified for the Death's Head Ring – the highest honour which Himmler could bestow upon members of his Black Order. Several non-Germans were decorated with the *RK*, but there were no female recipients.

It is worthy of note that the vast majority of Knight's Cross holders wore only their original award pieces and never purchased so-called 'duplicates' for front-line use. Unlike the *EK1*, the *Ritterkreuz* had to be taken off when changing uniform and so could very easily be moved from one order of dress to another. The private sale of replacements for lost or damaged Knight's Crosses was expressly forbidden as early as 22 October 1941, after which date all duplicates were available only upon application through official channels. However, several photographs testify to the fact that a significant number of soldiers newly awarded the *Ritterkreuz* wore an Iron Cross 2nd Class around the throat, or even in rare cases an *EK1* pinned

14. Senior Grades of the Iron Cross.
From top to bottom:
Knight's Cross with Oakleaves;
Knight's Cross with Oakleaves, Swords and Diamonds;
Grand Cross

through the knot of the neck tie, pending the presentation ceremony when the *RK* was formally bestowed. This practice became increasingly common towards the end of the war.

During the early campaigns of 1939–40, it became apparent that a still higher decoration was called for, and on 3 June 1940 Hitler instituted an oakleaf cluster to be attached above the Knight's Cross. The Oakleaves, or *Eichenlaub,* device was roughly circular in shape and measured 20 mm in diameter. It featured three vertical silver oakleaves, the middle one superimposed upon the other two. The reverse was smooth and slightly concave (never hollow or flat) and bore a suspension loop and hallmark. When awarded his Oakleaves, the recipient simply removed the original suspension loop from his *RK* and replaced it with the cluster. The original short-lived intention was that the Oakleaves, like those to the Order *Pour le Mérite* during the First World War, would be presented only to senior officers in recognition of tactical battles won, and the first award duly went to *Generaloberst* Eduard Dietl in July 1940, for his direction of the capture of Narvik. During the Second World War, 882 clusters were presented, eight of them to non-Germans. *Luftwaffe* Major Walter Nowotny received the decoration in 1943 for destroying 189 aircraft. Naval *Kapitänleutnant* Siegfried Wuppermann earned it by sinking four destroyers, five tankers, a submarine and a torpedo boat in a three-month period. In the Army, *Waffen-SS* and other ground forces, personal bravery of the highest order, or outstanding leadership, had to be demonstrated before any recommendation for the cluster could be considered. Hitler personally scrutinised all recommendations and, in most cases, presented the awards himself at Führer Headquarters. Moreover, recipients were given maximum publicity in the press and on the radio. In the upper social circles, a *Ritterkreuz mit Eichenlaub* would open a great many doors normally closed to men of humble backgrounds.

The introduction of a higher-ranking golden version of the Oakleaves was considered early in 1941, but was not progressed. Instead, on 21 June that year, significantly the day before he invaded Soviet Russia, Hitler created as a new incentive to his forces a successive grade of the *RK* to be known as the Oakleaves and Swords, or *Eichenlaub mit Schwertern.* This comprised a device identical to the silver oakleaf cluster but with the addition of two crossed swords below it. The suspension loop was also much longer, so that the swords hung well above the upper arm of the cross and never overlapped it. A total of 159 awards of the Swords was made during the war, the first being presented on the date of institution to *Luftwaffe Oberstleutnant* Adolf Galland for his sixty-ninth air victory in the west. There was only one foreign recipient, Japanese Grand Admiral Isoruku Yamamoto, architect of the attack on Pearl Harbor, who was posthumously awarded the *EK2, EK1, RK*, Oakleaves and Swords simultaneously in 1943. As with the Knight's Cross, the private sale by commercial firms of duplicate Oakleaves and Swords attachments was strictly prohibited in October 1941. From then on, all official-issue pieces were produced by Godet of Berlin and were supplied only through government channels.

On 15 July 1941, Hitler upgraded the *RK* still further by instituting the Oakleaves, Swords and Diamonds (*Eichenlaub mit Schwertern und Brillanten*), usually called simply the Diamonds. This award was similar to the Oakleaves and Swords device, but was encrusted with 45–50 diamonds of

15.   *The Star of the Grand Cross of the Iron Cross.*

different sizes. Only twenty-seven awards of the Knight's Cross with Oakleaves, Swords and Diamonds were made during the war, the first being on 16 July 1941 to *Luftwaffe Oberst* Werner Mölders, commander of *Jagdgeschwader 51*, for his destruction of twenty-eight Russian aircraft in the first three weeks of the eastern campaign. The ever-changing nature of the presentation criteria is indicated by the fact that *Oberst* Hermann Graf qualified for the Diamonds in September 1942 by shooting down 172 enemy planes, while 22-year-old Major Erich 'Boy' Hartmann had to destroy 301 aircraft before he won the award in August 1944. Almost half of all Diamonds bestowed went to the *Luftwaffe*.

16. SS-Oberst-Gruppenführer *Sepp Dietrich wearing the Diamonds to the Knight's Cross which he received on 6 August 1944, for his command of 1st* SS-Panzer-korps *in Normandy.*

On 29 December 1944, Hitler created what was to be the highest gallantry decoration of the Third Reich, the Golden Oakleaves, Swords and Diamonds to the Knight's Cross. This award was identical to the Diamonds, but was produced in hall-marked gold and was to be restricted to a maximum of twelve recipients. The sole winner was the extra-ordinary *Luftwaffe Oberst* Hans-Ulrich Rudel, commander of *Schlachtgeschwader 2* 'Immelmann', who flew an astounding 2,530 sorties as a Stuka pilot on the eastern front. He personally destroyed 532 Soviet tanks (the equivalent of five armoured divisions), 150 anti-aircraft batteries, the battleship *Marat*, a cruiser, a destroyer, seventy landing craft and numerous other vessels. Rudel also scored nine aerial victories, a unique achievement while flying a dive-bomber. He survived being shot down more than thirty times, including six occasions when he crash-landed behind enemy lines, and once escaped after being captured by Russian troops. He was wounded five times. In the last weeks of the war he lost a leg in action but soon returned to his squadron and destroyed twenty-six Soviet tanks while flying with one foot, using a specially adapted rudder pedal! As the only holder of his country's highest bravery award, Hans-Ulrich Rudel still features in the record books as the most highly decorated combat soldier in history.

The senior grade of the *EK* was the Grand Cross or *Grosskreuz,* which had existed since 1813. Worn around the neck, it was identical to the *RK* but was much larger, measuring 63 mm across. The *Grosskreuz* was not a bravery award, but was intended solely for general officers whose strategy had a decisive effect on the course of the war. The only holder of the Nazi Grand Cross was Hermann Göring, who received it on 19 July 1940 in recognition of his *Luftwaffe*'s contribution to the *Blitzkrieg* across Western Europe and the rapid defeat of France. Like Blücher before him, he immediately incorporated the prestigious decoration into the design of his personal standard. A single Star of the Grand Cross exists, taking the form of an *EK1* rivetted on to an eight-pointed gilded silver star measuring 87 mm across. It was apparently intended to be worn on the left breast in conjunction with the Grand Cross, as a higher class, by the field marshal whom Hitler would decide had contributed most to the ultimate victory of the Third Reich. Similar awards had been made to Blücher after Waterloo and to von Hindenburg following the Battle of Amiens-Arras in March 1918. For obvious reasons, the Nazi star was never bestowed. It now resides in the US Military Academy Museum at West Point. In a similar vein, a planned Grand Cross in Gold with a gilded silver frame was considered but rejected by the *Führer* on the grounds that it did not conform to the Iron Cross tradition.

When the Iron Cross was reinstituted in 1939, a Bar was created for those who had been awarded the cross during the First World War and who were again awarded the same grade in the Second World War. The 1939 Bar to the 1914 *EK2* measured 31 mm across and took the form of a national eagle and swastika mounted on a frame bearing the date '1939'. Silver in colour, it had four prongs on the reverse and was worn with the 1914 *EK2* or on a piece of its black and white ribbon through the second buttonhole of the tunic. The 1939 Bar to the 1914 *EK1* was similar in design but had a wingspan of 44 mm. It was worn above the 1914 *EK1* on the left breast pocket. Only weeks after the Bar's institution, several generals were presented with both classes simultaneously, and in practice many holders of the 1914 Iron Cross who were still actively serving in the armed forces after 1939 received the Bar almost automatically. A number of variant Bars were ultimately produced, including small or 'Prinzen' types for wear with the *EK2* on the court-mounted ribbon, and *EK1* Bars soldered directly onto the upper arm of the 1914 cross.

On 9 March 1943, Dr Goebbels referred in his diary to plans for a 'next-of-kin badge' for presentation to the wives or mothers of soldiers killed in action. It was to take the form of a black ribbon with a small Iron Cross attached. The project never progressed, however, although the Iron Cross regularly featured on Nazi military grave markers and as a cancellation stamp in identity documents denoting the holder's death in battle.

Along with the steel helmet and jackboot, the Iron Cross became a symbol of the military forces of the Third Reich. It appeared on propaganda postcards, rostrums, flags and badges. Recipients

17.   *1939 Bars to the 1914 Iron Cross.*
Left: 2nd Class, mounted on its buttonhole ribbon;
Right: 1st Class.

painted it on their aircraft rudders, tanks and artillery pieces. Hotels were named after it, and songs extolled its glory. This mystique continued long after 1945, as exemplified by films and novels like *Cross of Iron* and *Black Cross*. As a result, the Iron Cross has arguably become the best-known military decoration in the world.

THE HONOUR ROLL CLASP

In July 1941, the Army High Command drew up a Roll of Honour to record gallant acts by soldiers who had already won the Iron Cross 1st Class but whose most recent brave actions did not qualify them for the *Ritterkreuz*. The Navy inaugurated a similar so-called Honour Table in February 1943, and the *Luftwaffe* did likewise with its Honour List. It was not until 1944, however, that a decoration was created to recognise those concerned outwardly. The Honour Roll Clasp, or *Ehrenblatt Spange*, was allied to the Iron Cross series in that it was always worn through the second buttonhole of the tunic, attached to a piece of 1939 *EK2* ribbon. All Honour Roll Clasps took the form of a wreath of oakleaves, about 24 mm in diameter. The Army version, instituted on 30 January 1944, featured a silhouetted swastika in the centre of the wreath, while

18.   The Army Honour Roll Clasp, attached as per regulations to a length of Iron Cross ribbon.

19.   Honour Roll Clasps of the Navy (left) and Luftwaffe (right).

the Navy clasp, dating from 13 May, had an anchor and swastika. The *Luftwaffe* clasp was established on 5 July, and featured a flying eagle. All of these clasps were stamped in high relief from a zinc-based alloy, and were gold-plated with polished highlights. Holders of the Honour Roll Clasp and the 1939 Bar to the 1914 *EK2* were not permitted to wear both from the second buttonhole, so the *EK* Bar tended to be worn on a ribbon above the left breast pocket, leaving the buttonhole free for the *Ehrenblatt Spange*.

The Honour Roll Clasp was a rare award, since it was not retroactive but was given only to those entered on the Roll from the beginning of 1944. Around 4,500 went to soldiers of the Army and *Waffen-SS*. Far fewer were presented to *Luftwaffe* personnel, and the naval version was bestowed least of all, with around forty recipients. Officially, the clasp ranked below the German Cross in Gold, but in fact it was held in higher regard.

THE GERMAN CROSS

Even with the various classes of the Iron Cross, Hitler felt that there was still the need for a decoration to recognise an accumulation of repeated or continuous military achievements, particularly at the front. On 28 September 1941, during the early stages of the assault on Moscow, he filled this perceived gap by creating the impressive star-shaped War Order of the German Cross, or *Kriegsorden des Deutschen Kreuzes*, usually termed the German Cross, or *DK*. As the name suggests, it was to be presented only during wartime. Hitler's original intention had been to call the new and overtly Nazi award the 'Order of the Swastika', but he was persuaded against this by the traditionalist *Wehrmacht* High Command, and so the 'German Cross' of the title was adopted instead to refer to the massive black enamel swastika which formed the centrepiece of the star. Significantly, the swastika was placed upon a red-bordered silver disc in the manner of the

NSDAP membership badge. There is no doubt that the design of the German Cross was such as to be a statement of the glorification of Nazism and its military might, at a time when the forces of the Third Reich were victorious on all fronts.

The *DK* came in two divisions, gold and silver, and was to be worn on the right breast pocket at all times. Only those who had already been awarded the *EK1* were eligible to be considered for the *DK* in Gold. However, it was an independent decoration and not a 'stepping stone' between the *EK1* and the *RK*. Many recipients of the Knight's Cross were never awarded the German Cross in Gold, while others received the latter months or even years after they had been decorated with the *Ritterkreuz*. This was because the German Cross was intended to recognise steadfast meritorious conduct over prolonged periods of time rather than occasional or single acts of valour. The *DK* in Silver was awarded only to those already in possession of the War Merit Cross 1st Class and was given for consistent long-term furthering of the war effort in a non-combatant capacity. The colour of the central laurel wreath alone distinguished the two divisions of the decoration.

Constructed from five main separate parts, riveted and pinned together, the earliest German Crosses were very heavy affairs, weighing 65 g, and could not comfortably or even safely be worn on field tunics, especially by those operating in tanks and other confined spaces. Lighter versions distinguished by hollow rather than solid rivets and weighing around 50 g were later produced, but these were less robust and more easily damaged. On 5 June 1942, therefore, an active-service version of the *DK* in Gold was authorised. It was the same size as the heavy metal award but was hand-embroidered in cotton, silk and aluminium threads. The wreath generally remained metal but was much lighter. The active-service version, which was sewn to the tunic, had a background edging appropriate to the service of the holder, i.e. Army field-grey, *Luftwaffe* blue-grey, Navy blue, or black for *Panzer* troops. Unlike the metal version, the cloth German Cross could be purchased openly from uniform retailers upon presentation of the relevant proof of entitlement. It was very popular with those at the front, and allowed them to keep their presentation pieces safely at home. During the last year of the war the cloth badge was often conferred in lieu of its metal counterpart.

20. *The German Cross.*
Top left: German Cross in Gold, by C.F. Zimmermann; Top right: German Cross in Silver, by Deschler & Sohn; Bottom: Active service version of the German Cross in Gold, with field-grey edging.

The first thirty-eight awards of the German Cross in Gold were made to Army officers and NCOs on 18 October 1941. Among the recipients were: *Oberstleutnant* Hans Källner, who went on to win the Knight's Cross with Oakleaves and Swords; *Oberleutnant* Georg Grüner; and *Oberleutnant* Hans-Henning Freiherr von Wolff. Both Grüner and von Wolff later earned the Knight's Cross with Oakleaves. Typical holders of the German Cross in Silver were Kurt Daluege, head of the uniformed police, and Prof. Dr Karl Gebhardt, the Chief *SS* Medical Officer. A total of 24,204 German Crosses in Gold were bestowed during the war, as opposed to only 1,114 awards in Silver. The exact breakdown of awards was as follows:

German Cross in Gold

Army	14,639
Navy	1,481
Luftwaffe	7,248
SS and Police	822
Foreigners	14

German Cross in Silver

Army	874
Navy	105
Luftwaffe	65
SS and Police	70

The gold and silver crosses could be worn simultaneously, although only two recipients of both grades, namely *Admiral* Paul Meixner and *SS-Gruppenführer* Odilo Globocnik, are known. All *SS* holders of the German Cross automatically qualified for the *SS* Death's Head Ring.

Around the same time as the active-service version was authorised, a special grade known as the German Cross in Gold with Diamonds was instituted by Hitler, to rank above the *Ritterkreuz*. A prototype produced by the Munich jeweller Peter Rath

22. SS-Gruppenführer *Odilo Globocnik inspecting Russian auxiliary anti-partisan troops on the Adriactic coast in autumn 1914. Globocnik wears both the German Cross in Gold and the German Cross in Silver on the right breast.*

21. *One of only twenty examples of the German Cross in Gold with Diamonds, produced but never bestowed.*

at a cost of 2,800 Reichsmarks was delivered to the Reich Chancellery in October 1942. Qualification criteria for this decoration, which had the golden wreath studded with small diamonds, have never been ascertained but it is believed that Hitler intended it as a personal reward for his most enduring and longest-serving combat troops. Although an illustration of the special grade appeared in the 1943 edition of Doehle's book *Die Auszeichnungen des Grossdeutschen Reichs*, few German servicemen knew that it existed and it was never bestowed. The twenty specimens ultimately produced remained locked in safes at the Chancellery and Klessheim Castle. It is entirely possible that Hitler decided to delay presentation of the special grade until the war had been won, perhaps with the intention of restricting its bestowal to a select few who had demonstrated the highest levels of continuous achievement throughout the entire conflict.

Meritorious Service Decorations

THE WAR MERIT CROSS

On 18 October 1939, the anniversary of the German victory over Napoleon at Leipzig in 1813, Hitler instituted the War Merit Cross, or *Kriegsverdienstkreuz*, usually known as the *KVK*. Over the next six years it was to be used as a means of recognising virtually every sort of service imaginable and was to become the most widely distributed of all German decorations. As early as 3 May 1941, Hitler instructed his service commanders that they should bestow far fewer War Merit Crosses in future, so as to retain the initial prestige of the

23. *The War Merit Cross.*
From left to right, top to bottom:
2nd Class with Swords, by Wilhelm Annetsberger (5 million awarded)
2nd Class without Swords (2 million awarded);
War Merit Medal (3 million awarded);
1st Class with Swords, by Bauer & Sohn (450,000 awarded);
1st Class without Swords, by Steinhauer & Lück (92,000 awarded).

24. *The Knight's Cross of the War Merit Cross with Swords.*

award. However, by 1944 distribution of the *KVK* was almost out of control, and, counting all grades, over 10 million were ultimately presented! The cross was open to anyone, male or female, who contributed to the war effort of the Third Reich, from front-line troops to staff generals, from Hitler Youths to aged industrialists, and from factory workers to polished academics. Non-Germans were also eligible, and even Jews working on special concentration-camp projects were numbered among the recipients. Combat soldiers tended to hold the *KVK* in low regard, referring to its wearers as being in 'Iron Cross training', and prior to 28 September 1941 the War Merit Cross could not be worn with a corresponding grade of the *EK*, which took precedence. Like those of the Iron Cross, the regulations governing the War Merit Cross were altered to suit the volatile wartime climate and new grades were introduced periodically.

Initially, the decoration consisted of a 1st and a 2nd Class, each with or without Swords. An award with Swords was used to recognise all types of general military merit, where the recipient's duties or branch of service were such that he or she could reasonably expect to be exposed to enemy fire (including aerial bombing). Qualifying service therefore ranged from the planning of successful military operations to the efficient maintenance of front-line vehicles and equipment and the meritorious performance of civil defence and security tasks. An award without Swords signified war service of a political, diplomatic, economic, industrial or generally non-military nature, where exposure to enemy fire was not routinely anticipated. It was possible to win, for example, the 2nd Class with Swords and thereafter the 1st Class without Swords, dependent upon the service performed. Interestingly, during the spring of 1940 the *KVK* was known colloquially as the 'Polish Order' since the first examples were distributed to soldiers and Baustab Speer workers for general merit in the Polish campaign of 1939.

The 2nd Class, better known as the *KVK2*, took the form of a bronze-coloured Maltese cross with a stippled finish to the arms. On the centre obverse was a mobile swastika surrounded by an oakleaf wreath and on the reverse the date '1939'. Awards with Swords had two large swords set transversely between the arms. The *KVK2*, which measured 48 mm across, was suspended from a ribbon in the colours of the *EK2* reversed. The maker's code number was usually stamped into the suspension ring. The youngest recipient of the *KVK2* was a 10-year-old Hitler Youth from Dortmund who received it for assistance rendered in the wake of an air raid. The War Merit Cross 1st Class, or *KVK1*, was identical in design and dimensions but was silver in colour. It had a plain reverse and was worn permanently on the left breast pocket, like the *EK1*.

In August 1940, the War Merit Medal (*Kriegsverdienstmedaille*) was instituted for award primarily to civilian industrial and agricultural workers, particularly those who exceeded production targets in munitions factories. It was also given

25. Reichsministers *Albert Speer and Dr Robert Ley with eight new recipients of the Knight's Cross of the War Merit Cross, Berlin 1944.*

to flak auxiliaries, Red Cross personnel and so on for two years' general service in support of the war effort. The medal bore a representation of the *KVK* without swords on the obverse, with the legend '*Für Kriegsverdienst 1939*' on the reverse. Once around 20 per cent of the staff of a firm engaged in war work were in receipt of the *Kriegsverdienstmedaille*, the company itself was awarded the *KVK1* and was allowed to display a silver bullion version of the decoration on its DAF factory flag.

At the same time as the introduction of the War Merit Medal, Hitler created the Knight's Cross of the War Merit Cross, or *RK des KVK*, to rank higher than the *KVK1*. The design of the Knight's Cross was similar to that of the *KVK2*, but larger and in hall-marked silver. It was worn around the neck. By the end of the war, only 178 awards with Swords and 52 without Swords had been conferred, which gave the *RK des KVK* an air of exclusiveness it did not really deserve, as it ranked below the Knight's Cross of the Iron Cross. The vast majority of these awards were made during 1944. It should be noted that while 230 Knight's Crosses of the War Merit Cross were bestowed there were only 224 recipients since six of them (Walter Brugmann, Julius Dorpmüller, Karl-Otto Saur, Albin Sawatzki, Walter Schreiber and Walter Rohlandt) each received two Knight's Crosses – one with and one without Swords.

Awards of the *KVK* tended to be made four times per year, on 30 January (the anniversary of the Nazi assumption of power), 20 April (Hitler's birthday), 1 May (Labour Day) and 1 September (the date of the outbreak of the Second World War).

The distribution of the Knight's Cross of the War Merit Cross among the various services and organisations was as follows:

53 – Armaments and War Production Industries
43 – Army
21 – Railway Service
13 – Agricultural Production
11 – *Waffen-SS*
11 – Navy
 9 – *Luftwaffe*
 7 – Foreign Ministry

7 – Ministry of Transport
7 – Ministry of Occupied Eastern Territories
6 – *Wehrmacht* High Command
6 – *Organisation Todt*
6 – Police and Security Services
6 – Merchant Navy
5 – *Reichsarbeitsdienst* (*RAD*)
5 – Science and Education
5 – Postal Service
5 – *NSDAP*, *NSKK* and Hitler Youth (*HJ*)
3 – Ministry of Labour
1 – Ministry of Economics

According to Armaments Minister Albert Speer, Hitler made a final addition to the War Merit Cross series in October 1944 by founding the Golden Knight's Cross of the War Merit Cross, with and without Swords. Very significantly, this grade was never formally publicised in the *Reichsgesetzblatt* or any other official orders. Speer indicated that it was to be identical to the *RK des KVK*, but gold-plated, and was to rank immediately above the Knight's Cross of the Iron Cross. Only two were said to have been awarded 'on paper' on 20 April 1945, but these never reached their alleged recipients, Franz Hahne and Karl-Otto Saur. Indeed, it is highly unlikely that any Golden Knight's Crosses were actually placed into production.

THE SPANISH CROSS

On 14 April 1939, the Spanish Cross, or *Spanienkreuz*, was created for award to members of the German Condor Legion which had served with the nationalist forces in the Spanish Civil War between July 1936 and March 1939. The Nazi assistance given to General Franco was to some extent only semi-official, on a voluntary basis, and so the Iron Cross had not been reinstituted in 1936 to recognise German bravery or military achievement during the conflict. As a result of this distinct short-coming (over 24,000 German troops served with the Legion and many of them performed acts which would have been worthy of at least an *EK2*), it was decreed that the new Spanish Cross was to be not only a campaign award but also a gallantry decoration. Several presentation ceremonies took place and all the recipients paraded through Berlin

26. *The Spanish Cross in Bronze with Swords. First bestowed in May 1939, awards of this decoration continued to be made until the late summer of 1940.*

on 6 June 1939, to the rapturous applause of the populace.

The Spanish Cross was divided into six grades:

1. Bronze with Swords   8,462 awarded
2. Bronze without Swords   7,869 awarded
3. Silver with Swords   8,304 awarded
4. Silver without Swords   327 awarded
5. Gold with Swords   1,126 awarded
6. Gold with Swords and
        Diamonds   28 awarded

27. *Left: The Spanish Cross in Gold with Swords and Diamonds;*
Right: The Spanish Cross for Next-of-Kin of the Fallen.

The decoration was manufactured principally by C.E. Juncker of Berlin and took the form of a large Maltese cross, with a mobile swastika superimposed upon a central disc. A *Luftwaffe* eagle, flying clockwise, was set between each arm of the cross and reflected the important part played by the Air force, whose members accounted for about 70 per cent of the Legion's manpower. Swords, if appropriate, were also positioned between the arms. The grade with diamonds had fourteen brilliant-cut stones set around the swastika. The *Spanienkreuz* was worn permanently on the right breast pocket, below the later German Cross if that was also held.

The Cross without Swords was given to non-combatant military personnel and civilian auxiliary staff for three months' service in Spain, while the version with Swords was presented to combatants. Whether the award was bestowed in bronze, silver or gold depended upon the rank of the recipient, or the extent of his service during the war. In general terms, the silver was presented to those who had actually fought an engagement with the enemy or who had won the Spanish Red Military Merit Cross, while the gold was reserved for senior officers, recipients of the Spanish War Cross and those who had demonstrated significant bravery in the field. No non-combatant personnel were deemed deserving of a gold cross, so the gold grade was not conferred without Swords.

The highest grade, with Diamonds, was viewed as being akin to the old Order *Pour le Mérite* and was bestowed upon the Legion's commanding generals and outstanding soldiers. The known recipients, most of whom were *Luftwaffe* 'aces' (i.e. with four or more aerial victories) were as follows:

Oberleutnant Wilhelm Balthasar
Oberleutnant Otto Bertram
Leutnant Wilhelm Boddem
Oberleutnant Karl Eberhard
Oberleutnant Wilhelm Ensslen
Leutnant Paul Fehlhaber
Hauptmann Werner Mölders
Hauptmann Rudolf von Moreau
Hauptmann Wolfgang Neudörffer
Oberleutnant Walter Oesau
Generalleutnant Wolfram von Richthofen
Leutnant Heinz Runze

Oberleutnant Adolf
  Galland

Hauptmann Harro
  Harder

Major Martin
  Harlinghausen

Leutnant Oskar Heinrici

Oberleutnant Max Graf
  von Hoyos

Oberleutnant Hans von
  Kassel

Hauptmann Günther
  Lützow

Oberleutnant Karl Mehnert

Hauptmann Wolfgang
  Schellmann

Hauptmann Joachim
  Schlichting

Oberleutnant Reinhard
  Seiler

General Hugo Sperrle

Oberleutnant Bernhard
  Stärcke

General Helmut
  Volkmann

Major Karl Wolff

It is believed that the twenty-eighth recipient was *Oberst* Wilhelm Ritter von Thoma, commander of the Legion's *Panzer* force.

Dr Oskar Dirlewanger, the notorious counter-guerrilla commander, served in Spain from April to October 1937 and from July 1938 until May 1939, winning the Spanish Cross in Silver with Swords as a result. He was the only man known to have sub-sequently worn the award with *SS* uniform. Dirlewanger doubtless spent much of his time in Spain learning various anti-terrorist and counter-insurgency tactics which he later perfected in Russia and Poland.

A smaller version of the *Spanienkreuz* in Bronze without Swords, suspended from a ribbon in the German and Spanish colours, was presented as a keepsake to the next-of-kin of those killed in action in the Civil War, or who later died of wounds sus-tained in the conflict. The parents of the above-named *Leutnant* Wilhelm Boddem, for example, received such an award when their son succumbed to his Civil War wounds in January 1940. Only 315 next-of-kin crosses were conferred, the prescribed order of precedence for relatives' eligibility being:

1. widow
2. oldest son
3. oldest daughter
4. father
5. mother
6. brother
7. sister

WEHRMACHT LONG-SERVICE AWARDS

Compulsory national service was reintroduced in Germany on 16 March 1935, and exactly one year later all professional members of the armed forces, i.e. excluding conscripts, became eligible for a new series of long-service decorations instituted by Hitler and designed by Professor Richard Klein of Munich. For four years' service, a matt silver medal was presented. On the obverse it bore a *Wehrmacht* eagle and the dedication *Treue Dienste in der Wehrmacht* ('Loyal service in the armed forces'). The reverse featured the figure '4', surrounded by an oakleaf wreath. For twelve years' service a similar medal, but in matt gold with a '12' on the reverse, was awarded. A silver cross bearing an eagle on a central disc on the obverse and the number '18' on the reverse was presented for 18 years' service, and a slightly larger gold-plated cross with '25' on the reverse was bestowed for serving that number of years. A special grade for forty years, created in

28. *The* Wehrmacht *4-Year Long Service Medal, with ribbon emblem denoting presentation to a member of the* Luftwaffe.

29. Wehrmacht *Long-Service Awards for 18 years (left) and 40 years (right), with spread-winged ribbon eagles for Army and Navy personnel.*

30. *This Army corporal's dress tunic displays a Marksmanship Lanyard, 4-Year Service Medal and German National Sports Badge.*

1939, was simply the twenty-five-year cross with the addition of oakleaves pinned to the ribbon. All ribbons were cornflower blue, the colour of Germany's national flower and traditionally symbolic of faithfulness. Each ribbon had a small appropriately coloured metal eagle attached, being either spread-winged (Army and Navy) or flying (*Luftwaffe*). No more than two long-service awards could be worn simultaneously. When three or four were held, the prescribed order of pairing was either the silver cross with the silver medal or the gold cross with the gold medal. When the *Wehrmacht* long-service awards first began to be distributed, they were retroactive and it was possible for a long-serving soldier to receive all the grades simultaneously. Exceptionally long service, beyond the scope of the crosses, was recognised by a certificate issued by the *Wehrmacht* High Command.

WEHRMACHT MARKSMANSHIP LANYARDS
On 29 June 1936, a series of Marksmanship Lanyards, or *Schützenschnur*, was created for exellence in shooting with the carbine, rifle or machine-gun. The lanyard was conferred in twelve grades, depending on levels of proficiency, and was worn with one end attached to a button under the right shoulder strap and the other end draped across the breast and hooked to the second buttonhole of the tunic. Artillery personnel were tested in the use of cannon, *Panzer* crews qualified by shooting tank

31. *Badge worn with the grade 5–8 Marksmanship Lanyard for tank crews, introduced on 19 December 1938 with a representation of the* Panzer Mk I *as its centrepiece.*

guns, and sailors had to demonstrate expertise in torpedo firing, deck gunnery and so on. The whole range of lanyards was revised on 19 December 1938, but distribution tailed off during the war. The lanyard was not a decoration in the true sense, but rather a proficiency badge. It is included here for the sake of clarification, since lanyard badges were very similar in appearance to the later War Badges, for which they are often mistaken.

SS Long-Service Awards

On 30 January 1938, it was announced that full-time members of the militarised formations of the *SS* were to be given their own long-service awards, modelled on those of the *Wehrmacht*. Eligibility was restricted to volunteer soldiers of the *SS-Verfügungstruppe*, *SS-Totenkopfverbände* and *SS-Junkerschulen*, all of which came under the umbrella of the *Waffen-SS* in 1939–40. Former service in the *Wehrmacht*, *Landespolizei*, *Freikorps* or *NSDAP* paramilitary formations counted towards the total years necessary to qualify for the new award, but in any case every prospective recipient had to have served a minimum of four years in an appropriate armed *SS* unit. Since membership of the armed *SS* did not count as national military service until 1935, in effect no one could be eligible for these decorations until 1939 at the earliest. Moreover, members of the *Allgemeine-SS* could not receive them at all, and their long *SS* service was later recognised by bestowal of the *NSDAP Dienstauszeichnungen*.

Following a design revision of the lowest grade on 21 October 1938, which gave it a unique obverse, the *SS* range comprised black- and bronze-toned medals for four and eight years' service respectively, and large silver and gold swastika-shaped 'crosses' for twelve and twenty-five years. The latter two grades were the first Nazi decorations to use the swastika as the main part of their designs and bore silver or gold bullion Sig-runes hand-embroidered into their cornflower blue ribbons. The official orders of 21 October 1938 also referred to the approved incorporation of machine-embroidered runes into *SS* ribbons, and shortly thereafter the *Ordenskanzlei* commissioned a sample length of 200 m of this new *SS* ribbon from the Munich firm

of Karl Loy. The width of the trial run was 35 mm and its Sig-runes were machine-embroidered in light grey cotton thread rather than being hand-embroidered in silver or gold bullion. However, none of this prototype ribbon was ever issued. It is likely that it was intended for use with the four- and eight-year medals only.

The *SS* four-year medal was not open to officers, but the other grades could be bestowed regardless

32. *SS Long-Service Awards.*
Left: 12-year decoration, with bullion Sig-runes embroidered into its special 50 mm ribbon. This unusually wide ribbon was designed to be folded so as to show the runes above the award when court mounted. Note also the distinctive elongated 'tear drop' suspension ring, again intended for court mounting;
Top right: 8-year medal, court mounted;
Bottom right: 4-year medal.

of rank. They closely paralleled prescribed armed *SS* service periods, as other ranks normally enlisted for four years and NCOs for twelve, with officers 'signing on' for twenty-five years' service. All grades featured the legend *Für Treue Dienste in der SS*. Every *SS* decoration had an elongated 'tear-drop' suspension ring which was designed to fit neatly over the hooks used on court-mounted ribbon bars. This form of suspension ring was unique to the *SS*.

Designed by Karl Diebitsch, the *SS Dienstaus-zeichnungen* were produced in some quantity during the spring of 1939 by Deschler of Munich and Petz & Lorenz of Unterreichenbach, but they were not widely distributed thereafter since *Waffen-SS* soldiers became eligible to receive the standard *Wehrmacht* long-service awards from the outbreak of the Second World War. While at least one *Wehrpass* survives recording an award 'on paper' of the *SS* four-year medal to a *Scharführer* of the '*Das Reich*' division in August 1942, *Waffen-SS* officers and men during the 1939–45 period consistently sported Army eagles, not *SS* runes, on their service ribbon bars. Indeed, pictorial evidence reveals only one prominent *Waffen-SS* officer, Otto Kumm, regularly wearing the runic ribbon of the twelve-year decoration during the war. No photographs at all are known to exist showing the four-or eight-year *SS* medals being worn on parade, and no one ever qualified for a twenty-five-year decoration. All the indications are that very few *SS* long-service awards of any grade were ever bestowed.

It is interesting to note that the twelve-year award was conferred upon *Reichsführer-SS* Heinrich Himmler early in 1939 although he was, technically speaking, not entitled to receive it, never having served the requisite period in a military *SS* unit!

SS Marksmanship Awards

Members of the armed *SS* were prohibited from wearing *Wehrmacht* marksmanship lanyards. On 26 January 1937, a draft order instituting an *SS* Shooting Badge (*SS-Schiessabzeichen*) was drawn up describing four classes of cloth insignia, featuring targets, to be worn on the lower right sleeve. A further draft order dating from November 1937 refers to the creation of an Armed *SS* Shooting Badge (*Schützenabzeichen der SS-VT*), in metal

form, for wear on the left breast pocket. To further confuse the issue, a blank citation for an *SS* Marksmanship Lanyard (*SS-Schützenschnur*) also exists. However, none of these projected proficiency badges was ever produced and there was no outward recognition of *SS* marksmanship.

THE 'FLOWER WAR' MEDALS

On 1 May 1938, Hitler instituted the Commemorative Medal of 13 March 1938, or *Medaille zur Erinnerung an der 13 März 1938*, usually known as the *Ostmarkmedaille*, or *Anschluss* Medal. Designed by Professor Puchinger of Vienna, it was awarded to those who prepared for or took part in the Nazi annexation of Austria. It was the first in a series of three medals celebrating the so-called 'flower wars', when invading German troops were greeted with floral tributes rather than gunfire and the Nazi regime scored some spectacular bloodless victories. The second in the series, the

33.   Left: The Anschluss *Medal;*
Right: The Memel Medal.

Medal of 1 October 1938, was awarded for participation in the occupation of the Czech Sudetenland, and a Bar, bearing a representation of Prague Castle, was authorised on 1 May 1939 for holders of the medal who were further engaged in the occupation of the rest of Czechoslovakia and the subsequent organisation of the Protectorate of Bohemia and Moravia. The last medal in the series commemorated the return of the Memel District from Lithuania to Germany. Each of these medals featured the same obverse design – a tall standing figure carrying a swastika banner (Germany) assisting a shorter figure with broken shackles (representing the 'freed' Austrians, Czechs and Memellanders) to mount a podium which symbolised the Greater German Reich. The *Anschluss* and Sudetenland Medals had on their reverses the dates *13 März 1938* and *1 Oktober 1938* respectively, each surrounded by the legend *Ein Volk, Ein Reich, Ein Führer* ('One people, one nation, one leader'), a favourite pre-war slogan which promoted Hitler's reunification policy. The Memel Medal had the reverse inscription *Zur Erinnerung an die Heimkehr des Memellandes, 22 März 1939* ('In commemoration of the return of the Memel district, 22 March 1939'). The *Anschluss* Medal was silver in colour and the others bronze. It is noteworthy that the *Blumenkrieg* witnessed the first use of the Nazi field post office system, a sure sign that Hitler was by then expecting full-scale war.

The original design for the *Anschluss* Medal, as described in the foundation decree, had Hitler's profile on the obverse and a large eagle and swastika on the reverse. However, this pattern was never produced, probably because it would have smacked of 'occupation' rather than 'liberation'.

The numbers of 'flower war' medals distributed were as follows:

Anschluss Medal	318,689
Sudetenland Medal	1,162,617
Prague Castle Bar	134,563
Memel Medal	31,322

Military units taking part in any of these occupations were authorised to carry streamers, in the colours of the appropriate medal ribbons, attached to their regimental and battalion standards.

34. An SS-Unterscharführer wearing the Anschluss Medal on the occasion of his wedding in 1939. Of particular interest is the fact that the award hangs from its ribbon of issue in the civilian manner, rather than being court mounted as was usually the case for uniformed organisations.

THE WEST WALL MEDAL

The German Defence Wall Decoration, or *Deutsches Schutzwall Ehrenzeichen*, usually called the West Wall Medal, was instituted on 2 August 1939 for bestowal upon designers, planners and over 600,000 workers who constructed the Siegfried Line and other defensive fortifications along the western border of Germany. Members of the armed forces who were stationed on these defences prior to May 1940 were also eligible for the bronze award, which featured a pillbox surmounted by a sword and spade. A second striking of the medal, this time in zinc, was made in October 1944 for distribution as a morale-booster to large forces of workers and soldiers then strengthening the defence lines along Germany's western and eastern borders. Around 200,000 zinc medals were handed out *en masse* to the entire membership of *Organisation Todt* construction units, and the exigencies of duty at that late stage of the war frequently resulted in the award being presented with a partially blank citation so that the recipient could fill in his own details! A Bar comprising an eagle over a sword and spade was authorised for those who had already received the bronze medal in 1939–40, but it was never produced.

35. *A West Wall Medal by Steinhauer & Lück, with beige paper packet of issue.*

THE *OSTVOLK* DECORATION

On 14 July 1942, at the suggestion of the *Reichsführer-SS*, Hitler created the *Ostvolk* Decoration for bestowal on over 1 million former Soviet citizens, including a vast array of Moslem tribesmen from the Caucasus, who were serving as volunteers in the *Wehrmacht*. They were at that time ineligible for the Eastern Front Medal and other German combat awards, and so had recently taken to manufacturing their own 'Mickey Mouse' medals, most notably the 2nd Siberian and 5th Don Cossack Cavalry Regiment Crosses. The latter had no official standing whatsoever, but highlighted the desire of these people for some type of decoration to recognise their efforts.

a

b

36. *Unofficial awards created during 1941–2 by pro-Nazi Cossacks serving with the* Wehrmacht:
(a) The 2nd Siberian Cossack Cavalry Regiment Cross, manufactured in bronze and fine enamels by Braga Kraus of Zagreb;
(b) The poorer quality 5th Don Cossack Cavalry Regiment Cross, bearing the name of the unit commander, Kononov, in Cyrillic characters.

The *Ostvolk Auszeichnung* came in two classes, a 1st Class in Gold and Silver and a 2nd Class in Gold, Silver and Bronze. The 1st Class was a 50 mm wide pin-back badge worn on the left breast pocket, while the 2nd Class was a 40 mm medal suspended from a ribbon in progressively lighter shades of 'Turkic green', with white edge stripes for the silver grade and red stripes for the gold grade. Designed by Elmar Lang of the Godet firm, the various divisions of the zinc-based decoration all took the form of an Islamic star bearing a traditional Russian sunflower surrounded by laurel leaves, and each could be with or without Swords. An award with Swords denoted bravery in battle and could be bestowed by the local army divisional commander or, in the case of anti-partisan units, by the senior *SS* and police officer in the area. The award without Swords recognised meritorious service and was conferred in Hitler's name by the Minister for the Occupied Eastern Territories.

The *Ostvolk* Decoration was like all other German military and civil awards rolled into one and could be presented not only for valour or merit but also for being wounded, for taking part in close combat, or for participating in a recognised campaign. Consequently, it was very widely distributed. All grades of the 2nd Class had to be held prior to award of the 1st Class. However, to complicate the issue still further, each grade of the 2nd Class could be conferred three times on a single individual

37.   *The* Ostvolk *Decoration.*
Top left: 2nd Class in Gold without Swords, by Wächtler & Lange;
Top right: 2nd Class in Silver without Swords, by Wächtler & Lange;
Bottom: 1st Class in Gold without Swords.
A neck version of this decoration carrying with it the Soviet-like title Held des Volkes, *or 'Hero of the people', was contemplated for award to pro-Nazi native generals, but was never instituted.*

38.   Generalmajor *Bronislav Kaminski, commander of the Russian People's Liberation Army, wearing the* Ostvolk *Decoration 1st Class in Silver with Swords below his Iron Cross. Kaminski was executed by the* SS *for looting committed in the Lodz area of Poland during the autumn of 1944.*

39. *Members of the* Osttürkischer Waffen-Verband der SS, *which comprised Muslims from the Turkestan region, kneeling before prayer in October 1944. The man in the foreground wears the Iron Cross 2nd Class and the* Ostvolk *Decoration 2nd Class in Bronze with Swords.*

(i.e. three Bronze, three Silver and three Gold), and multiple awards were often made and worn simultaneously, hanging from separately pinned on ribbons in the traditional Russian style. For example, *Oberst* E.N. Kononov, commander of the 5th Don Cossacks, received the 2nd Class in Bronze twice, the 2nd Class in Silver once and the 2nd Class in Gold once, before being awarded the 1st Class in Silver. After that, he was presented with a further 2nd Class in Gold! Females could also qualify for the decoration, the first such recipient being 19-year-old Marij Studenikova, a front-line nurse with the 1st Cossack Division. To facilitate the 'Eastern' manner of their wearing, which was unique among Nazi awards, all examples of the 2nd Class were delivered from the factory attached to specially sewn ribbons through which the suspension ring was

hooked. This necessitated the use of a relatively flimsy and easily bent aluminium ring, left unsoldered and open, for ease of pushing through prepunched holes in the ribbon.

Notable recipients of the *Ostvolk* Decoration 1st Class included the infamous *SS-Oberführer* Dr Oskar Dirlewanger, who commanded an anti-partisan brigade frequently used as a terror unit against civilians; Bronislav Kaminski, leader of the so-called Russian People's Liberation Army; and Boris Smyslovsky, commander of the German Army's 1st Russian Division. The 1st Class was usually accompanied by a token cash payment which was often far more welcome than the award itself, given the poor financial circumstances of the majority of Russian auxiliaries in the Nazi forces. Despite this latter incentive, however, the Eastern troops to whom this decoration was initially exclusively given soon felt slighted that no German ever appeared with one. Consequently, in November 1942 automatic eligibility for the 1st and/or 2nd Class in Silver with Swords was extended to German cadre personnel who already held the Iron Cross 1st and/or 2nd Class respectively. On 14 February 1944 the equivalent Silver grades without Swords were authorised for appropriate German holders of the War Merit Cross. It was not until mid-1944 that Russian volunteers in the *Wehrmacht* were given the general right to wear the Iron Cross, Wound Badges and other German awards. After that time, distribution of the *Ostvolk* Decoration tailed off as it had always been fairly unpopular, not least because of its tawdry appearance and poor-quality finish. Indeed, the *Ostvolk* Decoration was seldom worn by its German recipients, who considered it something of a 'native trinket'.

The firm of Wächtler & Lange alone manufactured hundreds of thousands of *Ostvolk* awards during 1942–4 and shipped them east for local distribution. A number of 2nd Class decorations were supplied with variant ribbons in red, yellow, green and blue. Perhaps these were meant to correspond with the various national badges employed by Armenians, Volga Tartars and the like but, in any event, they do not appear to have been issued. Citations accompanying the *Ostvolk* Decoration were frequently bilingual, in German and the first language of the recipient.

Campaign Honours and Wound Badges

Arm Shields

Commemorative campaign shields, or arm shields, were awarded in various forms to personnel who took part in specific campaigns and battles which were either particularly successful or notably gruelling. They were worn permanently on the upper left sleeve of the tunic and greatcoat, 7 cm below the shoulder seam and above any other insignia present. *SS* and police troops often wore campaign shields erroneously under their arm eagles, presumably in ignorance of the regulations or because they were simply adhering to the generally accepted principle that the national emblem should take precedence over all other uniform badges.

THE NARVIK SHIELD

The first campaign shield, the Narvik Shield, was instituted on 19 August 1940 for award to personnel who took part in the capture of the port of Narvik

*40.   Left: The Narvik Shield;
Right: The Cholm Shield.*

between 9 April and 9 June that year, thus depriving Britain of her last foothold in Norway and, indeed, mainland Europe. The battle, which witnessed the evacuation of the Norwegian king and his government, was a triumph of *Wehrmacht* inter-service co-operation, and the design of the new decoration, executed by Professor Richard Klein of Munich, reflected that fact. The shield featured an edelweiss (representing the Army's mountain troops under *Generaloberst* Eduard Dietl), an anchor (for *Kommodore* Bonte's destroyers) and a *Luftwaffe* propeller. It was awarded in silver to Army and Air Force recipients and in gold to members of the Navy. Like all other shields, the *Narvikschild* was hollow-backed and stamped from sheet metal. A few early issues were plated aluminium or steel, but most were in lacquered zinc. The first Narvik Shield was presented to Dietl by Hitler on 21 March 1941. In all, 2,800 were awarded to soldiers, 3,700 to sailors (including 2,671 to destroyer crews) and 2,200 to airmen. These troops had snatched victory from the jaws of defeat in the hardest-fought battle of the western campaign.

THE CHOLM SHIELD

The Cholm Shield was founded on 1 July 1942 for all military and police personnel who held the Russian fortress town of Cholm (or Kholm) against overwhelming odds between 21 January and 5 May 1942. The Soviets launched over a hundred mass infantry attacks and forty tank assaults against the small beleaguered German force, but it stood its ground until relieved. Its commander, *General-major* Theodor Scherer, received the Oakleaves to the Knight's Cross for his conduct of the town's defence. The 1st Battalion of Police Regiment 25, which took part in the fiercest of the fighting, was duly awarded the honour title 'Cholm', and Dr Goebbels produced a propaganda book on the siege entitled *Kampfgruppe Scherer – 105 Tage Eingeschlossen* ('Battle Group Scherer – Cut Off for 105 Days'). Designed by *Polizei Rottwachtmeister* Schlimmer, a participant in the battle, the Cholm Shield was produced from stamped steel or zinc, painted silver or field-grey. Only 5,500 were bestowed between 31 October 1942 and 1 April 1943, and many of the recipients subsequently died on the Eastern front. As a result, it was one of the rarest campaign shields, seldom seen worn.

THE KRIM SHIELD

The *Krimschild*, instituted on 25 July 1942, was by contrast the most widely issued shield. Around 250,000 were distributed to the troops under *Generalfeldmarschall* Erich von Manstein, who between 21 September 1941 and 4 July 1942 conquered the Crimea and captured Russia's Black Sea ports. During prolonged fighting around Sevastopol the Germans employed 'Big Dora', the largest artillery piece ever built, to penetrate the many underground Russian bunkers. However, they eventually had to resort to using poison gas to finally overcome the Soviet defenders in these impregnable subterranean strongholds. This was the only campaign of the Second World War to witness the deployment of chemical weapons. The Crimea Shield was stamped in sheet steel with a bronze wash. In recognition of the part played by Romanian divisions in the campaign, a special version in hallmarked gold was presented by von

41.   From left to right:
The Krim Shield;
The Demjansk Shield;
The Kuban Shield.

Manstein to Marshal Antonescu in Bucharest on 3 July 1943. That November, von Manstein had a similar gold shield given to him by his staff officers as a birthday present. It is worthy of note that at least one enterprising Russian jeweller cashed in on the Nazi occupation by producing silver and gold finger rings, bearing engraved representations of the design featured on the *Krimschild*, which he sold to German soldiers as souvenirs of their stay in the Soviet Union!

THE DEMJANSK SHIELD

The Demjansk Shield was authorised on 25 April 1943 for 96,000 members of the 2nd Army Corps under General Walter Graf Brockdorff-Ahlefeld who were cut off at Demjansk, 100 miles north-east of Cholm, on 8 February 1942. They broke out of the encirclement on 21 April, but fighting in the area continued until mid-October that year. Stiff resistance from the German units, especially battle groups 'Eicke' and 'Simon' of the *SS-Totenkopf* Division, committed three entire Soviet armies which the Russians desperately needed elsewhere. Amongst the many thousands killed during the battle was Hitler's old friend *SS-Gruppenführer* Paul Moder, then serving as a *Totenkopf Hauptsturmführer der Reserve*. The Germans were kept supplied by means of an airlift, hence the incorporation of an aeroplane in the design of the shield. The *Demjanskschild* was initially produced in brightly silvered steel or zinc and distribution commenced at the beginning of 1944. Examples manufactured from mid-1944 were given a dull field-grey finish for camouflage reasons.

THE KUBAN SHIELD

The Kuban Shield was founded on 20 September 1943, as a morale-booster for *Generalfeldmarschall* Ewald von Kleist and his men who were then fighting for their lives at the Kuban bridgehead on the Taman Peninsula between the Sea of Azov and the Russian naval base at Noworossijsk, a battle popularised by the novel and feature film *Cross of Iron*. The defence of the bridgehead began on 12 February 1943, but continuous onslaughts from the Soviet North Caucasian Front Army resulted in the order being given on 4 September to evacuate all German and Romanian forces from the area. Supported by the *Kriegsmarine*, they withdrew across the Straits of Kerch and the Kuban fell to the Russians on 9 October. The names of the most significant encounters fought during the campaign, '*Lagunen*' (the 'Lagoon Battles'), 'Krymskaya' and 'Noworossijsk', were impressed on the face of the shield, which was stamped from sheet steel or zinc with a bronze wash. The first awards took place during the second half of 1944. A unique example of this shield in hallmarked gold is reported to have been presented to von Kleist by his staff officers.

All of the above five shields, the only ones verified from wartime photographs as having definitely been issued and worn, were supplied with backings of woollen or rayon cloth appropriate in colour to the tunics to which they were attached. The reverse of each shield had prongs or edge tabs, generally four in number, which were pushed through the cloth and were then secured in place by being bent over a sheet steel or zinc backplate. Early shields, especially the *Narvikschild*, usually had this plate in its turn backed by cloth. Mid-war pieces tended to have cheaper paper backings over the plate, while later shields like the *Kubanschild* were generally issued with uncovered backplates. Recipients were issued with three to five examples of each shield, to allow for simultaneous display on dress tunics, field tunics and greatcoats. This meant that many more shields were made than were actually awarded. For example, given normal wear and tear and replacement of tunics, it is estimated that over 3 million Krim Shields would have been needed for use by the 250,000 holders of the award. Photographic evidence indicates that some shields, particularly the *Demjanskschild*, were occasionally pinned or sewn directly to the sleeve without the regulation backing. Presumably, this was intended to give a neater appearance.

THE LAPPLAND SHIELD

The *Lapplandschild* differed significantly from its predecessors. In February 1945 General Franz Böhme, commander of the 20th Mountain Army, which had been fighting a two-front war against the British in northern Norway and the Russians in

42. The Lappland Shield.

Lapland since September 1944, suggested to the Army High Command that a commemorative shield should be instituted to recognise the efforts of his men. It was not until 1 May, however, the day after Hitler's death, that approval for the award was finally given, and the chaotic situation in Germany at that time meant that normal production was out of the question. The 20th Mountain Army surrendered to the British in Norway on 8 May, and the Germans soon found that their captor, General Thorne, unlike most Allied commanders, allowed his prisoners to wear their military decorations. In view of this, Böhme's soldiers decided to make their shield themselves. Rough sketches were circulated amongst some survivors of the campaign and the design chosen reflected the fact that the Nazi regime was at an end. A federal eagle, without a swastika, surmounted the word 'Lappland' above a map of the Northern Cape. A number of awards were duly made 'on paper', with appropriate entries in the recipients' *Soldbuchs*, and a few crude shields may conceivably have been produced in prisoner-of-war camps. It is noteworthy that citations bestowing the *Lapplandschild* were made out in the name of General Böhme personally, rather than in the name of the Führer (by then *Grossadmiral* Dönitz) or the *Wehrmacht* High Command.

THE SARDINIA SHIELD

The so-called 'Sardinia Shield' was not a campaign award but simply a cap badge worn by selected members of the 90th *Panzergrenadier* Division, which had been stationed on the island. The shield was legitimised by an order of the divisional commander, who issued certificates permitting the wearing of the badge on the left side of the field cap. It took the form of a small map of Sardinia, surmounted by a sword with the words 'Olbia' and 'Cagliari'.

Cuff Titles

Cuff titles, or *ärmelbanden*, were distinctive items of Third Reich uniform insignia, having their origins in the nineteenth century. Worn 15 cm above the sleeve edge, they were used to denote membership of certain elite units, training establishments and so on, as well as participation in specific campaigns.

THE VON RICHTHOFEN AND BOELCKE CUFF TITLES

On 1 October 1935, the '*Jagdgeschwader Frhr. v. Richthofen Nr. 1 1917/18*' and '*Jagdstaffel Boelcke Nr. 2 1916/18*' cuff titles were created for wear on the right sleeve by personnel of the new *Luftwaffe* who had previously served in either of these prestigious units during the First World War. These cuff titles were not campaign decorations, but were classed as commemorative awards and had to be returned within three months of the holder's departure from the Air Force. Only 300 'Richthofen' and 75 'Boelcke' titles were ever conferred.

THE SPANIEN 1936–9 CUFF TITLE

Like the foregoing, this piece of insignia was not a campaign decoration and is again included only for the sake of clarification. It was introduced on 21 June 1939 as a unit 'tradition' or battle honour for wear by personnel of the 1st Battalion, *Panzer-Lehrregiment* and the *Heer Nachrichten-Lehrabteilung*. These formations traced their origins to '*Gruppe Imker*' ('Beekeeper Group'), the Army training component of the Condor Legion during the Spanish Civil War. The cuff title was machine-woven in red artificial silk with the legend *1936 Spanien 1939* picked out in gold thread. It was to be worn only with dress tunics, and was not

43.   The 'Spanien 1936–1939' Cuff Title.

to be used on the field or panzer uniforms. Few photographs showing the title in wear have ever come to light and it is likely that it was withdrawn shortly after introduction, possibly when the Condor Legion Tank Badge was given official status on 10 July.

THE KRETA CUFF TITLE

The Kreta Cuff Title was instituted on 16 October 1942 for award to all personnel who took part in the invasion of Crete in May 1941. The airborne capture of the island cost the Germans dear, but completed

Hitler's conquest of south-eastern Europe and gave him control of the vital eastern Mediterranean area. The title was worn on the left cuff of the tunic and greatcoat, and took the form of a sturdy white or cream-coloured linen cloth band measuring 33 mm in width, with the word 'Kreta' and two stylised acanthus leaf scrolls machine-embroidered in

44.   From top to bottom:
The Kreta Cuff Title;
The Afrika Cuff Title;
The Kurland Cuff Title.

yellow cotton thread. The borders, also of yellow cotton, were stitched separately onto the cloth base. The construction of the title was the same for all ranks, and every recipient received four examples to allow for simultaneous display on a selection of uniforms. Awards began during the first half of 1943 and ceased on 31 October 1944.

THE AFRIKA CUFF TITLE

On 15 January 1943, Hitler founded the Afrika Cuff Title as a campaign honour for service in the North African theatre of operations. Recipients had to have been in the zone for at least six months, or three months if incapacitated through tropical disease. The time requirement was waived if the soldier had been wounded in action, or had won the Iron Cross or some other bravery award. It had a soft light brown base cloth, almost velvety in texture, and silver-grey embroidery, and it was made in exactly the same way as the Kreta title. The 'Afrika' legend was in cotton thread for all ranks – there was no bullion version for officers. The title was worn on the left sleeve, above the Kreta band if that award was also held. The design featured two palm trees, one either side of the word 'Afrika', and the decoration is often referred to as the 'Afrika with palms', to distinguish it from the Army *Afrikakorps* and *Luftwaffe* Afrika Cuff Titles, which were formation badges rather than campaign awards. The Afrika Cuff Title saw distribution during mid-1943, after the Germans had been defeated in North Africa, so it was not usually worn with the tropical uniform. Its award to foreigners (i.e. the Italians) was expressly forbidden. Presentations ceased on 31 October 1944.

It is worth mentioning that before the institution of the Afrika Cuff Title, members of the *Afrikakorps* gave themselves their own commemorative 'award' in the form of a finger ring which attained widespread popularity amongst the earliest veterans of the desert campaign. The *Afrika Ring* was originally created by an imaginative German supplies officer, Robert Hoefle, who while walking through the bazaars of Tripoli in the spring of 1941 saw many troops visiting local shops and buying rings with various Arabic motifs as souvenirs. He commissioned one of the Arab silversmiths to produce

rings bearing the *Afrikakorps* tactical symbol of a palm tree surmounted by a swastika and the legend '*DAK* 1941', for sale in unit canteens. The design soon became very well known and a number of Arab jewellers were subsequently kept busy applying Nazi symbolism to existing stocks of rings for their many eager German customers. The rings continued to be made well into 1942 and some elaborate examples bore gold tooling, elephant or camel designs and so on. Most had Arab silver hallmarks, although a few were stamped with German marks as well. The *Afrika Ring* soon took on the status of a campaign commemorative, since most of its wearers were the men who first saw action with Rommel in the desert. It continued to be displayed proudly on fingers until the end of the war although, of course, it had no official standing whatsoever.

THE KURLAND CUFF TITLE

The last campaign *ärmelband* was instituted on 12 March 1945 as Hitler's final award to the German forces in the Second World War. It was authorised for the men of Army Group Courland, who had been fighting a ferocious war of encirclement in Latvia for over five months. The woven title was made from a grey-white linen and bore the word 'Kurland' in black thread, between the stag's head shield of Mitau, Courland's chief city, and the shield of the Grand Master of the Order of Teutonic Knights, German colonisers of the area in the thirteenth century. It was manufactured inside the Courland Pocket by the troops themselves, using a commandeered weaving mill at Kuldiga, and was cut short to conserve material so did not extend around the entire circumference of the left cuff. This complied with the General Order of 18 November 1944, which laid down that all cuff titles manufactured after that date had to be shortened to 22 cm for economy reasons. Distribution of the Kurland Cuff Title began on 20 April, and continued right up until after the capitulation. On 3 May Hitler's successor, *Grossadmiral* Dönitz, ordered the long-awaited evacuation of troops from the Courland peninsula. Thousands managed to escape in a Dunkirk-like operation, but many more were trapped and captured by the Soviets. Of those, only

45. Major *'Sepp' Brandner, highly decorated commander of an assault gun battalion, wearing the Kurland Cuff Title on his lower left sleeve.*

a small number survived the years of hunger, disease and forced labour that were to be their lot in Russian captivity close to the Arctic Circle. The Kurland Cuff Title is by far the rarest of the three campaign bands which were issued during the Second World War. Most recipients simply never took the trouble to sew the decoration to their tunics – they had far more pressing things on their minds at the time. Consequently, the majority of issued titles were discarded at the end of the war. It is noteworthy that Hitler had ordered Courland to be held as long as possible for a special reason: he hoped to use the peninsula as a springboard for a flanking attack against the Russians in the unlikely event he could persuade the Western Allies to change sides at the last minute and join his crusade against Communism!

Unit Cuff Titles as Awards

Unit cuff titles were normally worn by members of selected formations only for as long as they were assigned to them. However, an Army order dated 25 October 1944 permitted, by Hitler's authority, the award by divisional and regimental commanders of the cuff titles *'Grossdeutschland'*, *'Feldherrnhalle'*, *'Infanterie-Regiment List'*, *'Brandenburg'* and *'Generaloberst Dietl'* to individual soldiers of these units for valour or extraordinary performance. When conferred personally in this way, such titles were allowed to be worn permanently by the recipients, irrespective of their subsequent transfer to other formations.

46. *Commemorative finger rings.*
Left: Typical silver Afrika Ring, bearing the 'DAK 1941' tactical symbol in gold. The piece is double hallmarked, with both an Arab silver stamp and the German '800' equivalent;
Right: Russian silver ring, with a representation of the Krim Shield and the dates '1941–1943' engraved on its copper mount.

Campaign Medals

The Third Reich usually recognised participation in military campaigns by the award of arm shields and cuff titles rather than medals. However, there were two notable exceptions to this general rule.

THE EASTERN FRONT MEDAL, 1941–2

The most common of all Nazi campaign awards was the Medal for the Winter Battle in the East 1941–2 (*Medaille 'Winterschlacht im Osten 1941–2'*), commonly known as the *Ostmedaille*, or Eastern Front Medal. Ironically, the word *schlacht* may be translated not only as 'battle' but also as 'slaughter', an appropriate double meaning bearing in mind the huge losses suffered by ill-equipped German troops during that first winter on the Russian front. Instituted on 26 May 1942, the *Ostmedaille* was designed by *Unterscharführer* Ernst Krause of the *Leibstandarte-SS* 'Adolf Hitler' and was presented to all those who saw active service on the eastern front between 15 November 1941 and 15 April 1942. Two weeks at the front line or sixty days in a combat zone were the normal prerequisites for

47. *Left: The Eastern Front Medal, by Foerster & Barth;*
Right: The Blue Division Medal, by Deschler & Sohn.

48. This hammered aluminium photograph frame was probably made by a close family relation of the young SS-Scharführer shown, who was killed in Russia. His dates, 1919–1942, are clearly evident and his initials 'T.W.' are surrounded by swastikas, Sig-runes and other Nordic symbols. The fact that the dead man served with the 6th SS-Totenkopf Regiment means it is likely that he perished during the fighting at Demjansk. A piece of ribbon for the Eastern Front Medal, which would have been delivered posthumously to his next-of-kin, is mounted alongside his picture.

award, but these time qualifications were waived if the soldier concerned was wounded in the campaign.

This typified the German 'multiple award' process in respect of wounds which meant that, for example, a man might spend only a few days in action in the Crimea during the winter of 1941–2 but if he was seriously wounded in the process he would receive not only the Wound Badge in Silver or Gold but also the *Ostmedaille*, the *Krimschild* and the Iron Cross 2nd Class automatically, on account of the severity of the wounding and where and when it had taken place.

The Eastern Front Medal was stamped from a heavy grey zinc-based alloy and was dished in form with a concave obverse and convex reverse. The border and steel helmet were given a frosted silver finish while the remainder of the award was plated a gun-metal blue-grey. This often had a 'bubbled' appearance due to overheating of the lacquer coating during the manufacturing process. The medal was suspended from a very distinctive dark red ribbon with narrow white/black/white centre stripes. Its foundation decree stated that the red represented blood, the white was for snow and the black honoured the memory of the fallen.

Foreign auxiliaries became eligible for the *Ostmedaille* from 20 January 1943. The medal was held in very high regard and its ribbon was frequently worn from the second buttonhole, a position normally reserved for wartime bravery and merit decorations such as the *EK2* and *KVK2*. The ribbon was also very often placed in commemorative photograph frames by the relatives of men killed in action in Russia. Awards of the *Ostmedaille* commenced in July 1942 and continued to be made until October 1944, by which time over 4 million had been distributed.

The Blue Division Medal

Closely related to the Eastern Front Medal was the 'Commemorative Medal for the Spanish Volunteers in the Struggle Against Communism', usually known as the Blue Division Medal. Instituted on 3 January 1944, it was awarded as a campaign honour to members of the 250th Infantry Division which fought on the eastern front between June 1941 and October 1943. This unit was composed almost entirely of Spaniards, many of them Civil War veterans, who were permitted to serve as volunteers with the German Army in Russia. By allowing them to do so, General Franco was able to repay Hitler for the assistance given by the Condor Legion, while still maintaining Spain's neutral status. The unit took its semi-official title 'Blue Division' from the blue shirts of Franco's Falangist movement. As many as

45,000 Spaniards saw service in the east, before their units were disbanded by Franco to placate the Allies. The medal was finely produced in gilded zinc by Deschler of Munich, with an inferior version being manufactured in Spain. Each Deschler piece was coated with *mittelgold* lacquer made by the Herbig-Haarhaus firm of Köln-Bickendorf, which soon wore off, leaving a dull grey surface to the award.

Wound Badges

The Spanish Wound Badge

The so-called Spanish Wound Badge was created on 22 May 1939 for award to Germans wounded in the Spanish Civil War. It was identical in design to the earlier 1918-pattern Army wound badge, but featured a swastika on the side of the imperial steel helmet. All three grades of the badge were hollow-backed plated or painted brass. Only 182 black badges and one silver badge were conferred as a result of the Civil War, and there were no posthumous bestowals. However, the Spanish pattern continued to be issued to troops in Poland and on the western front until mid-1940, when stocks of the standard 1939 type became generally available. In this way, many thousands were awarded, including hundreds of the gold grade.

The 1939 Wound Badge

On 1 September 1939, Hitler instituted a new Nazi-pattern Wound Badge, or *Verwundetenabzeichen*, for presentation to military personnel wounded in action. It was ultimately one of the most common of all Third Reich decorations yet also one of the most highly prized, since it had to be 'bought with blood'. The 1939 badge, which in fact was not manufactured until mid-1940, was slightly different in design from its First World War and 'Spanish' counterparts, and took the form of an oval wreath of laurel leaves surrounding two crossed swords which were surmounted by an M35 steel helmet bearing a mobile swastika. It came in three classes – black, silver and gold – and was worn on the left breast pocket below any war badges held. There was no distinct naval version, as there had been in 1918.

The Wound Badge in Black (representing iron) was awarded to those wounded once or twice. It was initially stamped from sheet brass, painted matt or semi-matt black, and had a hollow reverse with a needle pin attachment. From 1942, steel replaced brass in its manufacture and as the war dragged on so the quality of the steel declined. As a result, the later badges were very prone to rust. The Wound Badge in Silver was conferred for three or four wounds, or for only one wound if it involved brain damage, facial disfigurement or the loss of a hand, a foot, an eye or hearing. This award was produced first from silver-plated brass then, after 1942, from lacquered zinc, and had a solid reverse with either a needle pin or a broad flat pin bar. The Wound Badge in Gold was a gilded version of the silver badge and was given for five or more wounds, or for a single wound if it resulted in blindness, 'loss of manhood' or total disability.

In addition to the Wound Badge, certain war badges and campaign decorations could be conferred in recognition of wounds sustained while serving with the relevant *Wehrmacht* branches or whilst engaged in the appropriate campaigns. Moreover, from 1 June 1940 recipients of the Wound Badge in Silver or Gold were also presented automatically with the Iron Cross 2nd Class if they did not already possess it. This pluralism meant that, for example, a sailor who lost a hand or foot in action while serving on an E-boat at the Kuban bridgehead would receive not only the Wound Badge in Silver but also the E-boat War Badge, the *Kubanschild* and the *EK2*, purely on account of the wound sustained. Multiple wounds were not uncommon amongst German soldiers, particularly on the eastern front, as exemplified by *SS-Obersturmbannführer* Boris Kraas, who was wounded sixteen times in four years! Even his luck ran out, and his final wound was fatal. Regulations dictated that, of the many serious and long-lasting illnesses commonly contracted by troops stationed in countries with extreme climatic conditions, only frostbite counted as a wound for the purposes of the badge.

All members of the *Wehrmacht* and their auxiliaries were eligible for the Wound Badge and, from March 1943, it was also distributed to uniformed civilians such as policemen, firemen, railwaymen and Hitler Youths seriously injured during air raids. Authority to award the badge was usually delegated to senior hospital doctors, who issued the relevant citations and bestowed the *EK2* on amputees and those most severely maimed. Military doctors could also promote selected wounded servicemen in their care, where return to active duty was unlikely and the promotion would serve as a morale-booster to other patients. It is interesting to note that Dr Goebbels referred in his diary entry dated 26

49. *From left to right:*
The 'Spanish' Wound Badge in Black;
The 1939 Wound Badge in Gold, by the Vienna Mint;
The 1939 Wound Badge in Silver, by the Vienna Mint;
The 1939 Wound Badge in Black, by Klein & Quenzer.

September 1943 to plans for a special *Total-Bombengeschädigten-Abzeichen*, to be awarded to those killed, wounded or made homeless as a result of Allied bombing. However, no such decoration was ever produced.

THE WOUND BADGE OF 20 JULY 1944

The rarest of all Nazi wound badges was the Wound Badge of 20 July 1944. It was awarded to staff officers and HQ aides who were present during the famous 'bomb plot' attempt on Hitler's life. All grades of the badge were made by the Juncker firm, in solid hallmarked silver, and bore the date *20 Juli 1944* and a facsimile of Hitler's signature on the obverse. It is important to note that the Wound Badge of 20 July 1944 was a personal gift from Hitler to those involved, and was presented in addition to, rather than instead of, the normal-pattern Wound Badge. It was intended to be a treasured one-off souvenir of a momentous historical event, and was never meant to be worn. Significantly, the elaborate award citation, while signed by Hitler, referred only to the relevant grade of 'the Wound Badge', not 'the Wound Badge of 20 July 1944'. *Generalfeldmarschall* Keitel and *Generaloberst* Jodl certainly did sport the distinctive 20 July badge on their tunics while in Hitler's presence thereafter, but photographs indicate that other recipients like

50. *The Wound Badge of 20 July, 1944.*

SS-Gruppenführer Fegelein continued to wear their regulation Wound Badges, not the 20 July version. Of the twenty-four people in the room when the bomb detonated, three (Berger, Brandt and Schmundt) were killed and only eight (Bodenschatz, Borgmann, Buhle, Hitler, Jodl, Scherff, von Puttkamer and Warlimont) injured. However, all twenty-four (except Hitler himself) received the Wound Badge of 20 July 1944, in a grade corresponding to any standard Wound Badge already held. No duplicates were issued. Presentation to the non-injured highlighted the purely commemorative nature of the badge.

War Badges

A uniquely German phenomenon, the war badge, or *Kriegsabzeichen*, had the effect of showing at a glance the degree to which any given soldier had combat experience. War badges of a sort were in existence in Germany prior to 1918, but after 1939 there was a real explosion in their creation, manufacture and distribution. By 1945 there were over forty different patterns for the *Wehrmacht*, and some of these were themselves divided into three classes, Bronze, Silver and Gold. Others were subdivided into grades by the inclusion of boxed numerals on the obverse of their designs. Though similar in appearance, war badges were distinct from qualification badges, which were given automatically on completion of specialist training. The war badge reflected participation in active service, rather than showing a particular skill which the wearer had mastered. Basically, the war badge consisted of an oval wreath of oak or laurel leaves enclosing a symbol representative of the branch of service concerned. The whole badge was normally surmounted by a stylised eagle and swastika, and different ranges of badges existed for all three services, the Army/*Waffen-SS*, the Navy and the *Luftwaffe*. Most war badges were worn permanently on the lower left breast pocket when in uniform, although the combat clasp, a senior form of war badge, was sported above the left pocket.

War badges could be solid or hollow-backed and were both die-struck and cast. The earliest awards were made from bronze, brass, nickel silver or Cupal (a lightweight but strong aluminium and copper sheeting), and were heavily plated in the appropriate colours. With new metal restrictions, 1942 saw the widespread use of greyish zinc-based alloys in their manufacture. Such badges were given a coloured lacquer, or were even painted, since plating would not adhere to the acidic zinc surface. The most common coating used in this connection was known as *Brennlack*, a lacquer containing powdered metal of an appropriate bronze, silver or gold colour. When the treated badge was baked in an oven, the lacquer was burned off leaving a thin metallic coating adhering to the surface of the award. If the oven heat had been too intense, this coating was left with a 'bubbled' appearance. Badges so treated soon reverted to their base slate-grey as the fragile coloured coating wore off, or was dissolved gradually by the acid in the metal. The standard of zinc alloys progressively declined, culminating in the poor-quality and malleable *Kriegsmetall*, or war metal, of 1944–5, which had a blue-grey hue. The term *Kriegsmetall* was one of the series of generic titles which saw certain common German words prefixed by the Nazis with *Kriegs* during wartime, to reflect the stoical and Spartan nature of the times. Others in the series included *Kriegsjahr* and *Kriegsorden*. *Kriegsmetall* therefore became symbolic of the adversity endured by the German people during the closing stages of the conflict.

War badges were usually struck from one piece of metal, but where two or more parts were involved these were riveted or soldered together. Some exceptionally rare examples were elevated for particularly distinguished recipients (normally holders of the Knight's Cross with Oakleaves) by being encrusted with small diamonds. These were constructed from hallmarked silver and were given as personal tokens of appreciation by the heads of the appropriate branches of the armed forces. Each war badge had a pin, hinge and catch on the reverse for securing to the tunic. These could be of two main types: a thin needle pin most often employed on Army and *Luftwaffe* badges; and a broad tapering pin bar which usually appeared on Navy examples and was always used on combat clasps. Either

pattern could be affixed vertically or horizontally to the badge. Naval specimens frequently had a 'top hook' in addition to the standard pin assembly, to keep the badge completely flush with the tunic pocket while working in the close confines of a ship. Less obtrusive embroidered or finely woven cloth versions of certain Navy and *Luftwaffe* badges were also permitted.

Conditions for the bestowal of a *Kriegsabzeichen* could differ enormously from badge to badge. Certain war badges were given in recognition of good conduct which did not merit the *KVK2*, while others could be given, in addition to the Wound Badge, for sustaining a wound while in action with the branch of service represented by the war badge concerned. Authority to award was delegated to regimental and battalion commanders, or their equivalents.

Army and Waffen-SS War Badges

THE CONDOR LEGION TANK BADGE

In September 1936 *Oberst* Wilhelm Ritter von Thoma, commander of the Condor Legion's *Panzergruppe* 'Drohne', a training unit, created a badge to be worn on the left breast pocket by his tank crews. It was at that stage simply a formation badge, with little or no official standing, and was produced locally by a firm in Spain. The design fea-

51. *The Condor Legion Tank Badge. This finely executed example in hollow brass, with an oxidised silver plating, is of the second pattern and was struck in Berlin during the spring of 1940.*

tured a large Prussian-style *totenkopf*, or death's head, over a Spanish tank, surrounded by oakleaves, and was in silver plate, although von Thoma had a badge made in solid gold for his own use. The *totenkopf* had been adopted by German *Panzer* forces in the First World War, hence its continued use in Spain. On 10 July 1939, after the successful conclusion of the Civil War, *Generaloberst* von Brauchitsch, Commander-in-Chief of the Army, gave his permission for the badge to be worn as a commemorative decoration by those who had served with the armoured units of the Condor Legion. An improved version of the award was struck in Berlin, and issued with appropriate certificates until mid-1940. Around 400 presentations were made. The Condor Legion Tank Badge continued to be worn by its surviving recipients throughout the Second World War, sometimes in conjunction with the later *Panzerkampfabzeichen*. At least one photograph exists showing both awards being sported simultaneously by an Army *Panzer* crewman who had also affixed large *SS*-pattern cap death's heads to both collar patches, thereby emphasising still further the prestigious *totenkopf* insignia.

THE ARMY PARATROOP BADGE

On 1 September 1937, the Army Paratroop Badge, or *Fallschirmschützenabzeichen des Heeres*, was created for award to Army paratroopers upon com-

52. *The Army Paratroop Badge.*

pletion of their training. It was therefore a qualification badge rather than a war badge, but is included here for the sake of overall completeness. To retain the Paratroop Badge, the recipient had to complete six jumps per year, thus demonstrating his continuing proficiency. When the Army parachute battalions transferred to the *Luftwaffe* on 1 January 1939, this aluminium award was cancelled, although holders could continue to wear it. The badge was resurrected in a zinc form in June 1943 for special forces men of the 15th (Parachute) Company, 'Brandenburg' Regiment, but it was seldom bestowed thereafter. It is worthy of note that the 1,000 or so qualified paratroopers of the *Waffen-SS* were trained by the Air Force and so received the *Luftwaffe* version of the paratroop badge, not the Army one.

THE INFANTRY ASSAULT BADGE

The Infantry Assault Badge, or *Infanterie-Sturmabzeichen*, was instituted on 20 December 1939 by von Brauchitsch to recognise front-line action on the part of infantrymen. It was awarded to all ranks in infantry and mountain infantry units who, as from 1 January 1940, took part in three assaults on three different days, armed only with hand-held weapons. It could also be given for counter-attacks, patrols which resulted in combat and the single-handed destruction of an enemy tank. Recommendations for award were made by company commanders, and the first two bestowals, symbolically to one enlisted man and one officer, *Oberleutnant* Wilhelm Körbel, were made by von Brauchitsch personally on 28 May 1940. From 1 June that year, the badge could be conferred in a bronze version upon members of motorised infantry formations. Hundreds of thousands had been distributed by the end of the war.

A rifle with fixed bayonet was chosen as the central feature of this decoration, for obvious reasons, and the simplicity of its design made the *Infanterie-Sturmabzeichen* something of a 'classic' among Third Reich awards. It is noteworthy that the badge was very similar in appearance to that worn on the Grade 5–8 Marksmanship Lanyard for tank crews, introduced on 19 December 1938 with a *Panzer* Mk I as the centrepiece. This has given rise

53. *From left to right:*
The Infantry Assault Badge;
The Tank Battle Badge, by Hermann Aurich;
The General Assault Badge, by Assmann & Söhne.

to speculation that the design of the Infantry Assault Badge may have been drawn up as early as 1938, with the original intention that it should be used on the Army's general Marksmanship Lanyard for non-tank crews.

THE TANK BATTLE BADGE

The Tank Battle Badge, or *Panzerkampfabzeichen*, was instituted by von Brauchitsch on 20 December 1939, with a *Panzer* Mk III as its central design. It was initially in silver only, for award to tank commanders, drivers, gunners and radio operators who took part in three armoured assaults on three separate days. From 1 June 1940, it was also given in a bronze version to *Panzergrenadiere* and associated medical personnel, and to armoured car crews.

On 22 June 1943, larger numbered Tank Battle Badges were introduced, since it had by then become apparent that the basic badge was insufficient to recognise the mounting number of actions that a *Panzer* crewman might have participated in. The new grades had one of the numerals '25', '50', '75' or '100' in a box at the base of the badge, to indicate participation in that number of assaults.

The following variants were duly authorised:

in silver for 25 actions
in silver for 50 actions
in silver for 75 actions
in silver for 100 actions
in silver for 200 actions (only one award known to
   have been made 'on paper')

in bronze for 25 actions
in bronze for 50 actions
in bronze for 75 actions
in bronze for 100 actions

Many *Panzer* crews soon qualified for these numbered badges by virtue of their involvement in the decisive Kursk offensive of July–August 1943, where 70 per cent of Germany's tanks on the eastern front were mustered and engaged the Soviets almost continuously over a seven-week period. Indeed, the numbered Tank Battle and General Assault Badges may have been created specifically as an incentive for Kursk participants, which would explain the lack of a numbered Infantry Assault Badge, as footsoldiers at Kursk were *Panzergrenadiere* rather than infantry proper. Eight out of ten *Panzer* crews were killed in action during the Second World War, so these badges were very hard-won.

It is interesting to note that Michael Wittmann,

who knocked out 138 enemy armoured vehicles and was the most successful tank commander of the war, was never photographed wearing a numbered *Panzerkampfabzeichen*. Even the pictures taken shortly before his death in August 1944 show him sporting the basic, unnumbered award. All photographs of the numbered versions being worn seem to date from September 1944 and later, which suggests that distribution of these badges, like their General Assault counterparts, did not take place until that time. Such a delay between the institution of a decoration and its actual manufacture and bestowal would not be unusual, particularly in wartime. The Silver version for 200 actions, while authorised very late in the war, was never actually produced.

THE GENERAL ASSAULT BADGE

On 1 June 1940, the *Sturmabzeichen*, or Assault Badge, usually called the General Assault Badge, was created for award to pioneer troops. It was later extended to other support personnel, including artillery, anti-tank and anti-aircraft crews. Criteria for award were the same as for the Infantry Assault Badge. The *Sturmabzeichen* comprised an eagle and swastika over a crossed bayonet and grenade, and was in silver only. On 22 June 1943, numbered General Assault Badges were introduced in the same manner and for the same reasons as the numbered Tank Battle Badges. The higher classes were slightly larger in size, with dark grey central features and silver or gold wreaths. They were made retroactive, with twenty-five actions being credited to those with fifteen months' front-line service. Again, actual manufacture and distribution of the numbered badges does not appear to have taken place until the autumn of 1944. Consequently, they were seldom awarded and were very highly prized.

THE ANTI-AIRCRAFT BADGE

The *Heeres-Flakabzeichen*, or Army Anti-Aircraft Badge, was instituted on 18 July 1941 for award to personnel of flak artillery units. It took the form of a *Wehrmacht* eagle surmounting an 88 mm gun, and was conferred on crews who had taken part in the downing of at least five enemy aircraft. Battery commanders received the badge when half of the men in their unit had been awarded it. The *Flakabzeichen* could be worn in conjunction with the General Assault Badge, which took precedence as it recognised the more dangerous business of attacking land targets.

THE TANK DESTRUCTION BADGE

The *Sonderabzeichen für das Niederkämpfen von Panzerkampfwagen durch Einzelkämpfer*, or Special Badge for the Single-Handed Destruction of a Tank, dated from 9 March 1942 and was made

54. *The Tank Battle Badge in Silver for 75 actions.*

55. *The General Assault Badge for 100 actions.*

56. *The Army Anti-Aircraft Badge.*

57. *The Tank Destruction Badge. It is interesting to note that the centrepiece of the award, a* Panzer *Mk IV, is incorrectly represented, having three upper wheels instead of four. The later Finnish version of this badge used a Russian T34 tank in its design, which may have been more appropriate.*

58. *Two highly decorated army infantry captains in relaxed mood, 1944. The officer on the left sports four Silver Tank Destruction Badges on his sleeve.*

retroactive to 22 June 1941. Worn on the upper right sleeve, the badge comprised a black *Panzer Mk IV* on a silver woven band with black edge stripes. It was given to those who knocked out an enemy tank or other armoured vehicle using only hand-held weapons, i.e. grenades, satchel charges, mines, *Panzerfauste* and the like, who had previously been recognised by an award of the Infantry Assault Badge or General Assault Badge. A badge was given each time a tank was destroyed, and on 18 December 1943 a gilt version, on a gold woven band, was instituted to signify the 'killing' of five tanks. Thus for three tanks destroyed, three silver emblems were worn. One gold badge meant five tanks destroyed, one gold and three silver signified eight tanks, and so on. On 15 April 1945, at Stadensen-Nettelkamp in northern Germany, *Oberleutnant* Friedrich Anding of the '*Grossdeutschland*' anti-tank battalion destroyed six British tanks and five armoured cars using *Panzerfauste*, thereby qualifying for two gold and one silver badges in a single day. He also won the Knight's Cross for this action. The most successful tank stalker in the *Wehrmacht* knocked out twenty-one tanks, and so wore four gold badges and one silver.

THE FRONT-LINE DRIVER BADGE

The Front-Line Driver Badge was instituted by Hitler on 23 October 1942 to recognise military drivers who maintained the upkeep and care of their vehicles under combat conditions. Worn on the left forearm, the award was made like a campaign shield and featured a steering wheel surrounded by a wreath of laurel leaves. It came in three grades, Bronze, Silver and Gold, with each successive class being presented as the qualifying conditions were met. Motorcycle messengers, for example, received the badge in Bronze for serving ninety combat days, in Silver for 180 combat days and in Gold for 270 combat days. Supply vehicle drivers had to serve 165, 330 and 495 combat days respectively, since they were in less danger. Combat days were defined as those when the driver came under enemy fire, was on particularly long assignments, encountered special road hazards or was subjected to uncommonly difficult weather conditions. The award

59. The Front-Line Driver Badge in Silver.

could be revoked if the recipient was later convicted of a driving offence or neglect of his vehicle.

THE CLOSE COMBAT CLASP

On 25 November 1942, at the height of the Battle of Stalingrad, Hitler created a new incentive for his footsoldiers in the form of the *Nahkampfspange* or Close Combat Clasp. This decoration comprised a small version of the *Sturmabzeichen* with a long spray of oakleaves and rays either side, and was worn 1 cm above the medal ribbon bar. It came in three grades, Bronze, Silver and Gold, for completion of fifteen, thirty and fifty close-combat days respectively. Combat days were reckoned as from 1 December 1942, and had to have involved actual hand-to-hand combat on foot, whether in attack or

defence. Company commanders were made responsible for recording such actions in their daily reports, and lists of participating soldiers were drawn up with a view to awarding the clasp. The following translation of a soldier's record is typical of those compiled for the fifteen actions required before bestowal of the Bronze decoration:

List of Close Combat Days

1.	4.2.43	Breakthrough at Schenschenkowo
2.	11.2.43	Breakthrough at Nowo-Wotalga
3.	13.2.43	Breakthrough at Paraskowaja
4.	14.2.43	Attack near Bereka
5.	15.2.43	Attack near Bereka
6.	7.3.43	Attack at Walki
7.	11.3.43	Attack at Charkow
8.	14.3.43	Attack at Charkow
9.	20.11.43	Fighting near Krakowtschina
10.	29.11.43	Fighting at Gerbarov
11.	4.1.44	Defence of Ossykowa
12.	27.7.44	Attack towards Verrieres
13.	19.8.44	Securing Aubry
14.	1.9.44	Breakthrough at la Chappelle
15.	22.12.44	Defence west of Stavelot

Qualification might therefore be built up over many months or even years on different battlefronts, taking account of absence from action because of wounds sustained and so on. Divisional commanders could authorise men severely wounded, with no opportunity to complete the requisite number of days, to be awarded the Close Combat Clasp in Bronze for ten combat days, in Silver for twenty days

60. The Close Combat Clasp.

and in Gold for forty days. Prisoners of war and those missing in action forfeited all right of claim to the clasp, although on at least one occasion an NCO received the Bronze grade following his escape from American captivity in November 1944. It must have been a significant feat, as the recipient, Hermann Drechsler of the 149th Grenadier Regiment, was also promoted to *Leutnant* and presented with the Honour Roll Clasp on account of the same escape.

The first awards of the Gold Clasp were made on 27 August 1944, when Hitler personally invested fourteen Army and *Waffen-SS* officers with it. Of those, two held the Knight's Cross and all wore the German Cross in Gold. Léon Degrelle, commander of the Belgian *SS* Brigade, was among this group and was given the Oakleaves at the same time as the Gold Clasp. By virtue of an order from Hitler dated 30 August 1944, all holders of the Close Combat Clasp in Silver were automatically to be awarded the Iron Cross 1st Class on account of their combat achievements, while future recipients of the Close Combat Clasp in Gold were also to be given the German Cross in Gold, if they did not already possess it. A total of 619 Gold Clasps were conferred by the end of the Second World War. Of these, Hitler presented fifty-three in ten separate ceremonies, while Himmler presented 106 and *General* Guderian thirteen. The remainder were bestowed at the front by senior divisional officers. Some recipients qualified for the Gold grade as early as mid-1943.

The Guerrilla Warfare Badge

The increasing ferocity of the behind-the-lines war against partisans in Yugoslavia, Russia, Poland, northern Italy, Greece and Albania necessitated the creation of a new decoration to reward those who had been engaged in it for a prolonged period. On 30 January 1944, Hitler instituted the *Banden-kampfabzeichen*, which translates literally as 'Bandit Battle Badge', but more accurately as Guerrilla Warfare Badge. It is generally known by collectors as the Anti-Partisan War Badge, which was the translation adopted in early English-language books on Third Reich insignia. Whilst it was open to members of all the German fighting ser-

vices and their foreign auxiliaries, the Guerrilla Warfare Badge was officially designated as a *Kampfabzeichen der Waffen-SS und Polizei*, or *Waffen-SS* and Police Battle Badge, and was the only war badge so described during the Third Reich. It was without doubt the hardest-won of all the war badges.

Award of the badge came under the auspices of *Reichsführer-SS* Heinrich Himmler, who had been made responsible for all anti-partisan operations in October 1942. Uniquely, Guerrilla Warfare Badge citations were made out in his name rather than that of Hitler. An order issued from Himmler's field headquarters on 1st February 1944 laid down the following:

1. The Guerrilla Warfare Badge is both a bravery and a merit decoration.
2. It is awarded in three grades, Bronze, Silver and Gold.
3. The Guerrilla Warfare Badge can be awarded to all officers, NCOs and men engaged with the German forces in counter-guerrilla operations.
4. The qualification for award is:
   (a) Bronze – 20 combat days for ground troops
   30 combat days for *Luftwaffe* crews
   (b) Silver – 50 combat days for ground troops
   75 combat days for *Luftwaffe* crews
   (c) Gold – 100 combat days for ground troops
   150 combat days for *Luftwaffe* crews

61.   *The Guerrilla Warfare Badge.*

5. For ground troops, a combat day is reckoned to be one during which they have taken part in close combat (man against man) with guerrillas. For *Luftwaffe* crews, a combat day is reckoned to be one during which they have been exposed to anti-aircraft fire from guerrilla forces. Being shot down counts as three combat days.

6. Combat days may be reckoned as from 1 January 1943.

7. The Guerrilla Warfare Badge supersedes the Close Combat Clasp for those engaged in the war against partisans.

8. It may be worn on the left breast of all *Wehrmacht*, Police, *SS* and *NSDAP* uniforms.

9. The badge is awarded with a citation.

10. Posthumous presentations of awards in respect of those who have qualified for them prior to being killed in action will be made to their next-of-kin.

Qualification for award was therefore very high, making the *Bandenkampfabzeichen* far more difficult to achieve than similar decorations like the Infantry Assault Badge. Even so, fair numbers of *SS* and police troops were eligible from the date of its inception, due to their long involvement in anti-partisan operations. For example, in late February 1944 *SS-Obersturmbannführer* Dr Oskar Dirlewanger requested delivery of 200 blank citations for the badge in Bronze, thirty in Silver and twenty in Gold so that he might prepare them for presentation to deserving soldiers of his 600-strong counter-guerrilla battalion.

Himmler quickly reserved the right to award the Gold badge personally, which is hardly surprising since it was the equivalent of winning the Close Combat Clasp in Gold (recognised by Hitler as the highest infantry decoration) twice! The *Völkischer Beobachter* of 21 February 1945 reported that 'The *Reichsführer-SS* yesterday presented the first Guerrilla Warfare Badges in Gold to four members of the *Waffen-SS* engaged in the fighting on the Adriatic Coast.' One of these recipients was *SS-Obersturmführer* Erich Kühbandner of the 24th *SS* Division, which had been raised specifically to combat partisans in the Carso and Julian Alps. While the badge was hard-won, however, Knight's Cross holder Hans Sturm, who was awarded the Bronze grade while serving with the army in Italy, stated after the war that he never wore it as he did not wish to be associated with the atrocities which it represented. Many of his comrades appear to have been like-minded, for it is hardly ever seen in wartime photographs depicting regular *Wehrmacht* personnel. The *Waffen-SS* and Police, on the other hand, held the Guerrilla Warfare Badge in high regard and displayed it proudly on every possible occasion, giving it precedence over all other war badges. They saw it as 'their badge', recognising their particular role in quelling rebellion behind the front lines.

62. SS-Obersturmführer *Erich Kühbandner as he appeared in the* Völkischer Beobachter *dated 21 February 1945. His newly presented Guerrilla Warfare Badge in Gold is displayed prominently for this publicity picture. It is noteworthy that Kühbandner, although a young man, held the* NSDAP *15-Year Service Decoration and the Honour Chevron of the Old Guard. Both of these were earned by virtue of his long association with the Hitler Youth.*

The design of the Guerrilla Warfare Badge was based on that of the insignia of the Silesian *Freikorps* of 1919 and featured a wreath of oak-leaves enclosing a sword with sunwheel swastika (representing the German and auxiliary forces) plunging into a hydra (the partisans). The badge has always been described in previous literature on the subject as featuring a nest of snakes, but that is not the case. Cursory examination confirms that the creature depicted is, in fact, a hydra with a single tail and five heads. The hydra was a fabulous and terrifying multi-headed sea serpent of Greek mythology, which was renowned as being almost impossible to destroy since its heads grew quickly back again if they were cut off. The parallel with the partisan forces, which sprang up vigorously time and time again, is obvious. At the sword's point was a death's head, which was doubly appropriate since it symbolised both the *SS* involvement and the deadly nature of the struggle which was being carried on. The absence of the usual armed-forces-pattern eagle and swastika from the design again emphasised the *SS* rather than *Wehrmacht* origins of the award.

It has been suggested that Himmler ordered the manufacture of ten Guerrilla Warfare Badges in gold-plated hallmarked silver with diamond-encrusted swastikas for presentation as personal gifts to those soldiers who won the Knight's Cross with Oakleaves while fighting partisans. However, no proof of the actual existence of such badges has come to light.

THE BALLOON OBSERVER BADGE

Large barrage balloons were widely used by the German Army for artillery-spotting on the Eastern front, where air opposition was not so effective as in the West. As the war progressed, however, this form of observation became ever more dangerous as the *Luftwaffe* lost its aerial supremacy, and on 8 July 1944 a new war badge, the *Ballonbeobachterabzeichen*, was instituted to recognise that fact. The decoration featured a balloon surmounted by a *Wehrmacht* eagle and was presented on a points basis, in Bronze for twenty points, Silver for forty-five points and Gold for seventy-five points. Points were based on the difficulty of the events involved with, for example, a forced parachute

63. *Approved design of the Balloon Observer Badge.*

jump from a balloon earning the observer ten points. The first Balloon Observer Badge in Bronze was bestowed on 12 December 1944 to *Oberwachtmeister* Willibald Sellner of 3rd Company, 12th Motorised Observation Battalion. However, it is not known whether the badge itself was ever presented with the surviving citation. In any event, no authenticated wartime photograph of this award being worn is known to exist. It may, in fact, never have been manufactured before the end of hostilities.

THE SNIPER BADGE

By mid-1944, Germany was well and truly on the defensive, and the time had come to reward those manning static positions which were subject to regular and intensive attack. The most effective of such personnel were snipers, who concealed themselves in trees, haystacks and the like 'picking off' enemy officers and men at will and creating a high degree of fear amongst opposing front-line troops.

On 20 August 1944, the *Scharfschützenabzeichen* was instituted to recognise the achievements of these specialists. The badge, which superseded an earlier Sniper Commendation Certificate, took the form of a cloth oval bearing an eagle's head, and was to be worn on the right cuff. It came in three grades, with a silver border for the 2nd Grade and a gold border for the 1st. Given the late stage in the war, it is highly unlikely that the Sniper Badge was distrib-

64. *The Sniper Badge in Gold.*

uted in significant numbers. None has been pho-tographed in wear.

The following excerpt from *Wehrmacht* Daily Order No. 11 of 4 November 1944 recommends appropriate levels of recognition to be given in respect of confirmed 'kills' by Army and *Waffen-SS* snipers, or by *Volkssturm* sharpshooters engaged in the static defence of the Reich. It is interesting not only from the point of view of the Sniper Badge but also because it clearly illustrates the integration of war badges with the Iron Cross and other awards:

No. of 'Kills'	Recognition/Awards
10	Iron Cross 2nd Class, *plus* mention in divisional orders, *plus* 7 days' leave
20	Sniper Badge 3rd Grade
30	Iron Cross 1st Class, *plus* mention in corps orders, *plus* 14 days' leave
40	Sniper Badge 2nd Grade
50	Honour Roll Clasp, *plus* mention in army orders, *plus* 21 days' leave
60	Sniper Badge 1st Grade
75	German Cross in Gold
100	Knight's Cross of the Iron Cross

During the winter of 1944–5, the periods of leave allocated were probably much more welcome than the decorations they accompanied!

Navy War Badges

THE U-BOAT WAR BADGE

The *U-Boots Kriegsabzeichen* was instituted on 13 October 1939, and was therefore the first war badge to be created during the Second World War. It fea-tured a Type VII submarine and was given to U-boat crews who completed two operational trips, or were wounded in battle. Over 80 per cent of U-boat personnel ultimately died in action, so the badge was very highly prized. A version in gilded silver with a diamond-encrusted swastika was presented by *Grossadmiral* Dönitz as a personal gift to his twenty-nine most successful submarine comman-ders, each of whom held at least the Knight's Cross with Oakleaves.

THE DESTROYER WAR BADGE

The *Zestörer Kriegsabzeichen* was created on 4 June 1940 exclusively for destroyer crews who had served at the Battle of Narvik. The following October, eligibility was extended to personnel on other destroyers and torpedo boats, and the badge could thereafter be awarded for participation in three engagements with the enemy, or for twelve operational patrols. It could also be given for being wounded, for serving on a ship sunk in action, or for taking part in special or successful operations. The central design of the award featured the Z21 *Wilhelm Heidkamp*, a 1936-class vessel com-manded by Knight's Cross holder *Korvetten-kapitän* Erdmenger and sunk at Narvik. An interesting recipient of this award was Karl Krause, Hitler's personal *SS* orderly, who served with the Navy on a destroyer in Norway. As a later *Waffen-SS Panzer* officer, he was the only man to wear the *Narvikschild* in Gold and the Destroyer War Badge with the black *SS* tank uniform.

THE MINESWEEPER WAR BADGE

The full title of this award was the War Badge for Minesweepers, Submarine-Hunters and Escort Vessels (*das Kriegsabzeichen für Minensuch-, U-Boots-Jagd-, und Sicherungsverbände*). Autho-rised on 31 August 1940, it was again given for par-ticipation in three operational sorties and could be presented for a lesser number if the man concerned

65. *Navy war badges.*
From left to right, top to bottom:
The U-Boat War Badge, by Karneth & Söhne;
The Destroyer War Badge, by Josef Feix;
The Minesweeper War Badge;
The Blockade-Breaker Badge, by Schwerin & Sohn;
The Auxiliary Cruiser War Badge, by Friedrich Orth;
The High Seas Fleet War Badge, by Schwerin & Sohn.

had been wounded, the ship sunk or the mission particularly successful. The badge could also be awarded for continued excellence in performance of duty over a six-month period, for especially hazardous duty in a mined area, or for completing twenty-five days of escort duty. The central feature of the award, an exploding water column, was inspired by a propaganda photograph which

appeared in the military publication *Fahrten und Flüge gegen England* during the summer of 1940.

THE BLOCKADE-BREAKER BADGE

The *Abzeichen für Blockadebrecher* dated from 1 April 1941 and was the only war badge recognising the efforts of primarily civilian personnel. It was given to crews of merchant navy vessels who:

- successfully broke through an enemy blockade
- sank an enemy ship
- scuttled their ship to avoid it falling into enemy hands
- survived being sunk by the enemy
- were wounded in action

The decoration featured a merchant ship breaking

66. Admiral *Oskar Kummetz wearing the High Seas Fleet War Badge below his 1914 Iron Cross 1st Class.*

67. *The Auxiliary Cruiser War Badge with Diamonds was bestowed no more than four times. This is the only known surviving example.*

shipping. The most successful of these were the *Atlantis*, *Komet*, *Kormoran*, *Michel*, *Orion*, *Pinguin*, *Stier*, *Thor* and *Widder*, all of which had been sunk by 1943.

The *Kriegsabzeichen für Hilfskreuzer* was created on 24 April 1941, and centred upon a Viking longship, the archetypal surface raider, on top of a globe. It was awarded for participation in a single long-distance voyage, or for being wounded. A version in gilded '900' silver with diamonds in the swastika was presented at least once, to Bernhard Rogge, Captain of the *Atlantis*, which sank twenty-five Allied ships. Rogge won the Knight's Cross with Oakleaves and was the most celebrated of all the auxiliary cruiser commanders. It is unclear whether the other three auxiliary cruiser captains who held the Oakleaves, Kaehler, Krüder and von Ruckteschell, also received the diamond-studded badge.

THE HIGH SEAS FLEET WAR BADGE

The *Flottenkriegsabzeichen* was instituted on 30 April 1941 to recognise the naval actions of German battleships and cruisers in the war against Great

through chains, and was presented in the name of the Reich Commissioner for Sea Travel, Karl Kaufmann, who was also *Gauleiter* of Hamburg and an *SS-Obergruppenführer*. It is interesting to note that during the 1920s, Kaufmann was expelled from the Nazi Party for wearing an Iron Cross to which he was not entitled!

THE AUXILIARY CRUISER WAR BADGE

This badge was also given to those serving on merchant vessels, but of an entirely different sort. Auxiliary cruisers were merchant ships crewed and armed by the Navy, which acted under the guise of cargo vessels and harassed undefended Allied

Britain. It was presented for twelve weeks' active service at sea, but could be given for a lesser period if the man concerned had been wounded or the ship sunk through enemy action. The badge was also awarded for leadership, or for participation in particularly successful naval engagements such as the sinking of HMS *Rawalpindi* and HMS *Hood*. All crew members of the *Scharnhorst* and *Gneisenau* received the badge, in view of the operational effectiveness of these vessels. Similarly, every sailor who was present on the *Tirpitz* when it was bombed by the British in Tromsö fjord on 12 November 1944 automatically qualified for the award.

THE E-BOAT WAR BADGE

During the war, the Allies referred to German torpedo boats as 'E-Boats' or 'enemy boats', and this term has now become the standard one used. In fact, the correct abbreviation so far as the Germans were concerned was *S-Boot* (for *Schnellboot*, or 'speed boat'). E-boat crews originally received the Destroyer War Badge but in 1941 the E-boat offen-

68. *The E-Boat War Badge, 1st pattern. The design of the replacement version introduced in January 1943 was basically the same, but depicted a longer vessel, which cut across the oakleaf wreath, and an enlarged eagle and swastika emblem.*

sive was considerably stepped up and on 30 May of that year the *Schnellboot Kriegsabzeichen* was instituted for torpedo-boat personnel. As usual, it was given for twelve sorties, being wounded, being sunk or participating in successful missions. In January 1943, the design of the badge was altered to incorporate the new E-boat recently brought into service with the *Kriegsmarine*. This design change of a war badge was unique.

A special grade of the E-boat War Badge, in hall-marked silver with a diamond-encrusted swastika, was presented by Dönitz to the following torpedo boat captains, each of whom held the Knight's Cross with Oakleaves:

Korvettenkapitän Georg Christiansen
Korvettenkapitän Klaus Feldt
Korvettenkapitän Friedrich Kemnade
Korvettenkapitän Bernd Klug
Kapitänleutnant Götz Freiherr von Mirbach
Kapitän zur See Rudolf Petersen
Kapitänleutnant Werner Töniges
Oberleutnant zur See Siegfried Wuppermann

It is interesting to note that von Mirbach attained his diamond-studded badge as commander of the E-boat flotilla which engaged and sank a number of US landing craft taking part in a practice 'dummy run' for D-Day off the south coast of England in April 1944. Over 900 American soldiers lost their lives in this episode, the so-called 'Battle of Slapton Sands', which remained a well-kept secret until the early 1980s.

THE COASTAL ARTILLERY WAR BADGE

The coastal artillery was composed of land-based naval personnel responsible for coastal defence and anti-aircraft batteries at *Kriegsmarine* bases. They received their own war badge, the *Kriegsabzeichen für die Marineartillerie*, on 24 June 1941. It was awarded on a points basis, like the other flak badges, with eight points being the qualifying level. Two points were given for each aircraft shot down by a battery, with one point being given if the victory was gained in conjunction with another battery. Searchlight and sound locator crews got half a point for each first detection. The badge could also be awarded for a single act of merit

69. *The Coastal Artillery War Badge, by C.E. Juncker.*

insufficient to warrant the *KVK2*, or posthumously for being killed in action.

THE U-BOAT COMBAT CLASP

A further award for U-boat crews was instituted on 15 May 1944. It took the form of a small U-boat War Badge with a spray of oakleaves on either side, and was worn above the left breast pocket. The *U-Boots Frontspange* was initially only in Bronze, and was given for long and continuous active service on submarines. Recommendations for award varied according to numbers of sorties, demonstrated personal bravery, risks taken and so on, and each bestowal had to be personally approved by Dönitz. On 24 November 1944, a higher grade in silver was authorised, to recognise even greater achievements. Citations for the Silver Clasp were normally signed by Admiral von Friedeburg, commander of the U-boat fleet.

70. *The U-Boat Combat Clasp, by Schwerin & Sohn.*

Luftwaffe *Qualification and War Badges*

The *Luftwaffe* utilised a number of badges which recognised qualifications rather than participation in active service. These were worn in the same way as war badges so, for the sake of consistency, they have been grouped together in this section.

THE AIRCREW BADGE

The *Fliegerschaftsabzeichen* was instituted on 19 January 1935, and comprised an oval horizontal oak and laurel wreath enclosing a flying eagle clutching a swastika. It was worn by all aircrew which, in effect, meant pilots and observers only since at that time the *Luftwaffe* was not permitted to have bombers and the largest aircraft in use were two-man biplanes. The badge was withdrawn early in 1936, so was never worn during the Second World War.

THE PILOT BADGE

At the beginning of 1936, Hitler announced the expansion and re-equipping of the *Luftwaffe* in direct contravention of the Treaty of Versailles. With new and larger types of aircraft, there was a requirement for a range of qualification badges to properly recognise the different crew skills involved. The Pilot Badge, or *Flugzeugführerabzeichen*, was instituted on 26 March 1936 and was similar in appearance to the Aircrew Badge, but with a vertical silver wreath enclosing a dark grey eagle and swastika. It was presented with the military pilot's licence on completion of flying training.

71. *The short-lived Aircrew Badge was the rarest of all* Luftwaffe *qualification awards, and was seldom seen being worn. Its design clearly influenced that of the later Pilot Badge.*

72. Luftwaffe *qualification badges.*
From left to right, top to bottom:
The Pilot Badge;
The Observer Badge;
The Combined Pilot-Observer Badge
(Göring wore a personalised version of
this award with the wreath in '585' gold
and the eagle in '800' silver);
The Retired Aircrew Badge;
The Glider Pilot Badge.

THE OBSERVER BADGE

Again instituted on 26 March 1936, the *Beobachterabzeichen* was conferred on observers, navigators and bomb-aimers after completion of two months' service with a non-operational squadron, or after five combat sorties. It could be awarded after only one mission if the man concerned had been wounded. The badge featured a large eagle alighting on a swastika.

THE COMBINED PILOT-OBSERVER BADGE

The *Gemeinsames Flugzeugführer- und Beobachterabzeichen* was created on 26 March 1936 and was identical to the Pilot Badge, except that the wreath was gold and the eagle silver. To some extent, it was a direct replacement for the Aircrew Badge, since it was awarded to those who had held both a pilot's and an observer's certificate for at least one year. A version of this award in solid gold and encrusted with diamonds was used by Göring as a personal decoration which he bestowed on particularly successful pilots and also on foreign dignitaries and political personalities. A unique dual presentation of diamond-studded badges was made

73. Luftwaffe *ace Adolf Galland wearing the Combined Pilot-Observer Badge with Diamonds presented to him by* Reichsmarschall *Göring on 17 August, 1940.*

to the test pilot Hanna Reitsch. When she became the first female to win the Iron Cross 2nd Class in March 1941, Göring acknowledged her achievement by giving her a miniature brooch-sized version of the Combined Pilot-Observer Badge in Gold with Diamonds. He later awarded her the full-sized badge, in yellow and white gold with 104 diamonds, on the occasion of her winning the Iron Cross 1st Class in September 1942. It is noteworthy that in 1944–5, *Oberst* Rudel wore the standard Pilot Badge and the Pilot-Observer Badge with Diamonds simultaneously. Clearly, the latter did not supersede the former.

THE RADIO OPERATOR BADGE
This badge had as its central design a flying eagle clutching lightning bolts in its talons. Also instituted on 26 March 1936, it was intended for radio operators, air gunners and flight engineers, and had the same award criteria as the Observer Badge.

THE RETIRED AIRCREW BADGE
The *Flieger Erinnerungsabzeichen* was authorised on 26 March 1936 for wear by personnel who had been honourably discharged from flying duties. First World War veterans were required to have served for at least four years as aircrew in order to qualify, while others had to have served a minimum of fifteen years, although this could be reduced if the man concerned had been 'grounded' due to injuries sustained in a flying accident. This award recognised flyers who, because of ill health, advanc-

ing age and the like were no longer permitted to go up in an aircraft and were transferred to administrative or other non-combatant duties. The badge may have been cancelled shortly after its introduction, for it was very seldom bestowed. It featured an eagle perched on a rock.

THE PARATROOP BADGE
The *Fallschirmschützenabzeichen der Luftwaffe* was instituted on 5 November 1936 for Air Force (and, later, *Waffen-SS*) paratroops who successfully completed six parachute training jumps and other required tests. In order to retain the badge, the holder usually had to requalify each year. However, under the terms of an order dated 2 May 1944, *Luftwaffe* administrators, medical and legal personnel qualified for the award on making a single combat jump, and could continue to wear it thereafter. The badge featured a gold diving eagle in a dark grey wreath. It is interesting to note that the first man to qualify for the badge, *Major* Bruno Bräuer, received his jump certificate, serial no. 1, as early as 4 July 1936. He was subsequently referred to by his men as 'Paratrooper No. 1'. During the last year of the war, the badge was distributed only

74. Luftwaffe *qualification and war badges.*
From left to right:
The Radio Operator Badge, by Imme & Sohn;
The Paratroop Badge;
The Flak Battle Badge, by Gustav Brehmer;
The Ground Assault Badge.

in its embroidered cloth form for reasons of practicality and economy, with accompanying citations making specific reference to the *Fallschirmschützenabzeichen in Stoff*.

THE GLIDER PILOT BADGE

Instituted on 16 December 1940, the *Segelflugzeug-führerabzeichen* comprised a black soaring eagle within a silver oakleaf wreath, and was presented with the military glider pilot's licence on completion of flying training.

THE FLAK BATTLE BADGE

The *Flak-Kampfabzeichen der Luftwaffe* was instituted on 10 January 1941 and comprised an 88 mm gun surmounted by an Air Force eagle. The badge was awarded on a points basis, with sixteen points being the prerequisite. Four points were given to flak battery members for each aircraft shot down, or two points if it was shot down in co-operation with other batteries. Searchlight and sound locator crews received one point for each first detection. As the war progressed, the requirements were modified, so that the badge could be conferred after three actions if at least one aircraft was downed, or after five actions if no aircraft was shot down. It could also be given for a single act of bravery or merit which did not meet the criteria for the *EK2* or *KVK2*. Battery commanders received the badge when at least half of the personnel under their command had won it. The Flak Battle Badge could also initially be given for participation in three engagements against land or sea targets, but following the institution of the *Luftwaffe* Ground Assault Badge the *Flak-Kampfabzeichen* was awarded only for anti-aircraft actions.

THE GROUND ASSAULT BADGE

The *Luftwaffe* encompassed a very large number of ground combat formations, notably the 'Hermann Göring' *Panzer* Division, twenty-two field divisions of infantry and, of course, paratroop battalions. Personnel of these units were originally made eligible for the Infantry Assault Badge, the General Assault Badge and the Tank Battle Badge of the Army, but on 31 March 1942 they received their own assault badge, the *Erdkampfabzeichen der*

Luftwaffe. The emotive design featured a thunder cloud with a large lightning bolt striking the ground. The badge was awarded for participating in three ground assaults on different days, and men who already held the Army badges in respect of such deeds were obliged to exchange them for the new *Luftwaffe* award.

THE AIR GUNNER BADGE

On 22 June 1942, a badge identical to the Radio Operator Badge, but without the lightning bolts, was created for air gunners, flight engineers and aircrew meteorologists who were not qualified radio operators. It had the same award criteria as the Observer Badge. On 25 April 1944, a version of the Air Gunner Badge with the colours reversed, i.e. with a black wreath and silver eagle, was authorised for air gunners who had taken part in at least ten operations, but who did not have the air gunnery certificate. This recognised the efforts of ground crew and others pressed into service as *ad hoc* air gunners during emergency situations.

THE OPERATIONAL FLYING CLASP

The *Frontflugspange* recognised service with front-line *Luftwaffe* squadrons, and was instituted on 30 January 1941. The clasp comprised a spray of oak-leaves either side of a symbol representative of the type of squadron involved, and was worn above the left breast pocket. It came in three grades, Bronze for twenty operational flights, Silver for sixty and Gold for 110.

Initially, three different clasps were authorised:

- for fighters, with a winged arrow pointing upwards
- for bombers, with a winged bomb pointing downwards
- for reconnaissance, air-sea rescue and meteorological squadrons, featuring an eagle's head with a large eye

On 19 November 1941, a new variant was created for transport and glider squadrons, and featured a flying eagle. On 13 May 1942, a fifth type was authorised for long-range fighters and air-to-ground support squadrons, and had the winged arrow pointing downwards.

A series of pendants, comprising gold stars with

75. *Operational Flying Clasps.*
From top to bottom:
In Gold, for Short-Range Fighter crews;
In Silver, for Long-Range Fighter crews;
In Bronze, for Bomber crews;
In Silver, for Reconnaissance, Air-Sea Rescue and Meteorological crews;
In Gold, with 500 mission pendant, for Transport and Glider crews.

laurel leaves either side, was introduced on 26 June 1942. These were suspended beneath the central part of the Gold clasp and signified the following:

- 250 missions for reconnaissance and night-fighter crews
- 300 missions for bomber, air-sea rescue and meteorological crews
- 400 missions for divebomber, long-range day-fighter and air-to-ground support crews
- 500 missions for fighter and transport crews

The variance in these gradings was intended to reflect the level of danger faced by the crews concerned.

On 14 August 1942, the central wreaths of fighter clasps were blackened to denote service with night fighters. A sixth form of the *Frontflugspange*, with crossed swords as the centrepiece, was authorised on 12 April 1944 for air-to-ground support squadrons. This came a few days after *Oberst* Rudel, the famed tank-busting Stuka pilot, had received the Diamonds to the Knight's Cross for completing over 1,800 successful sorties on the eastern front. His achievement no doubt prompted the institution of the new clasp. Air-to-ground support crews previously in receipt of the long-range fighter clasp were obliged to exchange it for the new type.

On 29 April 1944, the star pendants were replaced by boxed numerals rising in increments of 100. These ranged from 200 to 2,000, the latter being a special diamond-encrusted gold and platinum version given to Rudel upon completion of his 2,000th combat mission. Werner Mölders had also

76. *The Operational Flying Clasp for Transport and Glider crews.*

77.   *The highest awards won by* Oberst *Hans-Ulrich Rudel, including no fewer than five diamond-encrusted pieces. Of particular note are: the Golden Oakleaves, Swords and Diamonds to the Knight's Cross (centre); the Combined Pilot-Observer Badge with Diamonds (lower left); and the Operational Flying Clasp in Gold and Diamonds with 2,000 mission pendant for Air-to-Ground Support crews (bottom).*

been presented with a diamond-studded fighter clasp prior to his death in an air accident on 21 November 1941, although in his case the bejewelled badge was purely a personal gift from Göring, in recognition of Mölders's status at that time as the most highly decorated man in the *Wehrmacht*.

An operational flight was deemed to be one which penetrated enemy territory to a distance of at least 30 km, or one during which contact was made with the enemy in the air. Any flight which lasted more than four hours counted as double. Operational flights with different types of squadron could be added together towards the award of a clasp. Aircrew kept logbooks, which were checked and certified, and were automatically awarded the clasp or pendant by their unit commanding officer when the designated number of operational flights was reached.

The history of this decoration is particularly interesting when viewed against that of the European air war as a whole. When the clasp was first introduced, the Battle of Britain was at its height and tactically the most important *Luftwaffe* squadrons were day-fighters and bombers. As the Allied air offensive against Germany intensified in 1942, night-fighters became crucial to the strategic defence of the Reich, while air-to-ground support on the Russian front was vital after mid-1943 to stem the mass tank and infantry assaults increasingly being launched against *Wehrmacht* positions. By 1944-5, the few *Luftwaffe* pilots and aircrew left flying were airborne virtually around the clock, typically taking part in several combat missions daily. It is therefore evident that the development of the Operational Flying Clasp clearly reflected Germany's changing fortunes in the air war.

Projected Decorations

A number of Third Reich military awards were approved and designed but never officially manu-factured or distributed. Most of these were created as morale boosters during the last months of the war, and existed on paper only since there was insufficient time or opportunity for their produc-tion. They have been extensively faked since 1945.

THE 1939–40 AND 1939–41 CAMPAIGN MEDALS
Commemorative campaign medals for the battles of 1939–40 and 1939–41 were planned, in bronze for combatants and iron for non-combatants, but were never issued. Trial strikes of the proposed medals were made by the Frankfurt firm of E. Ferdinand Wiedmann, and featured the *Wehrmacht* eagle, an Iron Cross, dates and the legend *Den Kämpfern für die Deutsche Freiheit* ('To the fighters for German

a　　　b　　　　c　　　　d

e

f

78. *Designs of Projected Decorations.*
(a) The 1939–40 Campaign Medal, officially approved but never issued;
(b) The Stalingrad Shield, considered but never sanctioned;
(c) The Warsaw Shield, officially approved but not produced;
(d) The Lorient Shield, never officially approved;
(e) The 'Metz 1944' Cuff Title, officially approved and probably embroidered in small quantities by the recipients themselves;
(f) The Aircraft Destruction Badge, approved but not manufactured.

freedom'). The intention of these awards was to recognise those who had participated in the conquest of Poland, western Europe, the Balkans and Russia. By the end of 1941, however, it was clear that the distribution of such 'victory medals' would have been premature, and their official institution was postponed, then shelved completely.

THE STALINGRAD SHIELD

Hitler seriously considered a shield for presentation as an incentive to those who were encircled at Stalingrad on the Volga between November 1942 and January 1943. Several designs were drawn up, including one by *Generalfeldmarschall* Paulus featuring the city's famous granary silo and the legend *Stalingrad – Wolga*. However, the ultimate crushing defeat of Paulus's 6th Army was a bitter blow and Germany's first major setback of the war, and the idea of a commemorative campaign shield was immediately shelved. As a result, the *Stalingradschild* never progressed beyond the drawing board, although a small so-called 'Stalingrad Cross' was authorised on 23 March 1944 for wear on the shoulder straps as a battle honour by members of the *Grenadier* Regiment '*Hoch- und Deutschmeister*'.

THE FRONT CROSS

In the 10 July 1943 edition of *Das Neueste*, the newspaper of the 2nd *Panzer* Army, it was announced that Hitler intended to institute a decoration called the *Frontkreuz*, or Front Cross, to recognise one year's front-line service. To that end, it was reported, a design competition had been organised inviting suggestions and sketches from the troops themselves. This information was doubtless received with some excitement, as the war artists Krause and Schlimmer, who were also combat soldiers, had achieved considerable publicity the previous year by virtue of having designed the *Ostmedaille* and Cholm Shield respectively. Various designs were duly submitted, but the whole concept fell through and the award was never sanctioned or produced. It is possible that this entire exercise was nothing more than a propaganda stunt, to keep up the morale of combat troops at the start of the Kursk offensive.

79. *On 10 July 1943, Leutnant Wilhelm Dempewolf, then serving on the staff of the 252nd Artillery Regiment, submitted this proposed design for a 'Front Cross'. It never progressed beyond the drawing board.*

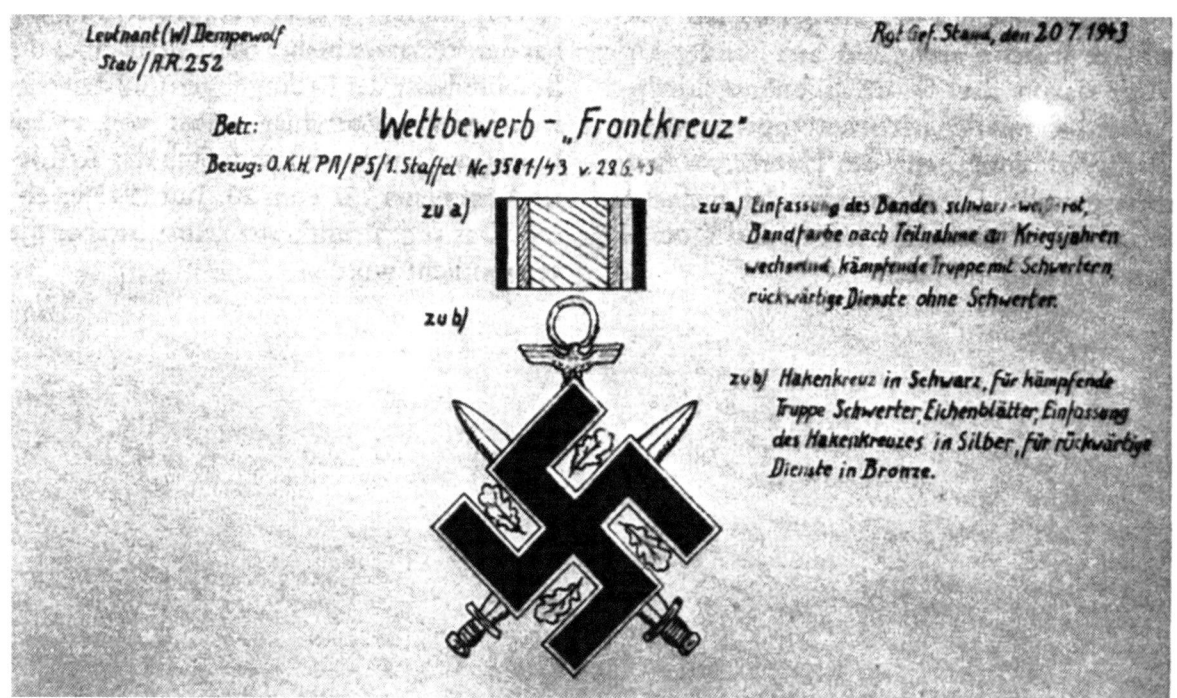

THE DECORATION FOR ETHNIC GERMANS

On 22 July 1943, *SS-Obergruppenführer* Werner Lorenz suggested in a report to Himmler that a *Volksdeutsche Opferkreuz* should be instituted to reward ethnic Germans who had been persecuted under Czech, Polish and other foreign rule before the war, or who had distinguished themselves in the cause of furthering Germanism abroad. Potential recipients included some 185,000 *Volksdeutsche* from all over Europe who had volunteered for service with the *Waffen-SS*. Himmler indicated that he would give due consideration to this suggestion when hostilities ceased. Consequently, nothing more was heard of the idea.

THE *SS* AUXILIARY CLASP

On 28 July 1943 a silver clasp in the form of *SS* runes superimposed over six oakleaves bearing the word *Helfen*, or 'Assistance', was instituted by Himmler as a proficiency badge for female *SS* auxiliaries. Women fulfilled various communications and other roles for the *SS*, particularly the *Waffen-SS*, during the war, acting as radio operators, telephonists and typists. They also staffed *SS* maternity homes, ran courses for the *Bund Deutscher Mädel* (*BDM*) and guarded female prisoners. The new decoration, called the *Silberspange der SS Helferinnen*, was to be open only to the minority of female assistants who met the rigorous selection criteria which entitled them to full *SS* membership, and who had served in the *SS* for at least two years. However, production may have been postponed pending the end of hostilities, for the clasp was apparently never manufactured. No photographs of it being worn have ever come to light, and no coverage was given to it in the *SS* newspaper *Das Schwarze Korps*. Evidence indicates that female *SS* auxiliaries deserving of special recognition invariably received the War Merit Cross 2nd Class.

THE MEMEL SHIELD

This shield was for some time rumoured to have been founded by *Generalleutnant* Dr Karl Mauss, commander of the 7th *Panzer* Division, when

80.   Designs of Projected Decorations.
From top to bottom:
The SS *Auxiliary Clasp, officially approved but never manufactured;*
The Luftwaffe *Close Combat Clasp, approved but not distributed;*
The Dunkirk Shield, never officially approved;
The Balkan Shield, approved but not produced.

81. Alleged design of the Memel Shield.

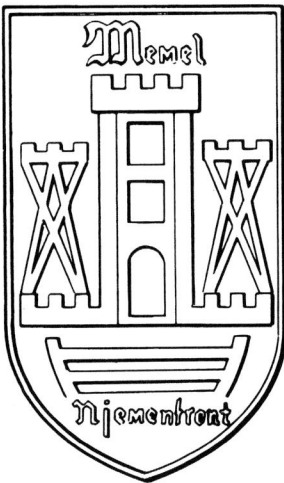

Memel was under siege by the Russians at the beginning of October 1944. However, when questioned about the alleged shield after the war, Mauss denied all knowledge of it. The Russian General Bagramyan captured the city after an operation lasting only two days (8–10 October), and the institution of a commemorative shield for so short an action would have been highly unlikely. Consequently, it is extremely improbable that any such shield was ever approved or made during the Third Reich.

THE METZ 1944 CUFF TITLE

A cuff title was instituted on 24 October 1944 to recognise the achievements of a battle group under *Generalmajor* Joachim von Siegroth which, between September and November that year, held the besieged city of Metz and thus brought to a halt the sweeping advance towards Germany of Patton's US 3rd Army. The band was to take the form of a black base with silver-grey edging and the legend 'Metz 1944', but it was never officially placed into production. A very small number of awards were made 'on paper' and von Siegroth apparently had at least one example of the cuff title custom-made for his own uniform. A few other survivors may have done likewise, but the vast majority of potential recipients were either killed in action or captured by the Americans. The psychological importance of this engagement, which was fought on the very frontier of Germany, can be gauged by the fact that *Gauleiter* Josef Bürckel, who held overall military responsibility in the area, was selected to become the first living recipient of the German Order at the height of the battle.

THE *LUFTWAFFE* TANK BATTLE BADGE

On 3 November 1944, the *Panzerkampfabzeichen der Luftwaffe* was instituted for award to tank crews and grenadiers of the 'Hermann Göring' *Panzerkorps*. It was in two types, silver and black, analogous to the silver and bronze Tank Battle Badges of the Army. Criteria for award were identical to those of the Army badges, and on 10 November 1944 numbered versions were authorised for twenty-five, fifty, seventy-five and 100 actions. The *Luftwaffe* Tank Battle Badge never saw production during the war, however, and long-serving Air Force tank crews were obliged to continue wearing their Army war badges. Nevertheless, several presentations were made 'on paper' only, the following translation of a surviving typed memorandum testifying to the fact:

> To *Unteroffizier* Gustav Kretschmer, 11th Company, 3rd *Fallschirmpanzer Grenadier* Regiment 'Hermann Göring'. In the name of the Supreme Commander of the *Luftwaffe*, I award you the *Luftwaffe* Tank Battle Badge with effect from 17 February 1945. To save paper and because of the ongoing combat situation, no formal certificate will be issued for the award. However, this document is valid in place of the certificate. I offer you my most sincere congratulations on the award.

The memorandum was signed by Kretschmer's company commander.

THE *LUFTWAFFE* CLOSE COMBAT CLASP

Dating from 3 November 1944, the *Nahkampfspange der Luftwaffe* was instituted to reward air force combat troops for participation in lengthy periods of hand-to-hand fighting. The clasp came in bronze, silver and gold and was similar in design to the Operational Flying Clasp with an eagle, bayonet and grenade as the centrepiece. Criteria for award were identical to those of the army

Nahkampfspange, to which *Luftwaffe* ground personnel had hitherto been entitled. The *Luftwaffe* Close Combat Clasp, although again awarded in small numbers 'on paper', never saw actual distribution and Air Force soldiers continued to receive the Army version until the end of the war.

THE NUMBERED *LUFTWAFFE* GROUND ASSAULT BADGE

On 10 November 1944, numbered versions of the *Luftwaffe* Ground Assault Badge were created, like the numbered General Assault Badges, with the numerals '25', '50', '75' and '100' to indicate the actions undertaken. These decorations were not put into production due to the late stage of the war. Numerous former *Luftwaffe* combat troops, includ-

ing *Generalmajor* Albert Henze, commander of the 2nd Field Division, stated after the war that they knew of no occasion when an award of the numbered badge had been authorised, even 'on paper'.

82.   *Designs of Projected Decorations.*
(a) The Luftwaffe *Tank Battle Badge;*
(b) The Numbered Luftwaffe *Ground Assault Badge;*
(c) The Luftwaffe *Sea Battle Badge;*
(d) The Navy Frogman Badge;
(e) The Navy Frogman Clasp;
(f) The Navy Combat Clasp.
All of these items were officially approved, but only the Navy Combat Clasp went into production. It was made on an ad hoc *basis in the de-Nazified form shown at (f) on board a few German ships during late April and early May, 1945.*

a

b

c

d

e

f

THE NAVY FROGMAN CLASP

A clasp designed by Ottfried Neubecker and comprising a sawfish surrounded by ropes was instituted on 13 November 1944 for presentation to frogmen and the crews of midget submarines, one-man torpedoes and other unconventional craft which formed the *Kleinkampfverbände*, or small battle units, commanded by Admiral Heye. The 'K-Men' saw action at Anzio in April 1944, and were thereafter engaged in various dangerous waterborne missions on all fronts. The clasp came in bronze, silver and gold for four, seven and ten actions respectively. However, production did not take place before the end of the war.

THE NAVY FROGMAN BADGE

A cloth arm badge comprising a yellow sawfish and rope with one, two or three swords denoting that number of actions was also instituted for K-Men on 13 November 1944. Again, it was not manufactured due to the late stage in the war.

THE NAVY COMBAT CLASP

The *Marine Frontspange* comprised an anchor, eagle and swastika with a spray of oakleaves either side, and was instituted on 19 November 1944 as a higher award for those who already possessed a naval war badge and who fulfilled a further five times the conditions required for the war badge. For example, in the case of the E-Boat War Badge, sixty sorties would be needed to qualify for the Combat Clasp. The *Frontspange* was never officially manufactured in its intended form, although a few rough versions, without the eagle and swastika, are reputed to have been produced on board the *Reiher* and other ships during early May 1945. Several

83. *The officially approved design for the Navy Combat Clasp, with eagle and swastika, which never progressed beyond the drawing board.*

awards were certainly made 'on paper' by *Fregattenkapitän* Heydel in Courland on 14 May and by Admiral Kreisch in Copenhagen on 15 May.

THE *LUFTWAFFE* SEA BATTLE BADGE

The *Luftwaffe* Sea Battle Badge was created on 27 November 1944 for award to *Luftwaffe* personnel serving on air-sea rescue launches, supply ships and other surface vessels. It was conferred on an accumulation of days at sea, with a 'sea day' equalling ten hours afloat. The necessary requisites for award were:

- sixty days at sea in the North Sea or Baltic Sea
- twenty days at sea in the more hazardous Mediterranean, Aegean or Black Sea
- ten days at sea if a successful rescue of downed aircrew was effected.

The approved design featured a ship with rigging and mast surmounted by a *Luftwaffe* eagle. While the badge was never produced before the end of the war, it was again certainly awarded in small numbers 'on paper'. One surviving citation, to *Oberstkapitän* Eberhard Künzel of the *Transportkorps Speer*, was presented on 15 March 1945 by the *Luftwaffe* General Officer Commanding in Italy, and was professionally printed by the latter's own headquarters staff. Another certificate, to *Oberfeldwebel* Bruno Freienstein, is dated 9 May 1945 and bears the signature of *Generalleutnant* Ernst-August Roth, Commanding General of the *Luftwaffe* in Norway.

THE WARSAW SHIELD

The Warsaw Shield was created on 10 December 1944 to recognise *SS*, military and Police personnel who crushed the Polish Home Army in the city between 1 August and 4 October that year. The battle was especially ferocious, taking the form of extended guerrilla fighting on a house-to-house basis, and no quarter was asked for or given. Sketches for the shield were drawn up by *SS-Oberführer* Prof. Benno von Arent, a creator of opera sets who had delighted Hitler with his theatrical designs for the Diplomatic Service uniform and who subsequently revelled in the title Reich Stage Manager! The approved design for the

Warsaw Shield featured an eagle (the German forces) choking a snake (the rebels). The eagle bore a swastika and *Warschau* 1944 on its chest. Dies were duly prepared, but they were reported destroyed in an air raid soon afterwards and no shields were ever produced.

THE LORIENT SHIELD

The Lorient Shield is said to have been approved as a local, unofficial award by *General* Wilhelm Fahrmbacher at the end of 1944, for men of his 25,000-strong garrison encircled since 7 August that year within the port of Lorient, a U-boat base in Brittany. The shield had no national standing and there is great doubt as to whether it ever existed at all, even in theory. The alleged design, featuring a helmeted soldier standing guard over a berthed submarine, is totally unlike anything of Third Reich vintage. A so-called alternative shield, comprising a standard identity disc stamped with the words *Festung Lorient 1944*, has not been positively confirmed either. Fahrmbacher's forces held out against bombardment until the end of the war. Significantly, *Admiral* Hennecke, the naval commander at Lorient, said after the war that he never knew anything about plans for a Lorient Shield during his time in the fortress. This item is more than likely the product of an over-active postwar imagination. However, there is a possibility that examples were distributed as commemorative unit Christmas presents to some of the garrison personnel, for retention as keepsakes.

THE DUNKIRK SHIELD

The Dunkirk Shield has a similar background to the Lorient and Memel Shields. It is supposed to have been created by *Admiral* Friedrich Frisius, Channel Coast Commander, for the 14,000 defenders of Dunkirk which, like Lorient, remained in German hands until the armistice. Over the years, a few bronze examples of this item have appeared, bearing a watchtower, waves, chain links and the inscription *Duenkirchen 1944*. They all measure only 32 mm × 40 mm, giving rise to the suggestion that they may have been intended for wear on the field cap as 'tradition badges', like the Sardinia Shield, a common practice amongst U-boat crews

and other naval personnel. Alternatively, the small shield could have been used on the shoulder straps, like the Stalingrad Cross. However, it is also possible that this piece is simply a postwar fabrication. It is worthy of note that, during the 1970s, several completely spurious campaign shields were produced in rusted steel, for the collector market. These included Afrika, Atlantik, Arnheim, Charkow, St Nazaire and La Rochelle shields. None of these existed, even as proposals, before 1945.

THE AIRCRAFT DESTRUCTION BADGE

Localised pennants acknowledging anti-aircraft batteries which were particularly successful in shooting down enemy planes were distributed throughout the war by the *Kriegsmarine*, and by *Luftgaue VII* and *XI* of the Air Force. On 12 January 1945, Hitler instituted a national badge for shooting down low-flying aircraft, the *Tieffliegervernichtungsabzeichen*. It came in two grades, gold and silver, and was identical in appearance to the Tank Destruction Badge except that the centrepiece was a black aeroplane. Unlike the pennants, the badge was to be given to those who downed a flying aircraft using only a rifle, sub-machine-gun or machine-gun under 20 mm in calibre. A silver badge recognised one plane destroyed, and a gold badge five planes. The award was conferred at least once 'on paper', by way of an entry in the *Soldbuch* of a member of *Sturm-Regiment 1*, who shot down a Russian Yak 2 aircraft, flying at a height of 50 metres, with his rifle near Jänkendorf on 3 May 1945. However, the decoration was never actually manufactured before the end of the war.

THE BALKAN SHIELD

Early in 1945, Hitler approved the institution of the *Balkanschild* to reward troops fighting both the Red Army and Tito's partisans. The somewhat unimaginative design, produced by Benno von Arent in March 1945, was akin to that of the *Krimschild* and comprised an *SS*-pattern eagle, the legend *Balkan 1944-1945* and a map of the Aegean archipelago. Three trial samples were made, one in bronzed zinc, one in silvered zinc and one in plain subdued zinc. The latter sample was chosen for economy and camouflage reasons, but due to the late stage in the war the Balkan Shield was never manufactured.

Non-Portable Awards

A significant number of Nazi military awards fall into the 'non-portable' category. This generic term is used to cover items which were not designed to be worn on the uniform in the usual way.

THE LUFTWAFFE HONOUR GOBLET

On 12 January 1940, aviation industry representatives presented Göring on his forty-seventh birthday with a specimen goblet and citation and urged him to revive the practice of awarding these to victorious aircrew, as had been done during the First World War. They also provided a fund totalling 50,000 Reichsmarks to cover goblet production costs. On 27 February that year, Göring duly inaugurated the *Ehrenpokal für Besondere Leistung im Luftkrieg*, or Honour Goblet for Distinguished Achievements in the Air War, bearing two fighting eagles on the obverse and a representation of the 1939 Iron Cross on the reverse. The goblet measured 20 cm in height and was constructed in two parts from silver or, after 1942, silver plate. The recipient's name was engraved around the base portion by the sole manufacturer of the award, the Berlin firm of Wagner & Sohn.

Unlike the First World War procedure when a goblet or, later, a small silver beaker was bestowed for each enemy aircraft destroyed in combat, the *Luftwaffe* Honour Goblet recognised various actions which did not merit the German Cross or Knight's Cross. It was awarded as a personal gift from Göring, and he often handed it over himself. It was given only to aircrew who already held the *EK1* and continued to distinguish themselves in battle. The first award went to *Oberstleutnant* Johann Schalk shortly after institution. Presentations tailed off after June 1943, and a *Luftwaffe* High Command memorandum dated 6 July 1944 referred to a goblet production lag due to war conditions and the fact that goblets would in future be sent direct to the recipients' relatives for safekeeping, as many had been damaged or lost in transit to front-line

squadrons. By 10 December 1944, when the last presentation was made, around 50,000 Honour Goblets had been authorised. However, it is believed that only 14,000 or so were actually produced and bestowed.

84.   *The* Luftwaffe *Honour Goblet.*

THE *LUFTWAFFE* SALVER OF HONOUR

On 15 June 1942, Göring created a new award, the *Ehrenschale für Hervorragende Kampfleistung*, or Salver of Honour for Distinguished Achievements in Battle. The large silver plate measured 28 cm in diameter and bore as its central motif the *Reichsmarschall*'s eagle with crossed batons surmounted by the name of the recipient and date of presentation. The Salver was the ground troops' equivalent of the Honour Goblet and was again bestowed by Göring on a personal basis for bravery in action which did not merit the German Cross or Knight's Cross. All paratroops, members of *Luftwaffe* field divisions and Air Force tank crews were eligible, provided they already held the Iron Cross 1st Class and the Ground Assault Badge or its equivalent. The Salver of Honour was a very rare award, and it is believed that fewer than 100 examples were conferred. As with the Goblet, presentations of the Salver declined sharply with the advent of the *Luftwaffe* Honour List in April 1943, and Honour Roll Clasp in July 1944, which were

85. *The* Luftwaffe *Salver of Honour.*

cheaper means of recognising the relevant achievements.

THE ARMY HIGH COMMAND COMMENDATION CERTIFICATE

In addition to the normal Army and *Waffen-SS* war badges and decorations, a special certificate of commendation signed by *Generalfeldmarschall* von Brauchitsch, Commander-in-Chief of the Army, was created after the invasion of Russia in June 1941, and could be presented for single acts of bravery. When Hitler assumed personal command of the Army at the end of the year, issue of this certificate ceased. It was conferred 1,322 times.

THE *FÜHRER* COMMENDATION CERTIFICATE

Around 20 December 1941, the *Führer* Commendation Certificate was introduced to replace

86. *The* Führer *Commendation Certificate awarded to* SS-Panzer *Reconnaissance Battalion 10 of the 'Frundsberg' Division on 1 August 1944.*

that formerly awarded by von Brauchitsch. The document was headed by a large eagle and swastika. A typical surviving example reads:

> *Ich spreche dem Oberleutnant Lothar Roessler für seine hervorragenden leistungen auf dem schlachtfelde bei Mal-Sapadenka am 24.1.1943 meine besondere anerkennung aus. Hauptquartier den 18.April 1943. Der Führer.* ('I express my special appreciation to *Oberleutnant* Lothar Roessler for his outstanding distinction on the battlefield at Mal-Sapadenka on 24 January 1943. Headquarters, 18 April, 1943. *Der Führer.*')

The certificate was signed by Hitler, or bore a facsimile of his signature.

The *Führer* Commendation Certificate was used to recognise acts such as the single-handed destruction of a tank or aircraft, until separate badges were instituted to acknowledge such feats. It could also be conferred on an entire unit, as was the case on 1 August 1944 when *SS-Panzer* Reconnaissance Battalion 10 of the 'Frundsberg' Division received the Certificate in recognition of its personnel having shot down three enemy aircraft by means of infantry weapons at Kurdwanowka on 6 April that year.

THE *REICHSMARSCHALL* COMMENDATION CERTIFICATE

Hermann Göring is known to have presented his own *Anerkennungsurkunde des Reichsministers der Luftfahrt und Oberbefehlshabers der Luftwaffe* to Air Force personnel for singular actions. An example dating from 25 June 1941 was issued jointly to four aircrew in recognition of their having sunk an 80-ton vessel in Sagunt harbour on 8 November 1938, during the Spanish Civil War.

THE *REICHSFÜHRER-SS* COMMENDATION CERTIFICATE

This document certainly existed, and is referred to in official *SS* orders, but its appearance and award criteria are shrouded in obscurity. The Certificate was issued personally by Himmler to members of the *SS* and police for 'distinguished personal actions and special achievements'. As the front-line troops of the *Waffen-SS* were eligible to receive the *Führer* Commendation Certificate and other awards for heroism in battle, it can reasonably be assumed that the *Reichsführer*'s Certificate related to personnel engaged in non-combatant duties and security tasks.

GAULEITER COMMENDATION CERTIFICATES

A number of *NSDAP Gauleitern* took upon themselves to issue semi-official certificates of commendation to citizens who distinguished themselves in civil-defence duties during air raids. A surviving example dated 24 December 1941 was presented by Hartmann Lauterbacher, *Gauleiter* of South Hanover-Brunswick, and bears the exhortation: *Alle für Einen – Einer für Alle!* ('*All for one and one for all!*')

THE FLAK AUXILIARY COMMENDATION CERTIFICATE

The *Anerkennungsurkunde für Luftwaffen-Helfer* dated from 1944–5 and was presented to Hitler Youths and others serving as auxiliary anti-aircraft gunners in the defence of the Reich. No further details are known.

WALL PLAQUES

A number of unofficial wall plaques were created by *Luftwaffe* divisional and other commanders to recognise merit in their own areas of jurisdiction. The plaques generally took the form of small metal plates, rectangular in shape, bearing a suitable design and inscription. They were intended to be hung from a wall, or stood on a desk. The following are known to have existed:

- *Plaque for Outstanding Achievement in Air District XI*. Instituted at the end of 1939 by *Generalleutnant* Ludwig Wolff, commander of *Luftgau XI* (Hamburg), in Iron and Silver versions. In January 1940, an Iron plaque went to *Gefreiter* Hall of Searchlight Transport Battery 112, who prevented the spread of a fire which occurred when a 70,000 litre petrol tank ruptured. In February 1942, *Oberfeldwebel* Nelke saved three aircrew from a German plane which crashed and burst into flames at Rechlin airfield, for which he received the plaque in Silver. These give an idea of the criteria for award. Only fourteen Silver plaques are known to have been bestowed during the period 1942–4. *Generalmajor* von Hippel, Commander of 3rd Flak Division, received both

versions, being awarded the Iron plaque on 24 December 1942 and the Silver one on 24 December 1943.
- *Plaque for Outstanding Merit in Air District II*. Instituted in 1941, this bore a sword and coat-of-arms.
- *Plaque for Special Merit in the Battle of Crete*. Authorised by *Generaloberst* Kurt Student, commander of *XI Fliegerkorps*, for those who distinguished themselves in the conquest of Crete during May–June 1941.
- *Ehrenschild der Kampfgruppe z.b.v. 105*. For merit in the 105th Special Bomber Group, this shield bore a map of Europe with the words *Narvik* and *Kreta*.
- *Plaque for Technical Merit in Russia*. *Generalfeldmarschall* Albert Kesselring, Commander of *Luftflotte 2*, instituted a plaque in autumn 1941 'in recognition of technical merit in the campaign against Soviet Russia'. At least one plaque was awarded, to an *Unteroffizier* in a motor-repair platoon. Further details are unknown.
- *Plaque for Outstanding Merit in Air District Kiev*. Instituted towards the end of 1941, this bore an eagle over the city of Kiev and was awarded to *Luftwaffe* personnel serving in the Ukraine.
- *Plaque for Outstanding Merit in Air District Kharkov*. For *Luftwaffe* personnel serving in the Kharkov area. Further details are unknown.
- *Plaque for Special Achievement in Air District XII/XIII*. Created by *General der Flakartillerie* Heilingbrunner in Autumn 1942. Further details are unknown.
- *Plaque for Outstanding Achievement in the 21st Field Division*. The 21st Field Division of the *Luftwaffe* was formed during the siege of Cholm, from various ground units, and was then known as the Meindl Division. In 1943, *Generalleutnant* Richard Schimpf instituted a plaque, designed by *Gefreiter* Schröder of the 1st *Luftwaffe* Field Regiment, to reward his men for special merit at Cholm and subsequent battles. Around 1,000 were manufactured, although only 400 were bestowed.
- *Plaque for Merit in Air District Finland*. Created in 1943 by the *Luftwaffe* commander in Finland, *General der Flieger* Schultz. Around 1,000 were made. Further details are unknown.

87. Luftwaffe *wall plaques.*
(a) For Outstanding Achievement in Air District XI;
(b) For Special Merit in the Battle of Crete;
(c) For Outstanding Achievement in the 21st Field Division;
(d) For Merit in Air District Finland;
(e) For Achievement in Air District Norway.

- *Honour Plaque of Air District Norway.* Manufactured in Oslo for bestowal by the *Luftwaffe* commander in Norway, *General* Wilhelm Harmjanz. Over 6,000 are believed to have been made, since surviving examples bear serial numbers ranging from 1268 to 6641. Awards ceased in December 1943.
- *Plaque for Outstanding Technical Achievement in the Southern Command.* Also created by *Generalfeldmarschall* Kesselring for merit in the technical branch of the *Luftwaffe*. The few known recipients included *Oberleutnant* Dr Hahn, commander of a transport unit of the Military

Railways Directorate in Florence, who received the plaque on 18 May 1944.

- *Plaque for Special Achievement in the South-East Theatre of Operations.* Instituted by *General der Flieger* Fiebig for merit in the Balkans. The plaque was manufactured by the firm of Pleuger und Voss in Lüdenscheid. No further details are known.
- *Plaque for Merit in Military Air District XXX.* Authorised by *General der Flieger* Waber in the autumn of 1944 for front-line *Luftwaffe* troops in the northern Balkans. The plaque bore heraldic shields with the names *Agram*, *Skopije*, *Tirana* and *Belgrad*. No further details are known.

a

b

88.   Luftwaffe *medallions.*
(a) The Medal for Merit in the Technical Branch of the Luftwaffe;
(b) The Medal for Merit in Air District Belgium-North France;
(c) The Medal for Merit in Air District West France.

c

- *Honour Plaque for Luftflotte 1.* No details are known.
- *Honour Plaque for Luftflotte 4.* No details are known.

In addition to the above, there were three *Luftwaffe* medallions which were akin to the plaque-type awards. These were as follows:

- *Medal for Merit in the Technical Branch of the* Luftwaffe. This non-portable medal bore Göring's head on one side and the Air Force eagle on the other and was given for technical achievements between 1940 and 1941. It was superseded by the German Cross in Silver.

- *Medal for Merit in Air District West France.* Instituted in the summer of 1944 by *General der Flakartillerie* Dr Weissmann. At least one is recorded as having been presented to a female auxiliary.

- *Medal for Merit in Air District Belgium–North France.* Instituted by *General der Flieger* Wimmer. Further details are unknown.

The majority of these *Luftwaffe* plaques and medallions were only very rarely bestowed. This was partly because some were created to recognise acts soon to be covered by official decorations. The Crete Plaque, for example, was rendered obsolete by the introduction of the Kreta Cuff Title, while those for technical merit were overtaken by events when the War Merit Cross began to be widely distributed for that purpose.

UNIT MEDALLIONS
Many semi-official and unofficial 'unit medals' were created by battalion and regimental commanders for distribution among their men, to acknowledge participation in specific campaigns which had not been recognised by national decorations. Although

89. *The Unit Medallion of the 269th* Luftwaffe *Reserve Flak Searchlight Battalion.*

often made with suspension hooks or rings, such medals were not authorised for wear and were simply commemorative souvenirs. They usually featured an inscription naming the unit concerned, and a design representative of that unit or of a particular campaign in which the unit had been engaged. The following are known to have existed:

- Panzer-Abwehr-Abteilung 39 – *Occupation of Prague.* The 39th Anti-Tank Battalion was the first German unit to be posted at Prague Castle after the occupation of Czechoslovakia, and later produced a bronze medal to celebrate the fact. It was distributed to all personnel who had actually served during the occupation.
- *4th Company, 7th* Panzer *Reconnaissance Battalion – 1939–40.* Two hundred medals were manufactured to reward members of this unit, part of the 4th *Panzer* Division, who took part in the conquest of France.
- *207th* Luftwaffe *Territorial Battalion – Christmas 1940.* This formation was disbanded at the end of 1940, and produced a medal to commemorate its existence. It comprised three anti-aircraft batteries based at Bad Saarow.
- *3rd Company, 7th* Panzer *Reconnaissance Battalion – 1941.* This unit distributed medals for participation in the opening of the Russian campaign.
- *4th Company, 7th* Panzer *Reconnaissance Battalion – 1941–2.* Two hundred medals were produced for unit personnel taking part in the opening of the Russian campaign, and the first winter on the eastern front.

- *40th* Panzer *Reconnaissance Battalion – 1940–2.* This unit was part of the 14th *Panzer* Division, and the medal commemorated its actions in France, Yugoslavia and Russia.
- *98th Mountain Regiment – Caucasus 1942.* The 13th Company of *Gebirgsjäger Regiment 98* produced a medal, bearing an edelweiss and mountain, to commemorate its actions in the Caucasus in 1942.
- *54th Mountain Signals Battalion – Caucasus 1942.* This was similar to the medal above.
- *Mountain Units – Arctic Front 1942–3.* This anonymous medal simply bore a mountain troop edelweiss badge and the legend *Eismeerfront 1942–43.*
- *64th Motorcycle Battalion – 1943.* This formation was part of the 14th *Panzer* Division. The battalion was created in May 1942 and within a year its personnel had won ten German Crosses in Gold, three Knight's Crosses and one set of Oakleaves. The unit was annihilated at Stalingrad.
- *1st Volunteer* Bersaglieri *Battalion.* This unit was formed by loyal Italian Fascists on 8 September 1943 under the name *Primo Battaglione Volontari delle SS Benito Mussolini.* The *SS* designation was later dropped. A commemorative medal featuring *SS* runes and the legend *Sempre Fedele al Duce e al Fuhrer* ('Always loyal to *Duce* and *Führer*') was produced and distributed to members as a commemorative. It hung from a green ribbon.
- *269th* Luftwaffe *Reserve Flak Searchlight Battalion.* Major Holtfort, commander of this unit which was based on the island of Sylt, used the profits from his staff canteen to pay a Bremen firm to make medals which he distributed to his men as Christmas presents at the end of 1943. They featured the *Luftwaffe* eagle on the obverse and unit name on the reverse, and were produced in aluminium.

UNIT CAP BADGES

A vast array of semi-official unit cap badges, such as the 'Grenadier' of the 26th *Panzer* Division and the well-known 'Greyhound' of the 116th *Panzer* Division, were produced and awarded by local commanding officers for loyal service in the forma-

90. The Unit cap badge of the 26th Panzer Division.

THE VOLKHOV STICK

The Volkhov Stick was yet another form of unofficial campaign commemorative and was given by enlisted men on the eastern front to the more popular of their officers, particularly after an award of the Knight's Cross, German Cross or other decoration. It took the form of a walking stick carved in varying qualities from assorted woods by the men themselves, or by local native Russian craftsmen commissioned for the purpose. The *Wolchowstock* usually featured swastikas, Iron Crosses, divisional, regimental or other suitable emblems, and sometimes campaign names. First used on the Volkhov front during the winter of 1941–2, these sticks were very highly prized by their recipients as they denoted the esteem in which they were held by their own men.

tions concerned. The qualification criteria varied from unit to unit, but the fact that these badges were usually accompanied by citations elevated them to the status of minor awards rather than simple formation insignia.

91. A typical Volkhov Stick, carved with a swastika and unit emblems. The chequerboard and stripe designs were characteristic of such pieces.

Foreign Decorations

During the war, Germany and her allies exchanged decorations as a matter of diplomatic course. Foreign soldiers fighting alongside the *Wehrmacht* were often presented with the Iron Cross for bravery on the battlefield, and German troops similarly received military awards from Italy, Romania, Finland, Hungary, Slovakia and so on. Consequently, a variety of non-German military decorations could be seen on German uniforms. It is not within the scope of this book to describe them in any detail, but a few examples follow to give a general idea of the selection involved.

92.   A typical selection of foreign decorations worn with German uniform.
From left to right, top to bottom:
The Croatian Order of the Crown of King Zvonimir 3rd Class with Oakleaves, on its traditional Austro-Hungarian style triangular ribbon;
The Italo-German Campaign Medal;
The Romanian Commemorative Medal for the Crusade Against Communism;
The Finnish Arctic Front Cross;
The Turkish War Decoration, by Boerger & Co.;
The Sports Badge of the Volksbund der Deutschen in Ungarn, *created in the spring of 1942 by pro-Nazi Hungarian citizens of German descent as their equivalent of the German National Sports Badge.*

The Croatian Order of the Crown of King Zvonimir was created in May 1941 in five classes. It featured a white trefoil upon which was superimposed a crown, with swords for military service and oakleaves for bravery. The following November, a similar decoration but black in colour, the so-called Order of the Iron Trefoil, was instituted as the highest award for members of the Croat armed forces. Many Germans, and even some of their Cossack auxiliaries, received these Orders for participation in the struggle against Tito's partisans. Holders included *Oberst* Kononov of the 5th Don Cossacks, and staff officers of the *SS* Division 'Prinz Eugen'.

The Italian government honoured the deeds of Rommel's *Afrikakorps* by instituting the Italo-German Campaign Medal early in 1942. The obverse of this very well-made bronze medal, which was struck by Lorioli of Milan, depicted the *Arco dei Feleni*, or 'Marble Arch', a massive monument erected on the Via Balbia, the coastal road between the provinces of Tripolitania and Cyrenaica, to celebrate the early Fascist victories. It was flanked by the Italian fasces and Nazi swastika, above the knot of the House of Savoy. Around the outer rim of the medal was the legend 'Italo-German Campaign in Africa', in both Italian and German. The reverse featured two armoured knights (Italy and Germany) closing the jaws (the Suez Canal) of a crocodile (the British Empire). The medal was suspended below the left pocket flap from a ribbon bearing the Italian and German colours. Following Italy's withdrawal from the war and subsequent surrender, a German Army order of 8 April 1944 prohibited the further wearing of Italian decorations, and specific mention was made of the *Erinnerungsmedaille für den Italienisch-Deutschen Feldzug in Afrika*. It is interesting to note that all known surviving award documents for this medal were issued to members of the *Luftwaffe*, including paratroops. Some of the citations rather curiously bear US watermarks, having apparently been printed on captured American paper stocks.

A common Romanian decoration was the Commemorative Medal for the Crusade Against Communism, instituted on 1 April 1942 as the predecessor of the German *Ostmedaille*. The ribbon was dark red with white edges, and had a distinctive central 'ladder' effect in the Romanian national colours, red/yellow/blue. No fewer than fourteen Bars were eventually authorised, including 'Crimea' and 'Stalingrad'. The medal was bestowed liberally upon German troops fighting alongside Romanians on the Russian front.

The Arctic Front Cross was given by Finland as a campaign honour for service in Lapland between 1941 and 1944. Convex in form, with a screw-back fitting, it was a small blue enamel cross bearing a map of the region, national flags and details of the principal battles of the campaign. Prior to September 1944, when Finland broke off relations with Germany, it was distributed to members of the 20th Mountain Army, a few of whom wore it as a commemorative badge. Use of the cross was officially forbidden in November that year, which may have prompted General Böhme to suggest an alternative award, the Lapland Shield.

Another award often seen on German uniforms during the Third Reich period was the very distinctive Turkish War Decoration, worn on the right breast pocket. It was instituted on 1 March 1915 by Sultan Mehmet Resat V for bravery or meritorious service during the First World War, and was in a single class taking the form of a large pin-back red enamelled star with silver border. The centre featured a silver crescent beneath the Sultan's cypher, the characters of which represented *El Ghazi*, or 'the victorious'. Below was the date '333' in Turkish figures, corresponding to 1915 on the Western calendar. The Germans referred to the decoration as the *Eisener Halbmond*, or 'Iron Crescent', since it was to all intents and purposes the Turkish equivalent of the Iron Cross. It was widely awarded to German troops serving in the Near East, and the Turkish government in fact contracted three Berlin firms, Boerger, Godet and Wagner to manufacture the award on its behalf. A buttonhole ribbon in red and white, similar in configuration to that of the 1914 Iron Cross, was authorised for use in the field and was also made in Germany. The Turkish War Decoration could regularly be seen on the uniforms of senior *Wehrmacht* officers during the Second World War, being worn below the German Cross or Spanish Cross if these were also held.

Other foreign awards bestowed upon German forces during the Second World War included the Slovakian War Victory Cross, the Order of the Star of Romania, the Bulgarian Military Order for Bravery in War, the Spanish War Cross, the Hungarian Signum Laudis Medal, the Finnish Order of the Cross of Liberty and the Azad Hind decoration of the Free Indian Provisional Government. Some of these were made in Germany and Austria by established companies like Juncker and Souval, while others were produced by authorised firms based in the countries concerned, for example Kraus of Zagreb in Croatia. German racial communities outside the Reich, and collaborationist parties in occupied Europe, also had their own plethora of pseudo-Nazi medals and badges, a few of which occasionally appeared on *Wehrmacht* uniforms. Most notable was the Belgian Rexist Decoration, worn unofficially by Walloon volunteers in the German Army from 1941 and approved by Hitler at the end of 1944.

Remarkably, foreign volunteers in the *Wehrmacht* were permitted to continue to sport decorations they had won many years before, even if the regimes which had bestowed them had been enemies of Germany at the time! For example, a number of Frenchmen serving with the Nazi forces in Russia wore medals they had earned killing Germans on the Western front in 1914–18. This apparent anomaly was in fact a deliberate policy, intended to cultivate the loyalty of soldiers in the conquered territories.

Order of Precedence of Military Awards

The official order of precedence of standard Third Reich military decorations is given below. In reality, certain awards were harder to win than others technically senior to them. For example, numbered war badges represented long and active service at the front which had usually resulted in an earlier award of at least the Iron Cross 1st Class. The Spanish Cross also undoubtedly deserved to be higher up the scale. Wartime decorations, or *Kriegsorden*, always took precedence over peacetime awards.

1. Grand Cross of the Iron Cross
2. Knight's Cross of the Iron Cross with Oakleaves and higher additions
3. Golden Knight's Cross of the War Merit Cross
4. Knight's Cross of the Iron Cross
5. Knight's Cross of the War Merit Cross
6. German Cross
7. Honour Roll Clasps
8. *Führer* Commendation Certificate
9. *Luftwaffe* Honour Goblet and Salver
10. Iron Cross 1st Class
11. War Merit Cross 1st Class
12. Iron Cross 2nd Class
13. Combat clasps
14. Numbered war badges
15. Wound badges
16. Tank Destruction Badge
17. Unnumbered war badges
18. Campaign shields and cuff titles
19. War Merit Cross 2nd Class
20. *Ostvolk* Decoration
21. Eastern Front Medal
22. War Merit Medal
23. Cross of Honour, 1914–18
24. Spanish Cross
25. Qualification badges
26. Long-service awards
27. Commemorative medals
28. West Wall Medal
29. Foreign decorations

2. Political and Civil Awards

While the perennial interest in Nazi medals and decorations undoubtedly focuses on combat honours, the Third Reich also boasted an extensive selection of non-military awards which can be clearly divided into two distinct groupings, political and civil. For the sake of consistency, each of these groups is again best covered separately and chronologically. However, it should be borne in mind that as Nazi Germany developed the Party and the State became inextricably entangled, amply demonstrated by the adoption of the *NSDAP* swastika banner as the country's national flag in September 1935. By the time the Second World War broke out, the distinction between Party and State had all but disappeared and the design and bestowal of national decorations reflected that situation.

Political Awards

THE 1929 NUREMBERG PARTY DAY BADGE

The first political decoration to be created by Hitler was instituted on 15 August 1929, to commemorate the Fourth Party Rally held at Nuremberg on 1–4 August that year. This rally was by far the largest and most spectacular to date, with over 60,000 participants, and as well as taking place on the tenth anniversary of the foundation of the *NSDAP* it was the occasion of street battles with Communists, the consecration of twenty-four new *Sturmabteilung* (*SA*) standards, and a patriotic ceremony in remembrance of the German dead of the First World War. More importantly, it marked a turning point in the fortunes of the Nazi party, which had been smashed at the polls the previous year but now began to secure the backing of big business. The 1929 Nuremberg Party Day Badge was manufactured by Ferdinand Hoffstätter of Bonn and could be worn by all those who had attended the event. Its central

93.   Nazi party awards.
From left to right:
The 1929 Nuremberg Party Day Badge;
The Brunswick Rally Badge, early round pattern in silvered iron;
The Brunswick Rally Badge, later oval pattern in nickel silver.

94. SA-Sturmführer *Horst Wessel wearing the 1929 Nuremberg Party Day Badge shortly after the rally. Twenty-two-year-old Wessel was shot through the mouth by Communists a few months later, and died of his wounds on 23 February 1930. He instantly became a Nazi martyr, and a marching song he had composed was adopted as the anthem of the* NSDAP.

ɦorſt Weſſel
† 23. 2. 1930
Sturmführer 5 im Gauſturm Berlin

design featured a Nazi version of the imperial *Garde du Korps helmet*, which had been sketched by Hitler seven years earlier in the Munich workshop of Otto Gahr. The helmet had been planned for use by *NSDAP* standard-bearers, but was never placed into production. While little more than a glorified 'day badge', this award was later viewed with high regard and was a favourite with many *NSDAP* leaders. A larger version in the form of a plaque was presented as a special souvenir to those who had been guests of honour at the rally.

THE BRUNSWICK RALLY BADGE

The second-oldest party award was similar in nature and commemorated participation in the *SA* rally at Brunswick on 17–18 October, 1931. This event took place in the wake of a failed anti-Hitler revolt by the north German *SA* and, being held significantly in the northern heartland, marked the national unification of the various brownshirt organisations whose poverty-stricken rank and file members were at last persuaded to give their support to the bourgeois party leadership in Munich. The loyalty of the Nazi paramilitary forces to Hitler alone, rather than to local *SA* commanders, was firmly established for the first time across the entire country. Another twenty-four new *SA* regiments were sworn in at the rally and the *Motor-SA* and *NSKK* were also set up. Two Nazis were killed and fifty wounded in fighting with political opponents during the event. The Brunswick Rally Badge was manufactured in two distinct versions, round and oval, and was normally hollow-backed. Its main producer was F.W. Assmann & Söhne of Lüdenscheid.

THE COBURG BADGE

On 14 October 1932, Hitler rather belatedly instituted the Coburg Badge for wear by veterans of the so-called 'Battle of Coburg' ten years earlier, when 800 Nazis, almost the entire party at that time, had defeated the local Communists in street fighting which came to be recognised as the first decisive victory of the *NSDAP*. The badge was again designed by Hitler himself, and only 436 names were entered on the official party award list as recipients. Among these were the most senior of the Old Guard, including Max Amann, Hermann Esser and Alfred Rosenberg. Until 1938, the simple bronze Coburg Badge ranked as the highest *NSDAP* decoration, since the holders were regarded as having been largely responsible for the birth of the Nazi movement.

THE *FRONTBANN* BADGE

The year 1932 also saw the institution by Karl Ernst, commander of *SA Gruppe Berlin-Brandenburg*, of a badge for wear by former members of the *Frontbann* organisation, which had existed during 1924 as a substitute for the then banned *SA*. The

95. *The* Frontbann *Badge*

96. *Nazi party awards.*
From top to bottom, left to right:
The Coburg Badge;
The Standard 1923 Gau *Badge;*
The Thüringia Gau *Badge;*
The Baden Gau *Badge, presented in Gold to those who had joined the* NSDAP *before 9 November 1923 and in Silver to those who had become members between February 1925 and October 1927;*
The Osthannover Gau *Badge, for those local Nazi party stalwarts with membership numbers below 100,000.*

Frontbann Badge, comprising a swastika, a steel helmet, the *Opfer-Rune* of self-sacrifice and the motto *Wir wollen frei werden* ('We want to be free'), was manufactured in limited numbers by Paul Meybauer of Berlin. However, it was never officially approved by Hitler and its use was subsequently prohibited. Ernst alone issued citations for the badge, which he called the *Traditionsnadel alter Kämpfer*, or 'Old Campaigners' Commemorative Pin'.

GAU BADGES, 1933

In 1933, the uniform of the *NSDAP* political leadership was adorned with proper rank insignia for the first time, and with this development came a flurry of accompanying decorations to reward active party veterans whose efforts during the *Kampfzeit*, or time of struggle, had culminated in the Nazi assumption of power. The basic political leader's uniform dated from the Battle of Coburg and had been instigated so as to reinforce the military nature of the *NSDAP*, and draw a clear distinction between its hierarchy and the civil politicians of the period. No fewer than 400 Nazis were killed and 40,000 wounded during street fighting between 1923 and 1933, and so Hitler, the ex-soldier, considered it only natural that his old campaigners should have their many years of loyalty acknowledged through the creation and distribution of military-style awards. These came to be known colloquially as the 'civil war badges of the *NSDAP*'.

The first batch of *Gau-Ehrenzeichen*, or Regional Party Decorations, appeared in June 1933, and the right to bestow them was vested in local *Gauleitern*. They were presented in recognition of outstanding service, normally to the 1,000 senior *NSDAP* veterans in each *Gau*. A single standardised badge, comprising a wreath of oakleaves enclosing a large black enamel swastika bearing the date '1923' or '1925', depending on whether the holder had joined the Nazi party before or after its temporary prohibition in 1924, was awarded by the *Gauleitern* of Bayreuth, Halle-Merseburg, Hessen-Nassau, Magdeburg-Anhalt, Mecklenburg and Sachsen. It was struck in '800' silver by the Mittweida firm of Rudolf Wächtler & Lange, and was particularly well executed. Fritz Sauckel of the

Thüringen *Gau* chose to design his own veterans' badge, again in '800' silver, which took the form of a stylised eagle and swastika and the legend *Für Treue – NSDAP Thüring*. The *Gauleiter* of Baden, Robert Wagner, followed suit and distributed Gold and Silver badges bearing a wreathed eagle and swastika over the words *Gau Baden*, with the Silver version also being produced in a smaller brooch form for female recipients. Meanwhile, Adolf Wagner's *Gau* München-Oberbayern was awarding a special badge to survivors of the 1923 Munich *Putsch*. Made locally by Deschler, it comprised a

98.   The Munich Gau *Badge.*

bronze swastika enclosed by a wreath with the motto *Und ihr habt doch gesiegt*, meaning 'The victory is yours'.

Yet another variant *Gau* Badge, approved by Otto Telschow of Osthannover, appeared in July 1933. It was struck in Gold, Silver and Bronze and featured a prancing horse over a swastika. Thus within six months of the Nazis coming to power, no fewer than ten different *Gau-Ehrenzeichen* had been created, taking the various grades into account. Moreover, *Gauleiter* Karl Roever of Weser-Ems awarded a Shield of Honour in plaque form to his veteran *NSDAP* comrades, while in other regions those who had been wounded in early street fighting received an elaborate certificate, the so-called *Ehrenurkunde der NSDAP für Verwundungen in Kampf*. It was apparent that a more easily recognisable form of insignia was urgently required to distinguish the Old Guard on a national basis.

97.   Dr Otto Hellmuth, Gauleiter *of Main-Franconia, wearing the Coburg Badge and Standard* Gau *Badge in 1933. A dentist by profession, Hellmuth joined the* NSDAP *in 1925 and was appointed* Gauleiter *three years later. He held that post until the end of the Second World War.*

THE GOLDEN PARTY BADGE
On 13 October 1933, the *ad hoc* nature of rewarding the Old Guard was at least partially resolved when Hitler introduced the Golden Party Decoration, or *Goldene Ehrenzeichen der NSDAP*, usually referred to as the Golden Party Badge. The first examples were bestowed on 9 November 1933, and badges duly went to all those who had given uninterrupted service to the Nazi party since its reformation in February 1925 and who held membership numbers below 100,000. The very early

NSDAP practice of allocating random numbers to new recruits so as to make the party appear larger than it actually was, combined with the restrictions of active and unbroken membership, limited the recipients to around 22,000, all of whom had joined the *NSDAP* before September 1930. If a holder subsequently resigned from the Nazi party, he forfeited the right to wear the badge.

Designed by Munich jeweller Josef Fuess, the *Goldene Ehrenzeichen* took the form of a basic Nazi party member's badge, with the addition of a white surround, soldered onto a gilded brass backplate with oakleaf border. The reverse usually bore the holder's *NSDAP* membership number, the maker's mark (Deschler or Fuess) and the *Ges.Gesch.* patent pending designation. A small hole through the brass backplate facilitated the escape of trapped gasses when the two main parts of the badge were being soldered together. The award came in two sizes, 25 mm diameter for wear with civilian clothes and 30 mm for the left breast pocket of military or political uniform. The 30 mm badge was supposed to be placed above all other breast decorations, but it was not always worn as per regulations. For example, *SS-Obergruppenführer* Sepp Dietrich usually sported his *Goldene Ehrenzeichen* on the flap of the left pocket rather than on the pocket itself, while Göring often wore his under the Iron Cross 1st Class and *NSKK-Korpsführer* Adolf Hühnlein sometimes displayed the badge on the right pocket flap, above his Blood Order ribbon.

For some reason, Hitler initially chose not to wear the Golden Party Badge himself. This may simply have been due to his inherent dislike for the overtly theatrical, demonstrated by the fact that he used only very few of the many decorations to which he was undoubtedly entitled, usually restricting himself to his 1914 Iron Cross 1st Class and Wound Badge in Black. Many of his other First World War awards and *NSDAP* and foreign decorations were never sported at all, in stark contrast to the heavily bemedalled chests of Göring, Mussolini and their like. In any event, Hitler at last decided to wear the *Goldene Ehrenzeichen* above his Iron Cross in 1936, and continued to do so thereafter.

From June 1937, the Golden Party Badge was used as the central design of a flag known as the *Fahne der Alten Garde*, which preceded the 500 senior party veterans on their annual tour of Germany. It thereby became totally representative of the Old Guard nationally, and superseded the *Gau-Ehrenzeichen*, which were no longer permitted to be worn with it.

In 1938, a slight variation of the *Goldene Ehrenzeichen* was instituted and subsequently awarded in small numbers for outstanding service to the Party or State, regardless of length of *NSDAP* membership. The obverse was identical to that of the veteran's badge, but the reverse featured a wider pin and had the membership number replaced by an engraved version of Hitler's signature or initials and the date of presentation. It was bestowed throughout the war, and deserving holders of the earlier veteran's badge were also eligible to receive it. For example, *SS-Oberst-Gruppenführer* Kurt Daluege, head of the Uniformed Police, received the standard Golden Party Badge for *NSDAP* veterans in 1933 and was awarded the higher-ranked version for outstanding service ten years later. Other notable recipients of the Golden Party Badge for outstanding service were *Generalfeldmarschall* Keitel (1939) and *Grossadmiral* Dönitz (1943). The final bestowal of this prestigious award was made on 27 April 1945, when Hitler removed his own Golden Party Badge, serial no. 1, from his uniform

99. *The Golden Party Badge, 30 mm version, by Deschler & Sohn. This example bears the holder's* NSDAP *membership number '88536' stamped into the reverse. Around 22,000 Golden Party Badges for veteran membership were bestowed, while the version for outstanding service was conferred only 650 times.*

and gave it to *Frau* Magda Goebbels in the Berlin bunker as a personal tribute to her loyalty. It was by then rumoured that Hitler had fathered *Frau* Goebbels's son Helmuth during a Baltic holiday in 1934, and it may therefore be particularly significant that Magda poisoned herself and her six children hours after Hitler's suicide on 30 April.

100. *Wilhelm Frick wearing the Blood Order in the prescribed fashion, 1935. Note also the 25 mm Golden Party Badge on his left lapel. Frick served as Hitler's Minister of the Interior between 1933 and 1943, and then as Reich Protector of Bohemia and Moravia. Found guilty of war crimes at Nuremberg, he was hanged on 16 October 1946.*

A so-called Special Golden Party Badge for Foreigners exists, without the usual inscriptions or oakleaf border and bearing a facsimile of Hitler's signature on the reverse. Made in gilded and enamelled silver, it is reputed to have been presented as a 'diplomatic gift' from the *Führer* to Axis dignitaries, including the Hungarian leader Admiral Horthy, before the advent of the Order of the German Eagle. However, this seems unlikely. No reference to such a badge has been found in contemporary literature, and no pre-1945 photographs of it being worn have ever come to light. It is probable that this insignia is a postwar creation, manufactured during the early 1960s when a great many 'rare prototype' medals, daggers and badges were being dreamed up for the collector's market. In a similar vein, existing solid gold versions of the Golden Party Badge, and another variant encrusted with diamonds and rubies, cannot be authenticated.

THE BLOOD ORDER

On 9 November 1933, when he was presenting the first Golden Party Badges, Hitler announced his intention to create an *Ehrenzeichen am Band vom 9. November 1923*, later known as the *Blutorden*, or Blood Order, to reward participation in the abortive Beer Hall *Putsch* exactly ten years earlier, when he and a group of almost 2,000 followers had attempted to seize power from the Bavarian government in Munich. The first published reference to the new decoration appeared on 15 March 1934, and indicated that to qualify for award a person had to have:

- taken part in the events of 8–9 November 1923, on the Nazi side; and
- joined the *NSDAP*, or an affiliated organisation, by 1 January 1932.

The Order took the form of a basic silver medal, chemically treated so as to produce a tarnished effect, with an eagle and *9.Nov. - München 1923-33* on the obverse. The reverse featured a swastika over the *Feldherrnhalle* monument, the legend *Und ihr habt doch gesiegt* (adopted from the earlier Munich *Gau* Badge), the issue number of the award, a '990' silver stamp and the designer's name, 'J. Fuess, München'. It was worn uniquely

101. *The Blood Order, with its distinctive case bearing the legend '8./9. November 1923'. Of particular note is the buttonhole stitched into the ribbon.*

102. *The reverse of a second-pattern Blood Order, showing the* Feldherrnhalle *monument, '800' silver stamp and '1627' issue number. This example was awarded to Karl Maas of Itzehoe on 2 May 1939.*

from the button of the right breast pocket, hanging under the pocket flap on a very distinctive red ribbon with narrow black and white borders. The ribbon was stitched closed and had a buttonhole sewn into the centre at the factory. Consequently, the award's silver suspension ring had to be left unsoldered and open so that the medal could readily be moved by the recipient from one piece of ribbon to another, in the event of ribbon damage.

The numbering sequence of early Blood Orders depended more upon the date of application for the award than the seniority or actions of the recipient. While Himmler, Dietrich, Graf and Hess not surprisingly received medals with low serial numbers (3, 10, 21 and 29 respectively), other notable 'frontline' participants in the *Putsch* were allocated much higher numbers. Schaub, Schreck and Maurice, for example, held Blood Order numbers 296, 349 and 495, while Jakob Grimminger, successor to Heinrich Trambauer as traditional bearer of the Blood Flag itself, had to be content with serial no. 714.

In November 1937, a special formalised windjacket uniform, based on the hotch-potch of garb worn by the Nazis during the 1920–3 period, was authorised to be worn by all holders of the Blood Order when taking part in the annual *Putsch* celebrations in Munich. This short-lived uniform fell out of use after the outbreak of the Second World War.

On 30 May 1938, the conditions for award of the *Blutorden* were widened, much to the chagrin of *Putsch* veterans, at the instigation of *Reichsleiter* Martin Bormann, who had long coveted the Order. It could henceforth be given also to *NSDAP* members who had rendered outstanding services to the party during the *Kampfzeit*, notably those who had:

- served at least a one-year jail sentence for political activity
- been severely wounded in street fighting

Moreover, all party members who lost their lives in the service of the *NSDAP* were now to be automatically awarded the Blood Order, retroactive to 1923. It was therefore posthumously bestowed upon Horst Wessel, Hans Maikowski and other Nazi 'martyrs'. The expanded award criteria necessitated the striking of around 1,500 new medals,

103.   Every year on 9 November, the holders of the Blood Order paraded through Munich in solemn commemoration of the 1923 Putsch. *This picture, dating from 1935, shows Hitler and his closest associates about to lead the procession.*

distinguished by the absence of the Fuess mark and a modification in silver content to the more durable '800' standard. Several senior party figures, including Bormann himself, qualified for the Blood Order as a result of the 1938 edict. Bormann now received the *Blutorden* because he had been imprisoned during 1924–5 for complicity in the murder of Walther Kadow, his own former schoolteacher, who had allegedly betrayed Albert Leo Schlageter, the Nazi 'martyr' in the Ruhr. As another example, Security Police chief Dr Ernst Kaltenbrunner was presented with the award on 6 May 1942 on account of his having been jailed in 1934–5 for organising the then illegal Nazi party in Austria.

Distribution of the *Blutorden* was carefully controlled by the 'Office of 9th November', a body set up under the direction of Christian Weber, holder of Blood Order No. 84, to look after the welfare of the Old Guard and to organise and oversee their anniversary gatherings at the Munich *Bürgerbräukeller*, *Feldherrnhalle* and

Königsplatz. One of the most honoured guests at these functions was Elenore Baur, also known as Sister Pia, a Nazi nurse who had tended the wounded during the Putsch and who was one of only a handful of female recipients of the Blood Order. It is noteworthy and perhaps ironic that seven ordinary party members, including another female, Maria Hinle, who were killed by the unsuccessful bomb attempt on Hitler's life during the beer cellar reunion on 8 November 1939, each received the *Blutorden* posthumously. In all, 436 posthumous awards were made, the last being to *SS-Obergruppenführer* Reinhard Heydrich in June 1942.

The *Blutorden der NSDAP* was steeped in a deliberately cultivated mystique which made it the most revered decoration of the Nazi party. It was proudly borne on every possible occasion by its 3,000 or so recipients, although Hitler typically restricted the use of his own award, serial no. 1, to the annual Putsch celebrations. The instantly recognisable Blood Order ribbon, a length of which was always worn doubly furled around the flap of the right pocket instead of on the usual ribbon bar, became a status symbol in the Third Reich and guaranteed the wearer special privileges wherever he went.

Amt des Reichsstatthalters

NS=Vermittlungsstelle

Wien, I., Burg, Reichskanzleitrakt

Fernruf: R-23-1-48

N. S.-Vermittlungsstelle
beim
Reichsstatthalter
2 1. SEP. 1938

Bci. :

Fragebogen

für die

**Betreuung und Vermittlung der Parteiinvaliden — Lebenslängl. Verurteilten —
Mindestens ein Jahr in Haft Gewesenen — Ehrenzeichenträger und Anwärter —
Blutordenträgeranwärter**

I. Personalien:

Familien- und Taufname: *Dr Zechner Karl-Heinz*

Tag, Monat und Jahr der Geburt: *16. 7. 1910*

Ort, Bezirk und Land der Geburt: *Schönwald bei Lautsch CSR*

Staatsbürgerschaft: *Deutsches Reich* Familienstand: *ledig*

Anzahl und Alter der Kinder:

Genaue Wohnanschrift: *Wien 1, Kühnring 1*
(Ort, Land, Straße und Hausnummer)

Fernmündlich erreichbar: *V 12580 /744*

II. Parteidaten:

Eintritt in die NSDAP: *1934*   Mitglieds-Nr.:

Ortsgruppe:

Letzte Funktion in der Partei:

Angehöriger einer Parteigliederung seit: *SS*
(SA, SS, NSKK, HJ, NS-Frauenschaft, BDM usw.)

Dienstgrad: *Unterstuhrmführer*

Angehöriger der österr. Legion (ja oder nein) ———   (von — bis)

Waren Sie politischer Flüchtling im Altreich? (ja oder nein) *ja*   (von — bis) *Nov. 36 bis Dez.*

Militärdienst (von — bis)   Charge:

Kriegsdienstleistung (von — bis)   , davon Frontdienst (von — bis)

104. *Following the publication of revised criteria for award of the Blood Order on 30 May 1938, newly prospective holders were required to complete a questionnaire outlining their claim to the award. This example relates to SS-Unterstof Dr Karl-Heinz* Zechner, *an Austrian, who qualified for the* Blutorden *by virtue of his having been imprisoned between November 1936 and December 1937 for political activities.*

105. *The Honour Chevron of the Old Guard.*

106. *This citation entitled Horst Schneider to wear the Honour Chevron of the Old Guard with his* Waffen-SS *uniform. Schneider qualified for the badge on account of his having been an early member of the Hitler Youth.*

THE HONOUR CHEVRON OF THE OLD GUARD

On 3 February 1934, the Honour Chevron of the Old Guard, or *Ehrenwinkel für Alte Kämpfer*, was authorised for wear on the upper right arm by all members of uniformed *NSDAP* paramilitary organisations who had signed up prior to 30 January 1933. While the chevron was a simple piece of insignia, comprising a downward-facing silver or gold stripe, it was classed as an award and was presented with a certificate. The Honour Chevron came to be regarded as another badge of the 'die-hard' Nazi, even though, for example, an 18-year-old *SS* recruit in 1939 would have been entitled to wear it purely on account of his having been a 10-year-old Hitler Youth in 1931.

THE *SS* DEATH'S HEAD RING

On 10 April 1934, Himmler instituted the *SS* Death's Head Ring, or *Totenkopfring der SS*, for presenta-

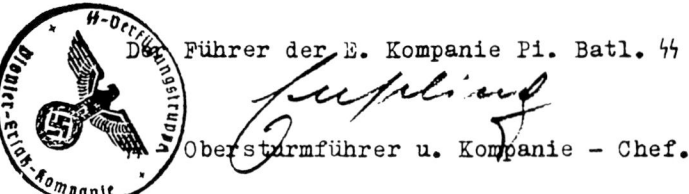

107. *The* SS *Death's Head Ring. This example was presented to* SS-Hauptsturmführer *Kurt Taschner on 9 November 1942.*

tion to his own Old Guard with *SS* membership numbers below 3,000. The ring, which had been distributed by the *Reichsführer* as a personal gift since 9 November 1933, now took on the status of an official *SS* honour and was presented with a citation. It comprised a massive band of silver oakleaves deeply embossed with a death's head and symbolic runes, and engraved inside with an inscription naming the recipient. Qualifications for award of the *Totenkopfring* were gradually extended until, by 1943, virtually all officers with over three years' service and *SS* holders of the Golden Party Badge, Coburg Badge and senior military decorations were eligible to receive it. Award of the ring could be withdrawn if the holder was punished for contravention of the *SS* discipline code. Around 14,500 rings were eventually awarded, with approximately 97 per cent of them going to officers. Only 350 or so went to NCOs, and around fifty to enlisted men, the majority of whom qualified as holders of the Golden Party Badge.

THE GOLDEN HITLER YOUTH BADGE

The next political decoration to be created was the Golden Hitler Youth Badge, instituted on 23 June 1934 by *Reichsjugendführer* Baldur von Schirach. Once again, it was an award for the Old Guard. It took the form of the normal *HJ* membership insignia with the addition of a wide gold border, and was intended to be a junior version of the Golden Party Badge. Generally known as the *HJ-*

108. *Nazi party awards.*
From left to right, top to bottom:
The Golden Hitler Youth Badge;
The Golden Hitler Youth Badge with Oakleaves;
The Berlin Gau *Badge, presented in Gold to the 30 founding members of the capital's branch of the* NSDAP *and in Silver to the 665 Berlin Nazis, including 41 females, who had joined the party prior to 1 June 1927;*
The East Prussia Gau *Badge;*
The Danzig-West Prussia Gau *Badge.*

Ehrenzeichen, or *HJ* Decoration, the badge was awarded to all members of the Hitler Youth who:

- had joined the organisation, or its predecessor the *Jungsturm Hitler*, prior to its first national rally at Potsdam on 2 October 1932; and
- had to their credit at least five years' service with the *HJ* or, if they had outgrown this, with some other *NSDAP* organisation like the *SA* or *SS*.

It could also be presented for an act of special merit within the Hitler Youth, irrespective of length of service. More than 13,000 *HJ-Ehrenzeichen* were issued, and they were permitted to be worn on military as well as political uniforms. In 1935, a far higher grade of the badge, with a border of gold oakleaves, was instituted as a national decoration for exceptional service to the Hitler Youth movement. No more than 250 were ever conferred, with recipients including such highly placed individuals as Himmler, Ley, Rosenberg and Todt. The award's prestige is indicated by the fact that it was often worn above the Golden Party Badge if that was also held. A unique version of the Golden Hitler Youth Badge with Oakleaves, manufactured from solid gold and set with diamonds and rubies, was gifted by the *HJ* leadership to von Schirach to mark the occasion of his thirty-fifth birthday on 9 May 1942, by which time he had become *Gauleiter* of Vienna.

GAU BADGES, 1935-6

Notwithstanding the introduction of the Golden Party Badge and the Blood Order, a number of *Gauleitern* still felt it necessary to create further *Gau-Ehrenzeichen* to reward their own Old Guard on a local basis. Josef Terboven presented decorations to the *NSDAP* veterans of Essen during the second half of 1935, to commemorate the tenth anniversary of the founding of the *Gau*. Manufactured by Hoffstätter of Bonn, the *Gau* Essen Badge took the form of a sword and two crossed hammers bearing the dates '1925' and '1935', and it was bestowed in hallmarked Silver and Silver-gilt grades depending upon extent of service. Three badges in 9 carat gold were given to Hitler, Göring and Dr Robert Ley. It is worthy of note that large quantities of a gilded aluminium version of the *Gau* Essen Badge were produced and sold as simple

commemoratives at the tenth anniversary rally. These are often confused with the awards proper. In October 1936 the *Gauleiter* of Berlin, Josef Goebbels, followed suit by contracting Lauer of Nuremberg to produce the *Gau-Ehrenzeichen* Berlin in Silver and Gold. The Gold class was reserved for the founding members of the capital's

109. Johannes Engel, founder of the Nazi factory workers' organisation, in his uniform as honorary SS-Brigadeführer, *1944. The Berlin* Gau *Badge in Silver is worn prominently alongside the Golden Party Badge. Also of note is the fact that Engel's War Merit Cross 1st Class is without Swords, while his Knight's Cross of the War Merit Cross has them.*

110. The Essen Gau Badge (left), alongside the larger and much more widely distributed 10th Anniversary Rally Badge (right), with which it is often confused.

branch of the Nazi party, and only thirty were ever awarded.

The prestige of the *Alter Kämpfer* was enhanced still further on 6 November 1936, when Deputy *Führer* Rudolf Hess issued a decree on behalf of Hitler elevating the earliest of the so-called Civil War Badges of the *NSDAP*, the Coburg Badge, the 1929 Nuremberg Party Day Badge and the Brunswick Rally Badge, to the status of national decorations, which meant that they could henceforth be worn on all military and civil uniforms as well as on those of the *NSDAP*. Authority to verify entitlement to the Coburg and Nuremberg awards was vested in local *NSDAP Kreisleitern*, while *SA-Standartenführer* were empowered to certify possession of the Brunswick badge.

THE *RZM*

During 1936–7 the *RZM* or *Reichszeugmeisterei*, a body which had been set up as early as 1 April 1929 to supervise the production and pricing of all Nazi party uniform items, was effectively reorganised by Richard Büchner and began to extend its influence into the realm of political awards. The basic functions of the *RZM* were to see that *NSDAP* contracts went to Aryan firms and to ensure that the final products were of a high standard, yet priced to suit the pocket of the average party member. It also acted as a clearing house between manufacturers on the one hand and wholesalers and retailers on the other. On 16 March 1935 contract numbers were introduced and awarded to every *RZM*-approved company, and after that date *RZM* numbers were supposed to replace makers' marks on all *NSDAP* accoutrements, although this directive took some time to work its way through the system. The Lüdenscheid firm of F.W. Assmann & Söhne, for example, which initially received the *RZM* contract number 17, regularly used its company logo alone or in conjunction with the '*RZM 17*' designation well into 1936. By the following year, the list of firms approved by the *RZM* had grown so considerably that it had to be divided into the following groups, depending upon function:

A – *Ausrüstung*: Equipment maker
B – *Baumwolle*: Cotton fabric manufacturer
D – *Dienstkleidung*: Service clothing producer
G – *Grosshandel*: Wholesaler
H – *Handelsvertreter*: Maker's agent
K – *Kleidereinzelhandel*: Clothing retailer
L – *Leder*: Leather goods maker
M – *Metall*: Metalware manufacturer
W – *Wolle*: Wool fabric producer

Each group was in turn subdivided into product categories, with those for metalware manufacturers being:

M1 – Insignia (except day badges)
M2 – Subcontractors
M3 – Emblems (standard tops etc.)
M4 – Belt buckles
M5 – Uniform fittings
M5a – Buttons
M5b – Side hooks
M5c – Snap hooks
M5d – Other metal fittings
M6 – Aluminium goods
M7 – Daggers
M8 – Metal accessories (tent pegs etc.)
M9 – Day badges
M10 – Musical instruments

New codes were then issued, prefixed by the relevant category designation. So far as the makers of *NSDAP* badges and political decorations were concerned, the designation was always 'M1'. Thus the Assmann logo and *RZM* code 17 were replaced by '*RZM* M1/17' on all of the firm's Nazi party insignia except day badges, which carried the company's 'M9' category code of '*RZM* M9/1'.

At the end of the day, only the more common and widely issued *NSDAP* decorations came to bear *RZM* marks. These were primarily Hitler Youth awards which were made by a number of different firms for local presentation and sale via authorised dealers holding the *RZM*'s 'E16' licence. Higher honours such as the Coburg Badge, Blood Order and Golden Party Badge were produced on single contract from the Party Chancellery, under strictly controlled conditions for centralised distribution, and could not be obtained locally. So far as they were concerned, that procedure negated the need for the more general quality control measures which the *RZM* applied to the production of cap badges, belt buckles and so on. Senior political decorations therefore continued to feature manufacturers' or designers' names, or no makers' marks at all, since they were not processed through the *RZM* system.

THE EAST PRUSSIA *GAU* BADGE

The sole new *NSDAP* award of 1938 was instituted by Erich Koch, *Gauleiter* of East Prussia, who that year distributed a silver *Gau* Badge to reward the 1,000 senior *Alter Kämpfer* in his area. Manufactured by Wächtler & Lange, the decoration featured an eagle and swastika over the East Prussian coat of arms.

NAZI PARTY LONG-SERVICE DECORATIONS

On 20 April 1939, Hitler created a series of awards known as the *Dienstauszeichnungen der NSDAP*, or Nazi Party Long-Service Decorations. These comprised a bronze cross for ten years' service, a silver and blue enamel cross for fifteen years, and a gold and white enamel cross for twenty-five years. Unusually, all three grades could be worn simultaneously. Each decoration was made in three parts, with an eagle and swastika on the obverse and the

111. NSDAP *Long-Service Decorations for 15 Years (left) and 10 years (right).*

legend *Treue für Führer und Volk* ('Loyal to leader and people') on the reverse. The qualification for award was to have served the requisite number of years in an active capacity in any of the *NSDAP* uniformed organisations, including the Corps of Political Leaders, *SA*, *SS*, *NSKK*, *NSFK*, *NSBO*, *NSKOV*, *DAF*, *HJ*, *Deutsches Jungvolk* (*DJ*), *BDM* and *Jungmädel* (*JM*). So far as membership of a youth organisation was concerned, eligibility was restricted to adult officers. Presentations were made twice annually, on 30 January and 20 April, with the first awards being bestowed in 1940. Service prior to 30 January 1933 counted as double.

112. *The* NSDAP *25-Year Long Service Decoration.*

In other words, a man who joined the *SA* in 1925 and kept up his active membership thereafter, breaking only for *RAD* or military duties, would have qualified for the twenty-five-year decoration in 1943. The *Dienstauszeichnungen der NSDAP* ranked behind *Wehrmacht* long-service awards, but before national commemorative medals. A small number of women were eligible to receive the decoration, in which case it was worn around the neck, like the Mother's Cross, or from a bow on the left breast. While the crosses themselves were usually unmarked, the principal manufacturer of this award is known to have been Wilhelm Deumer of Lüdenscheid, whose *RZM* code 'M1/120' appears on many surviving presentation cases. Two variants of the twenty-five-year decoration exist, one with a neck suspender and the other with a pin-back fitting. These are considered to be prototypes of special grades for meritorious service which were never approved for general production, being superseded by the German Order.

THE DANZIG CROSS

The city of Danzig and its immediate surroundings was removed from Germany after the First World War and placed under the protection of the League of Nations as a Free City. However, the German nationalist movement inside the territory retained considerable influence and strength, and in June 1933 Danzig elected a Nazi-dominated government. From then on, it modelled itself closely on Hitler's Reich. On 1 May 1939, *Gauleiter* Albert Forster instituted a *Gau-Ehrenzeichen* Danzig-Westpreussen for presentation to his local *NSDAP* veterans. The new *Gau* Badge featured a swastika surmounted by the twin crosses and coronet of Danzig, and the legend *Alter Kämpfer*. Probably no more than 300 bestowals of this decoration were made before it was withdrawn and replaced by the *Danziger Kreuz*, or Danzig Cross, again created by Forster.

The Danzig Cross was instituted on 31 August 1939 and comprised a white enamel cross bearing the Danzig arms in gold. Designed by Benno von Arent, the decoration came in two classes: a 60 mm convex pin-back 1st Class; and a 43 mm 2nd Class worn from a ribbon. The *Danziger Kreuz* was bestowed in recognition of meritorious service in the building up of the Nazi party within the Free City. Most awards were made at a ceremony on 24 October 1939, during which eighty-eight 1st Classes and 253 2nd Classes were conferred. The commanding officer, staff officers and company commanders of the *SS-Heimwehr Danzig*, the city's 'SS Home Guard', were all awarded the Danzig Cross 1st Class, while every platoon commander received the 2nd Class and lower ranks a commemorative lapel badge. This acknowledged the *Heimwehr*'s actions in securing Danzig for Germany during the first days of the Second World War.

THE WARTHELAND *GAU* BADGE

Gau Posen was created from scratch on 26 October 1939, following the dissolution of Poland, and three

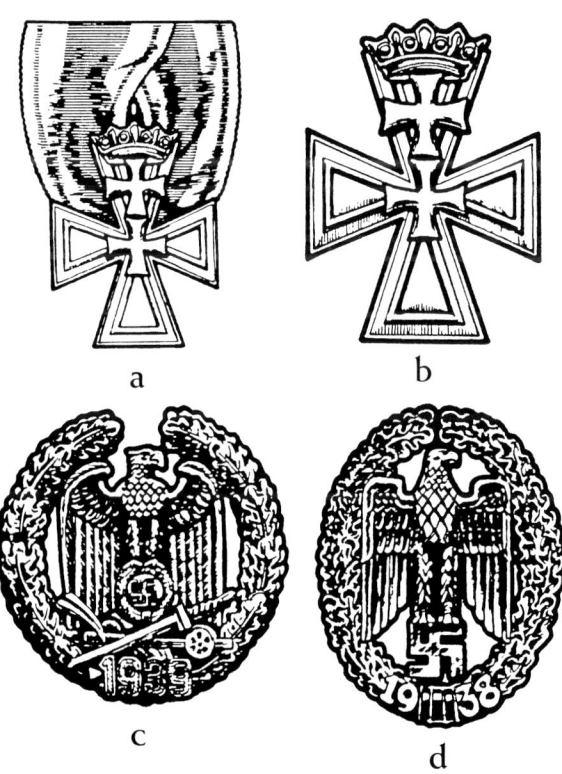

113. NSDAP *awards.*
(a) The Danzig Cross 2nd Class;
(b) The Danzig Cross 1st Class;
(c) The Wartheland Gau *Badge;*
(d) The Sudetenland Gau *Badge.*

months later was renamed *Gau* Wartheland after the River Warthe which ran through it. The new *Gauleiter* was Arthur Greiser, formerly Forster's deputy in Danzig, and shortly after taking office he felt obliged to institute his own Wartheland *Gau* Badge comprising a wreathed eagle and swastika over a sword, plough and the date '1939'. It was awarded in very limited numbers for meritorious service rendered during the foundation of the *Gau*. The only known photographs of this extremely rare decoration being worn date from 1943, when it was seen on the tunic of *SS-Obergruppenführer* Wilhelm Koppe.

THE GERMAN ORDER
At the end of 1939, Deputy *Führer* Rudolf Hess published proposals for a revised range of *NSDAP* decorations, principally to recognise war service, comprising:

- the basic Party Badge (already looked upon as a 'badge of honour' for wear by all Nazi Party members)
- a new Silver Party Decoration (to be bestowed for merit upon the recommendation of *Reichsleitern* or *Gauleitern*)
- the Golden Party Decoration (already being awarded for special merit in the cause of National Socialism)
- a new Golden Party Decoration on a Runic Star (not further described)
- a new Grand Cross of the Golden Party Decoration (as the highest *NSDAP* award)

Trial samples were struck by the Deumer firm, but Hess's proposals were apparently not progressed further at that time. However, when *Reichsminister* Dr Fritz Todt, designer of the *autobahn* system and the Siegfried Line defences and a member of the Nazi party since 1922, was killed in an air crash shortly after leaving *Führer* Headquarters at Rastenburg on 8 February 1942, Hitler almost immediately introduced an *NSDAP* Order, which he ranked as the party's highest honour. He bestowed it posthumously upon Todt on the occasion of the latter's state funeral three days later. The new award had evidently been designed and manufactured well before Todt's death and seems to have been based

114.   The neck cross of the German Order, without Swords. Several undocumented and unauthenticated variants of this mysterious decoration exist.

on Hess's suggested Grand Cross of the Golden Party Decoration.

By 1942, Hess had been disgraced and his somewhat clumsy designation was never used. The award was subsequently known by a multitude of slightly different titles, including the National German Order, the Golden Cross of the German Order and the Chancellery German Order, all of which took account of Hitler's personal desire that it should be called simply the German Order, or *Deutscher Orden*, a term previously used when referring to the Teutonic Order of the Middle Ages.

Believed to have been designed by Benno von Arent and manufactured by Wilhelm Deumer, the German Order took the form of a black enamel cross with gold eagles between the arms. The centrepiece was the Golden Party Badge and a facsimile of Hitler's signature appeared on the reverse, reinforcing the personal nature of the award. The entire cross was surmounted by a large gold laurel wreath, crossed swords, an eagle and

115. *Adolf Hitler adds the German Order to the many decorations displayed on Reinhard Heydrich's funeral pillows, 9 June 1942.*

oakleaves, and it was to be hung around the neck from a distinctive ribbon identical to that of the Blood Order, but wider. Apart from Dr Todt, the only known recipients were:

9 June 1942 – *SS-Obergruppenführer* Reinhard Heydrich (posthumous)

22 June 1942 – *NSKK-Korpsführer* Adolf Huhnlein (posthumous)

8 May 1943 – *SA-Stabschef* Viktor Lutze (posthumous)

3 October 1944 – *Gauleiter* Josef Bürckel (committed suicide in November 1944)

7 October 1944 – *Generalmajor* Rudolf Schmundt (posthumous)

24 February 1945 – *Reichsarbeitsführer* Konstantin Hierl

12 April 1945 – *Gauleiter* Karl Hanke (murdered several weeks later)

19 April 1945 – *Gauleiter* Karl Holz (killed in action the following day)

28 April 1945 – *Reichsjugendführer* Artur Axmann

Dönitz, Himmler and Speer were also considered for the award, but so far as can be ascertained never received it. For obvious reasons, this decoration came to be known somewhat melodramatically as The Order of the Dead. No photographs of it being worn have ever come to light, although it was clearly pictured, perhaps significantly without a ribbon, on the funeral pillows of Todt and Heydrich.

116. *The German Order.*
(a) Neck cross with laurel leaves and swords, as photographed on the funeral pillows of Todt and Heydrich;
(b) Breast cross without swords, approved but never conferred.

a

b

It is likely that Hitler intended to use the German Order primarily as a means of personally acknowledging ongoing services to the *NSDAP*, thereby negating the need for further awards of the Old Guard's Blood Order and Golden Party Badge, aspects of which were incorporated into its design.

117. No photographs showing the German Order in wear are known to exist. This artist's impression of Gauleiter Karl Hanke illustrates how he would have worn the neck cross bestowed upon him on 12 April 1945.

However, since the Order is known to have been manufactured in at least two classes and six different versions, both with and without swords, it is also possible that he contemplated a postwar extension of its scope to make the German Order the principal state award for services of a more general nature which were not already covered by some specific decoration or medal, i.e. a sort of elevated peacetime version of the War Merit Cross. In any event, no further presentations were made, or award criteria published, and the history of the *Deutscher Orden* remains shrouded in obscurity. It is worthy of note that the Order and ribbon have been exquisitely reproduced in strictly controlled quantities since the 1960s, with fakes changing hands for astronomical sums.

THE SUDETENLAND *GAU* BADGE

The last political decoration of the Third Reich was the Sudetenland *Gau* Badge, instituted by *Gauleiter* Konrad Henlein in January 1944. Designed by Franz Moser and Otto Zappe, the gold and silver insignia featured an eagle and swastika above the black/red/black Sudeten colours and the date '1938', reflecting the year of the *Gau*'s foundation. The decoration was to be awarded annually on 1 October, and the first and last presentation ceremony duly took place on 1 October 1944, with badges being bestowed on a very limited basis to a selected few of those who had pioneered Nazism in Czechoslovakia during the 1930s, or who had performed particularly meritorious work in the *Gau* during the war. Recipients included *SA-Stabschef* Wilhelm Schepmann, and the widow of Sudeten Nazi 'martyr' Hans Knirsch.

Civil Awards

While most civil decorations of the Third Reich were created after Hitler's assumption of power, a few predated the advent of Nazism.

THE GERMAN NATIONAL SPORTS BADGE

The German National Sports Badge was instituted as early as 1913, and underwent several design changes which culminated in 1937 with the addition of a swastika below the '*DRL*' monogram of the *Deutscher Reichsbund für Leibesübungen*, or German National Physical Training Union. This finely made award came in three classes, Bronze, Silver and Gold, and was given for regularly demonstrated proficiency in swimming, jumping, running, weight-throwing, cycling and so on. A cloth version was authorised for wear on the athletics shirt, and a small silver variant with the initials 'RJA' ('*Reichs Jugendsport Abzeichen*') was presented to qualifying schoolchildren. Vast numbers of the *DRL* Sports Badge were ultimately bestowed, with 95,000 presentations in 1938 alone. On 18 November 1942 an additional class, with a gold wreath and silver

118. *This* NSKK-Sturmführer *wears the pre-Nazi version of the German National Sports Badge, below insignia denoting his participation in the Upper Bavarian* SA *and* SS *ski competition held at Bad Tölz in 1933.*

119. *Left: The German National Sports Badge, by Hermann Wernstein;*
Right: The National Youth Sports Badge for female schoolchildren, by Hermann Wernstein. The male version of this award took the form of a stickpin, rather than the brooch shown.

monogram, was instituted for war-wounded civilians and members of the armed forces who in spite of considerable disabilities managed to attain high standards in the various test exercises. This development highlighted the fact that Nazi Germany placed great emphasis on physical fitness across the entire spectrum of its population, with members of all military, political and civil uniformed organisations being encouraged to win and wear the *DRL* Sports Badge.

THE RED CROSS DECORATION
Another pre-Nazi award which Hitler allowed to continue was the Red Cross Decoration, instituted

120. *The Red Cross Decoration.*
Top: The Star of the Grand Cross;
Bottom left: 1st Class;
Bottom right: Medal.

in 1922 by the President of the German Red Cross. During the early period of the Third Reich, the Red Cross Society and the Order of St John were the main social-welfare organisations tending to the needs of the German people in times of hardship. While the so-called *Johanniter Orden* bestowed by the latter body was a private award, the Red Cross Decoration came to be regarded as a state-approved means of recognising significant contributions in this area of work. After design changes in 1934 and 1937, it eventually took the form of a gold and white enamel cross surmounted by a black eagle and swastika with a Red Cross shield in the centre. The award, which was manufactured principally by the

Berlin firms of Gebrüder Godet and Alfred Stübbe, came in all the usual international grades, from a Grand Cross to a Medal, to allow for every level of service. In the days before the advent of the Order of the German Eagle, the Red Cross Decoration was conferred liberally on 'friendly' foreigners with whom the Reich wished to curry favour. Such recipients included Mussolini, Princess Olga of Yugoslavia and the mother of King Farouk of Egypt.

THE EAGLE SHIELD OF GERMANY

The *Adlerschild des Deutschen Reiches*, or Eagle Shield of Germany, also made its first appearance in

121. Police Oberst *Dr Nozleff (right) wearing the Cross of Merit of the German Red Cross below his left breast pocket. He is accompanied by* SS-Oberführer *Otto Steinhäusl, Police President of Vienna, who took part in the Austrian Nazi* Putsch *of 1934 and was consequently awarded the Blood Order in 1939. He died the following year.*

122. The Eagle Shield of Germany.

123.   Equestrian badges.
From left to right:
The German Horseman's Badge;
The German Horse Driver's Badge;
The German Young Horseman's Badge.

1922. This non-portable award, devised by President Ebert and comprising a detachable round 110 mm bronze medallion mounted on a pedestal, came to supersede the civil division of the Order *Pour le Mérite* and was given to academics whose intellectual creations had benefited the German people. The Nazi eagle and swastika became the centrepiece of the medallion in 1934, and approval for bestowal thereafter rested with the *Führer* personally. The holder's name and achievements were cast into the reverse of each piece. By 1943 only sixty Eagle Shields had been presented, with recipients including the composer Richard Strauss and the Nazi historian Dr Erwin Kolbenheyer.

EQUESTRIAN BADGES, 1930–2

On 9 April 1930, the German National Federation for the Breeding and Testing of Thoroughbreds instituted the *Deutsches Reiterabzeichen*, or German Horseman's Badge, in the form of a mounted rider enclosed by an oakleaf wreath with the letter 'R' at the base. The badge came in three classes, Bronze, Silver and Gold, and was awarded for success in horse-racing or at tournaments, or for outstanding equestrian achievement. The following month the Federation introduced the German Horse Driver's

Badge, depicting a man in a two-horse chariot, which was similarly presented in three classes for success in trotting and other appropriate competitions. The German Young Horseman's Badge, awarded to boys under the age of seventeen who demonstrated proficiency in horsemanship, was instituted in July 1932 and was a small round bronze version of the *Deutsches Reiterabzeichen*. All of these equestrian badges were later afforded the status of national decorations by Hitler, and over 100,000 were eventually distributed.

THE GOETHE MEDAL FOR ART AND SCIENCE

The last pre-Nazi civil award which continued to be presented during the Third Reich was the Goethe Medal for Art and Science, founded in 1932 to reward outstanding achievement in the Goethe centennial year. It was initially intended to be a one-time award, but President von Hindenburg retained it as a national medal and this practice was carried on by Hitler. The *Goethe-Medaille für Kunst und Wissenschaft* took the form of a 70 mm non-portable silver medallion with a profile of Goethe on the obverse and the German eagle on the reverse. The holder's name was engraved around the edge, beside the stamped silver hallmark '835' and maker's abbreviation 'PR.ST.M.B.', denoting the Berlin mint. Recipients included well-known personalities prominent in the fields of literature, medicine, architecture, engineering and exploration. By 1943, when the last figures were published, a total of 467 Goethe medals had been awarded.

124. *The Goethe Medal for Art and Science.*
Top: Obverse;
Bottom: Reverse.

125. *Civil awards.*
(a) The Life-Saving Medal;
(b) The Life-Saving Medallion;
(c) The Anhalt *Badge;*
(d) The Steel Helmet Veterans' Decoration.

LIFE-SAVING AWARDS

Following Hitler's appointment as Chancellor on 30 January 1933, the first national civil decoration to be instituted was the Life-Saving Medal, or *Rettungsmedaille*. Based on a Prussian award dating back over a century, the medal was created on 22 June 1933 to recognise those who had saved human life at the risk of their own. The obverse bore a federal eagle, complete with swastika after 1937, while the reverse featured the legend *Für Rettung aus Gefahr* ('For rescuing from danger'). The medal with its yellow and white ribbon was very rarely issued, partly due to the fact that a larger non-portable medallion of similar design was available for life-saving of a lesser degree. On 25 September 1933 the German Life-Saving Association, or *Deutschen Lebensrettungsgesellschaft*, which was concerned solely with swimming and water safety, followed suit by creating its own special badge for saving the life of an endangered person in the water. This silver insignia depicted a wreathed eagle standing on a rocky island surmounted by the letters *'DLRG'*.

THE ANHALT BADGE

On 30 September 1933, the State of Anhalt issued an award commemorating the foundation by Konstantin Hierl in 1928 of the Anhalt *Arbeitsdienst*, or *AAD*, which was the forerunner of the Nazi National Labour Service, the *Reichsarbeitsdienst*, or *RAD*. The Anhalt Badge took the form of a swastika enclosing the monogram *AAD* and came in Bronze, Silver and Gold grades. It

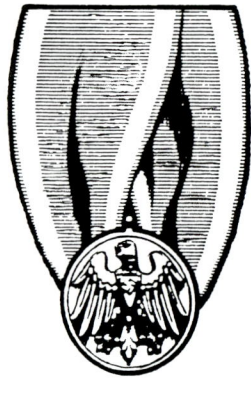

a

b

c

d

was bestowed according to length of service, and a version bearing the date '1932' was reserved for the Old Guard of the *AAD* and *RAD*. The Anhalt Badge received semi-official recognition by Hitler and was permitted to be worn only with the *RAD* uniform.

THE STEEL HELMET VETERANS' DECORATION

November 1933 saw the introduction by the Steel Helmet War Veterans' Association of a badge for its long-standing members. The *Stahlhelm* had supported Hitler during his struggle for power, and the new award was allowed to be worn on all types of uniform during the next two years until the dissolution of the Association. The *Ehrenzeichen Alte Garde des Stahlhelm* was a black enamel disc featuring a silver steel helmet over two oakleaves above the date of the holder's enrolment in the organisation. These dates ran from 1918 (seventeen recipients) to 1932. The reverse of each award bore the maker's mark of Steinhauer & Lück, the wearer's unit designation, his precise date of joining, the *Ges.Gesch* patent pending stamp and a silver hallmark.

THE *SA* SPORTS BADGE

On 28 November 1933, *SA-Stabschef* Ernst Röhm created the ubiquitous *SA* Sports Badge, which took the form of a Roman sword superimposed over a swastika within an oakleaf wreath. This bronze decoration, which looked very much like the Coburg Badge, was to be given for athletic prowess and was initially restricted to members of the *SA* and *SS*. Its reverse bore the legend *Eigentum d. Chefs d. Ausbildungswesens*, or 'Property of the Chief of Training Staff', indicating that the badge would be 'on loan' to the recipient only for so long as he could demonstrate the required standard of fitness. Hitler quickly saw the benefits of using such an award to encourage the physical development of the male population as a whole, and on 15 February 1935 he decreed that the *SA-Sportabzeichen* was to be given national status, expanded to include Silver and Gold grades, and opened to the public at large. The upgraded badge was distinguished by the inscription *Eigentum des SA-Sportabzeichen-Hauptstelle*, or 'Property of the *SA* Sports Badge Department', on the reverse. In January 1939, with the entire country on a general war footing, the designation of the decoration was changed to *SA-Wehrabzeichen*, or *SA* Defence Badge, and the emphasis was thereafter placed on military sports. The property mark on the back was revised yet again, this time to read *Eigentum der Obersten SA-Führung*. All able-bodied German males were challenged to earn the award, which now took on a greater significance than ever before as it encouraged potential combatants to train in military-related areas.

The test exercises for the *SA-Wehrabzeichen* had to be passed regularly in order to retain the badge, and were divided into three groups as follows:

- Physical exercises
    - 100 metre sprint
    - Long jump
    - Shot putting
    - Long-distance throwing
    - 3,000 metre run

- Military exercises
    - 25 kilometre route march with pack
    - Rifle shooting
    - Grenade throwing
    - 200 metre obstacle course in gas mask
    - Swimming or cycle speed test
    - First aid

126. The SA *Sports Badge, by Werner Redo.*

- Field exercises
    - Map reading
    - Judging terrain and estimating ranges
    - Signalling
    - Reconnaissance

- or Seamanship
    - 25 minute row
    - Casting line
    - Knotting
    - Morse and semaphore
    - Compass/navigation

The Bronze badge was given to men under thirty-five years of age who passed all the tests within a period of twelve months. The Silver version went to men under thirty-five who passed the tests annually for five consecutive years, or to men between thirty-five and forty who passed the tests once within twelve months. The Gold badge was given to men over forty who passed the tests within a year. A variant bearing an anchor on the obverse was created for the *Marine-SA*, but appears to have been seldom, if ever, awarded.

SA Sports Badges earned prior to the outbreak of the Second World War bore issue serial numbers on the reverse. However, this practice ceased for economy reasons in 1939. By the end of 1943, over 2,500,000 *SA-Wehrabzeichen* had been bestowed. Miniatures were authorised for wear on the left lapel of civilian clothes, and woven versions could be sewn to the athletics vest. A personalised candidate's booklet, specifically devoted to the recording of the tests required for the badge, was kept up to date as necessary, and upon successful completion an official award document contained within it was endorsed and signed by the issuing authority.

LÄNDER AWARDS, 1933–4

The months following the institution of the *SA* Sports Badge witnessed the creation of a selection of state, or *Länder*, decorations to reward local Fire Service personnel. The first of these dated from 21 December 1933 and took the form of a pin-back silver badge depicting an old-fashioned fireman above a blazing house. It was given by the then Prussian Minister of the Interior, Hermann Göring, in recognition of an act of bravery or special merit

127. *The Bavarian State Medal for 25 Years' Service in Industry. This and similar* Länder *awards were superseded on 30 January 1938 by the Faithful Service Decoration.*

or, alternatively, for twenty-five years' service in the Prussian Fire Brigade. In April 1934, the states of Baden and Hanover began to bestow their equivalent decorations, and Hesse, North Rhineland and Thüringia followed suit. Around the same time, the Chamber of Industry and Commerce of the state of Anhalt issued a medal *Für Treue in der Arbeit* ('For loyal work'), paralleled by the Bavarian State Medal for 25 Years' Service in Industry, the East Thüringian Medal for Loyal Work and the Badge for 25 Years' Service to the Economy of Pfalz Province. All of these *Länder* awards were short-lived, however, for Hitler replaced them with newly created Reich-level decorations of his own.

THE *BDM* AND *JM* PROFICIENCY CLASPS

On 28 April 1934, Baldur von Schirach instituted the *Bund Deutscher Mädel Leistungsabzeichen*, or League of German Girls Proficiency Clasp, to be awarded to girls between the ages of fourteen and twenty-one who successfully passed tests in first aid, nursing, home economics, athletics and political ideology. It was, therefore, to some limited

128. *Left: The* BDM *Proficiency Clasp;*
Right: The JM *Proficiency Clasp.*

extent a junior female version of the *SA* Sports Badge, and was presented in two classes, Bronze and Silver, and three subdivisions, namely Grades A, B and C, depending upon marks scored in the various examinations. The Clasp comprised the letters '*BDM*' inside a rectangular metal frame surmounting a 29 mm length of red/white/red ribbon.

The reverse bore the the maker's *RZM* code and the award serial number. It was worn on the left breast of the *BDM* uniform and around 200,000 examples were eventually bestowed. A very similar clasp, taking the form of the letters '*JM*' in silver on a red ribbon, was given to girls between the ages of ten and fourteen who belonged to the *Jungmädel* organisation and passed tests akin to those of the *BDM*. Approximately 70,000 were awarded. It is interesting to note that these female youth awards predated, even if only by a few weeks, their male counterparts.

THE *HJ* PROFICIENCY BADGE

In June 1934, von Schirach instituted the *HJ Leistungsabzeichen*, or Hitler Youth Proficiency

129. *The so-called Death's Head Swimming Badge was awarded by the German Swimming League for completing three hours' continuous and unaided swimming in the open sea. The accompanying photograph shows it being worn by a Cologne-based member of the naval branch of the Hitler Youth.*

Badge, which was thereafter to form the basis of all *HJ* boys' training. This badge took the form of a Nordic Tyr-Rune, symbolic of leadership, and could be awarded in Iron (i.e. black), Bronze or Silver depending upon the age of the recipient. Each of these grades was in turn subdivided into three levels of proficiency, again characterised as A, B or C. The tests leading to an award of the *HJ Leistungsabzeichen* revolved around sports, athletics, shooting, route marching, map-reading, camouflage and so on. There was originally also a test on political knowledge, but that was dropped during the war when the emphasis switched entirely to paramilitary training. The badge was supposed to be worn on the right breast pocket, but wearing on the left was also commonplace. By the end of 1943, over 350,000 awards had been made.

Notwithstanding the predominance of the *HJ* Proficiency Badge amongst youth decorations, a number of approved sports associations were permitted to continue the distribution of their own proficiency badges. For example, the German Cycling

130. Youth Proficiency Badges.
From left to right, top to bottom:
The HJ *Proficiency Badge in Silver, by Steinhauer & Lück;*
The HJ *Proficiency Badge in Black, by Karl Wurster;*

The DJ *Proficiency Badge, by Wilhelm Deumer;*
The HJ *Leader's Sports Badge, by Gustav Brehmer;*
The German Youth Cyclist's Badge, by Lehmann & Wunderberg.

Association, or *Deutscher Radfahr Verband*, which was affiliated to the *NSDAP*, awarded the *Deutsches Jugend-Radfahrabzeichen* to young cyclists who passed designated tests.

THE *HJ* EXPERT SKIER BADGE

Around the same time as the *HJ Leistungsabzeichen* was created, the Hitler Youth Expert Skier Badge, comprising a 60 mm silver disc enclosing an edelweiss, skis, an enamelled *HJ* diamond and the legend *HJ Ski Führer* made its first appearance. It was the largest of all the youth awards and was intended as a qualification badge for ski instructors in the *HJ*, *DJ*, *BDM* and *JM*. The sole manufacturer was Wittmann of Munich. The *Skiführerabzeichen* was probably withdrawn shortly after its introduction, since no photograph of it being worn has come to light. It was most likely replaced by the later *HJ-Schiwart* Cuff Stripe, a form of miniature cuff title, which was authorised for wear by those supervising Hitler Youth skiing courses.

RIFLE ASSOCIATION AWARDS

The year 1934 also saw the German Rifle Association, or *Deutscher Schützen Verband*, fall under the control of the *NSDAP*. Hundreds of local shooting clubs had been established long before the advent of the Third Reich and were considered by Hitler to have great potential in the field of paramilitary and pre-military training. Shooting contests

131. *The HJ Expert Skier Badge.*

132. *A selection of typical Rifle Club awards. From left to right:*
A cross presented as 5th prize at a D.Sch.V. shooting contest held at Esserden in 1936;
A badge for the winners in a rifle competition organised in 1940 by the Kyffhäuser Association for War Veterans;
A medal presented at a shooting contest between former imperial light infantrymen held at Hagen on 2 and 3 September 1933.

were gala events at which competitors took their marksmanship very seriously, and club uniforms were normally worn during the proceedings. The *D.Sch.V.* was soon given overall responsibility for instituting and rendering a new Nazified series of prize-winners' decorations which had no fixed pattern and were often designed locally for single events. They were commonly suspended from ribbons in green and white (the colours of the Rifle Association), blue (for loyal service) or red, white and black (the national colours). Due to the unofficial nature of these awards, Dr Frick, the Reich Minister of the Interior, published regulations governing their wear, to the extent that they could be worn only on the shooting uniform when *en route* to and from, and while at, events run by the Association. The wearing of *D.Sch.V.* shooting medals with military uniform or civilian clothing was strictly forbidden.

THE DANZIG RED CROSS DECORATION

On 13 December 1934, the Supreme Council of the Danzig Red Cross instituted a decoration to recognise special merit in serving the welfare needs of the local population. It featured the Danzig arms with swastika, a Red Cross and the inscription *Rotes Kreuz der Freien Stadt Danzig*. Two lesser grades, a Cross of Merit 1st Class and 2nd Class, were given for twenty-five years' and ten years' service respectively in the Danzig Red Cross. These long-service awards were innovative, since the national German

Red Cross Society did not reward long service on the part of its own staff. They had to wait until 1937 for a similar series of decorations.

THE *TENO* DECORATION

On 20 April 1935 the *Ehrenzeichen der Technischen Nothilfe*, or *Teno* Decoration, was created to reward longstanding members of the Technical Emergency Service. This organisation had been formed in September 1919 as a voluntary strike-breaking force of right-wing tradesmen and technicians, and under the Nazis it evolved into a massive auxiliary police corps controlled by the *SS*. The bulk of *Teno*'s domestic work came to be of an air-raid defence nature, dealing with breakdowns in public services and utilities caused by bomb damage. In addition, front-line construction and repair units known as *Tenokommandos* operated with the *Wehrmacht* during the Second World War. The new bronze award was limited to veteran members who had joined *Teno* between 1919 and 1923, and it took the form of an eagle surmounting a swastika, a cogwheel and the letters '*TN*'. Each badge was numbered on the reverse and bore the logo of the manufacturer, Wilhelm Fühner of Pforzheim. In June

133.   The Danzig Red Cross Decoration.
(a) Decoration for Special Merit;
(b) Cross of Merit 1st Class, for 25 years' service;
(c) Cross of Merit 2nd Class, for 10 years' service.

a

b

c

134. *The* Teno *Decoration.*

1936, the short-lived *Teno* Decoration was replaced by a series of black and yellow cuff titles, or *Jahresbanden*, each bearing laurel leaves and one of the dates 1919–1923. The Decoration was rein-

stated on 1 May 1944 as a merit badge, but was seldom bestowed thereafter.

THE *DJ* PROFICIENCY BADGE

On 26 September 1935, boys between the ages of ten and fourteen who were members of the *Deutsches Jungvolk* were granted their own proficiency badge. They had previously been eligible for the *HJ Leistungsabzeichen* in Black, but the new award reflected the recently enhanced status of the *DJ*. It was presented for demonstrated proficiency in general academics, athletics, field exercises and air-rifle shooting, and took the form of an aluminium Sig-rune enclosing a swastika surmounted by the legend *Für Leistung im DJ*. Cloth versions were produced for wear with the sports kit, and a half-size metal miniature was authorised for use on the left lapel of school uniform and civilian clothes. By 1943, when the last reliable figures were made available, almost 153,000 awards of this finely produced insignia had been conferred. It is remarkable that even with such a very junior decoration every piece was stamped on the reverse with the award serial number.

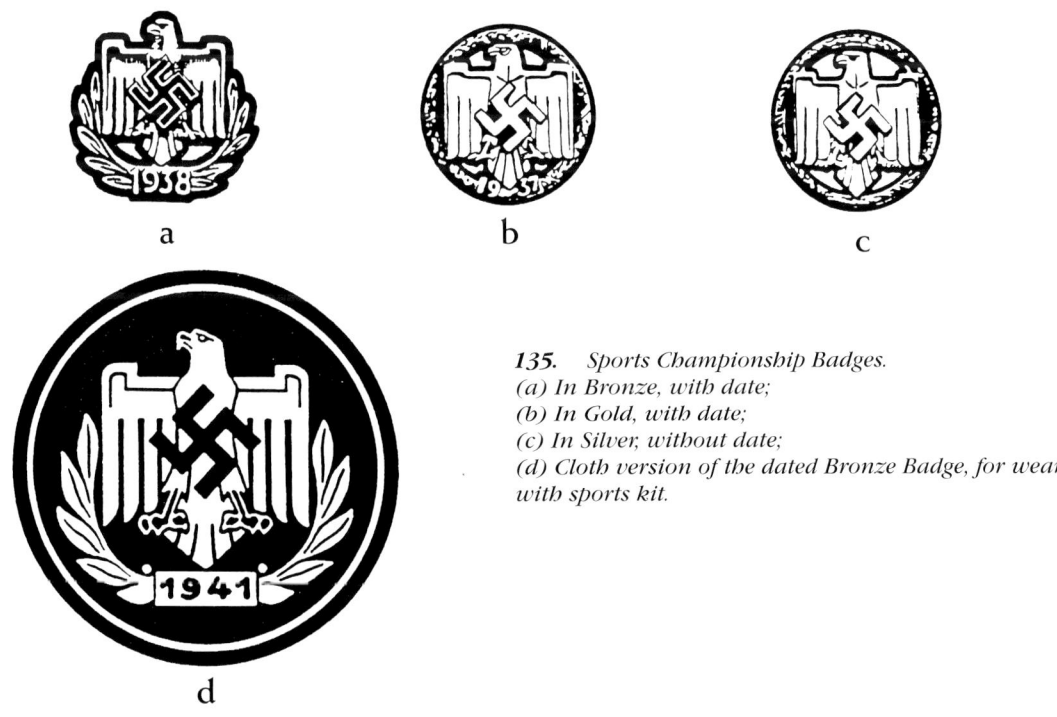

a

b

c

d

135. *Sports Championship Badges.*
(a) In Bronze, with date;
(b) In Gold, with date;
(c) In Silver, without date;
(d) Cloth version of the dated Bronze Badge, for wear with sports kit.

SPORTS CHAMPIONSHIP BADGES

On 14 November 1935 the National Socialist Physical Training League, predecessor of the *DRL*, instituted championship badges or *Meisterschaftsabzeichen*, to recognise achievements in the general sports field. These awards were small stickpins designed for wear with civilian clothing only, and were graded as follows:

- Bronze with date – worn for one year only, in recognition of excellence in a single sport
- Bronze without date – permanent award for excellence in multiple sports
- Silver with date – worn for one year only, by runners-up in a single German national championship athletic event
- Silver without date – permanent award for excellence in representing Germany in international competitions
- Gold with date – permanent award for national champions in sports events

The *Meisterschaftsabzeichen* continued to be bestowed by the *DRL*, retaining their original central design of a square-winged eagle with a swastika on its chest.

THE OLYMPIC GAMES DECORATION

The sporting theme of Nazi awards reached its climax on 4 February 1936, with the institution of the *Deutsches Olympiaehrenzeichen*, or Olympic Games Decoration. The 11th Olympiad had been planned since the Weimar period and the main events were held in August 1936 in Berlin, with the earlier Winter Games taking place at Garmisch-Partenkirchen near Munich. Hitler used the spectacle to show off his new order to the world in grand style, and the power and magnificence of the Third Reich in its high summer shone through the classic cinema feature film which Leni Riefenstahl made of the games. The *Olympiaehrenzeichen* was not a contestants' award, but was intended to recognise the considerable 'behind the scenes' work which went into the preparation of this political and propaganda coup. Recipients therefore included Riefenstahl, Himmler and other senior *SS* officers who were responsible for the policing and security of the event, foreign diplomats representing the

participating nations, architects who designed the Olympic stadium and so on.

The convex award, drawn up by Prof. Waldemar Raemisch, was very modernist in design, comprising what can only be described as a five-armed Maltese cross in white enamel over a five-armed

136. *The Olympic Games Decoration.*
Top: 1st Class;
Bottom: 2nd Class.

137. The Olympic Games Medal, mounted on a bow for wear by a female.

gold sunburst, surmounted by a stylised eagle and swastika and the five Olympic rings. From a distance, it resembled the star-shaped Nordic Hagall-Rune. The 1st Class (767 recipients) was suspended around the neck while the 2nd Class (3,364 awards) was worn from a ribbon on the left breast. Citations presented to German winners featured Hitler's domestic title *Der Führer und Reichskanzler*, whereas those for foreigners were signed in the name of *Der Deutsche Reichskanzler*. A silver medal, bearing the national emblem, Olympic rings and date '1936', was distributed to 55,000 minor officials, journalists and commentators who rendered lesser services which contributed towards the smooth running of the games.

The *DRL* commissioned an entirely separate series of medals in Gold, Silver and Bronze for the victors in the various sporting competitions of the Olympiad, and a non-portable medallion featuring the famous Olympic bell was given by the organising committee to all the athletes and general workers involved as a commemorative keepsake.

POLICE EXPERT MOUNTAINEER BADGES

During the summer of 1936, the *Gendarmerie Alpinist* and *Hochalpinist* badges were created for presentation to members of the Rural Police qualified as expert mountaineers. Both insignia were produced by Klein of Vienna and their designs incorporated the Nazi Police eagle, an ice pick and an edelweiss wreath. Mountain gendarmes operated in the Alps of Bavaria and the Tyrol and were adept in various alpine skills. The highest levels of proficiency were required to reach 'expert' status so, consequently, very few of these badges were ever bestowed.

HJ MARKSMANSHIP BADGES

On 20 August 1936, the first in a series of Hitler Youth Marksmanship Badges was instituted by Baldur von Schirach. It comprised a black and silver target surmounted by the *HJ* diamond and two crossed rifles, and was given for shooting fifteen small-calibre rounds proficiently in prone, kneeling, supported and unsupported positions. By the end

138. Hitler Youth Marksmanship Badges.
From left to right:
Badge for HJ *Marksman;*
Badge for HJ *Sharpshooter;*
Badge for DJ *Marksman.*

of 1943, a total of 273,545 Marksmanship Badges had been distributed. The *DJ* version of the same award, which bore a white Sig-rune in place of the *HJ* diamond and was bestowed for air-rifle shooting, had been conferred no fewer than 580,872 times by the end of 1943. In 1938, the *HJ* badge was upgraded by the addition of Sharpshooter and Champion Shot levels, with silver and gold oakleaf surrounds for which the required score points were considerably increased. Over 31,000 awards of the Sharpshooter Badge and 800 of the Champion Shot Badge were eventually made.

THE MINE RESCUE DECORATION

On 13 November 1936, the *Grubenwehr Ehren-zeichen*, or Mine Rescue Decoration, was instituted to recognise the completion of fifteen years' service with the *Grubenwehr*. It could also be given for an act of bravery, for being invalided as the result of an injury sustained in the line of duty, or for outstanding general service to the rescue corps. Initially the award took the form of a round pin-back badge with a crossed hammer and pick, surmounted by an eagle and swastika and the legend *Für Verdienste um das Grubenwehrwesen*. This pattern was soon superseded by a smaller silver

medal of like design, suspended from a yellow ribbon with black and white edges. The majority of *Grubenwehr Ehrenzeichen* were bestowed upon rescue personnel engaged in the vast coalfields of the Saar territory, recently restored to the Reich after years of French occupation. The medal underlined the vital importance placed upon mining by the Germans, who had for long given their miners special privileges, including impressive dress uniforms.

THE NATIONAL SENATE OF CULTURE BADGE

On 28 November 1936 the first 125 awards of a new decoration for members of the National Senate of Culture were bestowed. The *Reichskultursenat*, established a year earlier, co-ordinated activities in the fields of art, music, the theatre, films, literature, the press and radio broadcasting, and was headed by Dr Goebbels. Its membership included Alfred Rosenberg, Albert Speer, Leni Riefenstahl, Education Minister Bernhard Rust, the architect Hermann Giesler, sculptors Arno Breker and Josef Thorak, Authors' Association President Hanns Johst, composer Richard Strauss, and conductor Wilhelm Furtwängler. There were also a number of overtly political and non-professional appointees to the

139.　*The Mine Rescue Decoration.*

140.　*The National Senate of Culture Badge.*

Senate, such as *SA-Stabschef* Viktor Lutze, who could not by any stretch of the imagination be considered an intellectual or cultural figure, and Economics Minister Walther Funk, who was admitted solely on the grounds that his department received many of the art treasures confiscated from Jews 'in lieu of payments due to the State'.

The badge to honour the Senate's membership was designed by Professor Richard Klein and comprised a sixteen-point gilded oval star enclosing a cream-coloured enamel disc bearing an eagle atop a swastika and Greek column, surrounded by the designation *Reichskultursenat*. The reverse featured an award serial number, '*Silber* 900' hallmark and the maker's details 'Deschler München'. A stickpin miniature with the abbreviated legend '*RKS*' was also authorised for wear on the left lapel of civilian clothes. All Nazi-approved authors, musicians etc. were soon obliged to join the *Reichskulturkammer*, or National Chamber of Culture, which was supervised by the Senate and ultimately had over 100,000 members, including 15,000 architects, 14,300 painters, 2,900 sculptors, 6,000 designers and 2,000 art publishers and dealers. Among them were many postwar favourites like Herbert von Karajan and Elisabeth Schwarzkopf. The Chamber had its own stickpin sporting the initials '*RKK*', but this was merely a membership badge, not a decoration. In a similar vein, a so-called National Film Honour Ring was presented by Goebbels as a personal gift to those who promoted the Third Reich's cinema industry.

NATIONAL FOOD ESTATE AWARDS

At the beginning of December 1936, the National Food Estate, or *Reichsnährstand*, to which all farmers and other food producers were required to belong, established a series of awards in Aluminium, Iron, Bronze, Silver and Gold for ten, twenty, thirty, forty and fifty years' service respectively. These were approved and presented on a regional basis, with varying designs encompassing both medals and badges, but all included the *Reichsnährstand* emblem of a swastika surmounted by a sword and ear of barley, often with an eagle holding a scroll bearing the organisation's motto *Blut und Boden* ('Blood and soil'). In addition, there were medal-

141.   The National Food Estate Medal. This example was awarded to farmers in Pomerania.

lions given for special achievement in milk production, cereal crop cultivation and animal husbandry. The wearing of Food Estate decorations was severely restricted, normally being limited to the holders' attendance at agricultural shows.

THE FIRE BRIGADE DECORATION

The last civil award to be created during 1936 was the *Feuerwehr Ehrenzeichen*, instituted on 22 December. It superseded the old *Länder* decorations given to Fire Brigade personnel and came in two very distinct grades, namely a 2nd Class for twenty-five years' service and a 1st Class for bravery or special merit. The latter was initially a large pin-back award, but after a short time reverted to being suspended from a ribbon like that of the smaller 2nd Class. The very impressive and original design, by military artist Herbert Knötel, featured a white enamel cross enclosing a black swastika surrounded by bright red flames, with silver or gold borders depending on class.

During the war, bravery at fires caused by air raids tended to be rewarded with bestowal of the Iron Cross or War Merit Cross with Swords, and even as late as September 1944 only 147 awards of the 1st Class Fire Brigade Decoration had been made. Tens of thousands of the 2nd Class were duly distributed to long-serving firemen, so much so that by the end of 1944 it was felt necessary to authorise an oakleaf cluster with the numeral '40' to denote that number of years' service. The cluster was never manufactured, however, due to the circumstances of the time. It is ironic that one of the principal makers of the *Feuerwehr Ehrenzeichen*, the firm of Glaser & Sohn, was based in Dresden, a city almost completely destroyed by firestorm bombing in February 1945.

142. *The Fire Brigade Decoration 2nd Class, by Foerster & Barth.*

THE GERMAN NATIONAL PRIZE FOR ART AND SCIENCE DECORATION

On 30 January 1937, Hitler instituted the most coveted of all the Third Reich's civil awards, the German National Prize for Art and Science Decoration, or *Ehrenzeichen des Deutschen Nationalpreises für Kunst und Wissenschaft*. Classed as the highest peacetime honour, the National Prize was created as a Nazi substitute for the Nobel Prize, which the *Führer* had forbidden German citizens to accept only one month before, and was a tax-free cash sum of 100,000 Reichsmarks. The accompanying Decoration comprised a massive breast star in platinum featuring the golden head of Athena on a red enamel field, four gold eagles and swastikas, and forty diamonds totalling no less than 10 carats in weight (compared to under 2 carats for the diamonds to the Knight's Cross). The star was so heavy that fourteen rivets were required to hold it together and, according to Speer's memoirs, recipients had to have special supports fitted to their dinner jackets in order to wear it. Each decoration was accompanied by a wide red and white silk sash, heavily embroidered with eagles and swastikas, in the manner of the Grand Cross of an Order. The first four awards of the National Prize for Art and Science were made on 7 September 1937, to:

- Prof. Paul Ludwig Troost, Hitler's favourite architect and designer of the House of German Art, the Martyrs' Monument at the *Feldherrnhalle*, the *Führer* Building and the Temple of Honour, all in Munich (posthumous)
- *Reichsleiter* Dr Alfred Rosenberg, author of *The Myth of the 20th Century* and racial philosopher of the *NSDAP*
- Prof. August Bier and Dr Ferdinand Sauerbruch, jointly, for their contributions to medicine and surgery
- Prof. Dr Wilhelm Filchner, for achievements in the exploration of Antarctica and Tibet

Presentations were thereafter to be restricted to three per year, and on 7 September 1938 further awards were made to:

- Dr Fritz Todt, designer of the Siegfried Line and *autobahn* system

- Prof. Dr Ferdinand Porsche, for his development of the Volkswagen motor car
- Prof. Dr Ernst Heinkel and Prof. Willy Messerschmitt, jointly, for their work in aircraft design and production

No more bestowals were made after the outbreak of the Second World War and so there were only ever nine recipients of this prestigious decoration, making it one of the rarest and most exclusive awards of the Third Reich. It is noteworthy that Rosenberg and Todt never wore the National Prize Decoration while in uniform and, indeed, no photographs of it being sported by any of the holders have ever come to light. The precious diamond-encrusted star and ornate sash were probably worn only with evening dress on the most formal of civil occasions.

144. Reich Minister of Propaganda Dr Josef Goebbels speaking with Heinkel, Messerschmitt, Porsche and Todt on the occasion of their being presented with the German National Prize for Art and Science, 7 September 1938.

143. The German National Prize for Art and Science Decoration.
Left: Star;
Right: Sash.

SPORTS AWARDS, 1937

In February 1937, three more sports badges were instituted in the wake of the Olympic Games. The Heavy Athletics Badge took the form of a *DRL* eagle surmounting a set of weights, over a shield depicting two wrestlers. It was presented for proficiency in boxing, weight-lifting etc. Full-time officers of the National Socialist Riding Corps (*NSRK*), the equestrian branch of the *SA*, were afforded the opportunity of winning a new award showing a mounted *SA* man enclosed by an oakleaf wreath with the *SA* insignia at the base. This so-called German Expert Horseman's Badge, or *Deutsches Reiterführerabzeichen*, was intended to recognise a meritorious pass in *NSRK* riding tests and the ability to instruct others in horsemanship, and could only be given to *NSRK* members already in possession of the *SA* Sports Badge. The third new decoration, the Badge for the Care of Horses, comprised an oval wreath enclosing a representation of a man running alongside a horse, and was given for long service in stables, stud farms or other equestrian establishments, or for repeated success at horse shows or tournaments. None of these badges was widely distributed.

145. *The German Expert Horseman's Badge.*

WEHRMACHT CIVILIAN AUXILIARY BADGES

From 20 April 1937, a lapel badge in the form of a gold eagle with outstretched wings surrounded by an oval oakleaf wreath, very like the Nazi Police emblem, was presented to civilian employees of the Army and Navy for twenty-five years' service. A similar award, comprising a small gold winged swastika within an oakleaf wreath, was authorised for civilians working with the *Luftwaffe*. These insignia were short-lived, however, being superseded by the ubiquitous Faithful Service Decoration nine months later. Civilian workers in the aircraft industry also had their efforts recognised in the spring of 1937 by the institution of a *Treuewerkabzeichen*, or Loyal Work Badge, in Silver and Gold. It took the form of a swastika shield surmounted by an eagle with a 'T' and an Opfer-rune (symbolic of self-sacrifice) on its chest. The *Treuewerkabzeichen* was cancelled soon after the outbreak of the Second World War, when aircraft factory workers' achievements began to be rewarded by the War Merit Cross and Medal.

THE ORDER OF THE GERMAN EAGLE

On 1 May 1937, Hitler created the Order of the German Eagle, or *Orden vom Deutschen Adler*, as a diplomatic award to be conferred only upon 'friendly' foreigners. The badge of the Order was a classic white enamel Maltese cross with eagles and swastikas set between the arms. Several fairly convoluted revisions were later made to the statutes governing the grades and titles of the Order, with the final definitive arrangement being as follows:

- Grand Cross in Gold with Diamonds – an eight-pointed 90 mm gold and diamond-encrusted breast star and 100 mm sash/66 mm badge
- Grand Cross in Gold – an eight-pointed 90 mm silver-gilt breast star and 100 mm sash/66 mm badge
- Grand Cross – an eight-pointed 80 mm silver breast star and 90 mm sash/60 mm badge
- 1st Class – an eight-pointed 80 mm silver breast star and 90 mm sash/50 mm badge
- 2nd Class – a six-pointed 75 mm silver breast star and 50 mm neck cross
- 3rd Class – a 50 mm neck cross

- 4th Class – a 48 mm pin-back breast cross
- 5th Class – a 45 mm breast cross worn from a ribbon
- Silver Medal – a 38 mm medal
- Bronze Medal – a 38 mm medal

Each of these grades, except the Grand Cross in Gold with Diamonds which was uniquely given to Mussolini, could be bestowed with or without Swords. Swords signified military merit and were

146. *The Grand Cross in Gold of the Order of the German Eagle.*
Top: Sash and badge;
Bottom: Star

147. *Mussolini with Hitler in September 1937. The Duce wears the Stars of the Order of the German Eagle and the Red Cross Decoration on his left breast.*

148. *The Order of the German Eagle, 1943 classes.*
From left to right, top to bottom:
2nd Class neck cross and breast star, with Swords;
3rd Class neck cross, without Swords;
Star to the Grand Cross, without Swords;
4th Class, without Swords;
Silver Medal, without Swords;
Silver Medal, with Swords.

affixed centrally on the stars and crosses or to the suspension loops of the two medals. Notable recipients of the higher classes of the Eagle Order included General Franco, Admiral Horthy of Hungary, the US aviator Charles Lindbergh and Henry Ford of motor-car fame. Most foreign diplomats working in Germany received one of the lesser grades, depending on their rank. Hitler's Foreign Ministers, von Neurath and von Ribbentrop, were also admitted to the Order, being given the Grand Cross in Gold, although in their particular cases it was referred to as a 'Special Grade'.

Most examples of the enamelled awards were marked '900', indicating silver content, and '21', the code number of their manufacturer, Godet & Co. The latter firm was famed for its quality products, having formerly been the Imperial Court Jeweller and maker of the *Pour le Mérite* and similar high-grade Orders. The Silver and Bronze medals were struck at the state mints in Berlin and Vienna. In general terms, the Order of the German Eagle fulfilled its role in 'greasing the rails' of Nazi diplomacy. It is noteworthy that it was one of only a few Third Reich awards to be graded, for reasons of expediency, on truly international lines, i.e. Knight Grand Cross/Knight Commander/Commander/Officer/Member. Hitler habitually rejected such old-fashioned courtesy rank titles out of hand, as meaningless vestiges of Germany's defunct royal past, but he was obliged to retain this familiar international format for his diplomatic Order. During the Second World War, the Eagle Order medal was used to reward foreigners working in Germany, being given

149. *Constantin Freiherr von Neurath, Hitler's first Foreign Minister, wearing the Special Grade of the Order of the German Eagle which he received on 20 April 1939.*

150. *The Order of the German Eagle, 5th Class with Swords. This cross was originally the '3rd Grade' of the Order, becoming the '5th Class' by virtue of statute revisions published on 27 December 1943.*

for two years' general service or for an act of special merit.

RED CROSS LONG-SERVICE AWARDS

Almost three years after the institution of long-service awards by the Danzig Red Cross, four national decorations were authorised on 1 July 1937 to recognise veteran sisters and matrons of the German Red Cross Society (*DRK*). They comprised slim silver neck crosses, with or without oakleaves, for twenty-five and ten years service respectively as

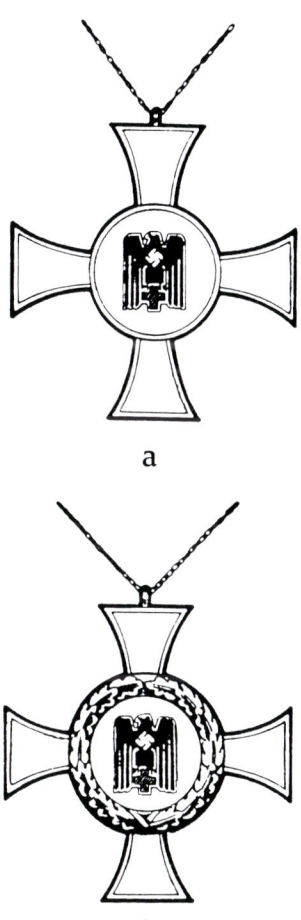

a

b

151. *Red Cross Long-Service Awards for Sisters and Matrons.*
(a) For 10 years' service.
(b) For 25 years' service.

a sister, and similar gold crosses for matrons and senior matrons. Each piece bore an enamel *DRK* eagle, swastika and red cross in the centre, and was suspended from a thin chain around the neck. The *Schwestern Kreuz* was worn in addition to the usual range of membership and qualification badges distributed to nursing staff by the Red Cross.

THE GERMAN ACADEMY FOR AERONAUTICAL RESEARCH DECORATION

On 21 January 1938 the German Academy for Aeronautical Research was founded, under the Presidency of Hermann Göring, to comprise selected individuals, both German and non-

152. *The Presidential Chain of the German Academy for Aeronautical Research, worn by Hermann Göring.*

German, who had made significant contributions to the advancement of aviation. Membership was very restricted, and a new decoration was approved for wear as a badge of office, like that of the *Reichskultursenat*. It took the form of a flying eagle clutching a swastika, surrounded by an angular oakleaf wreath, and was not unlike the *Luftwaffe* Pilot Badge. Göring wore the new insignia in real gold on a presidential chain around his neck, while ordinary, honorary and supporting members of the Aeronautical Academy wore it in gold, silver or bronze pin-back or stickpin versions. The Academy also bestowed a non-portable medallion, known as the Hermann Göring Commemorative Medal, upon individuals who furthered the cause of aviation through their own original and ground-breaking research. The obverse of the medal featured Göring's profile, and the reverse an eagle standing on top of a globe. The sole recorded recipient was Air Defence Chief Prof. Ludwig Prandtl, a physicist and pioneer of aerodynamics, who gave his name to the Lanchester-Prandtl Wing Theory.

THE FAITHFUL SERVICE DECORATION

On 30 January 1938, Hitler instituted a range of awards to recognise loyal civilian service to the German people. The most ubiquitous of these was the *Treudienst Ehrenzeichen*, or Faithful Service Decoration, designed by Richard Klein, which superseded the old *Länder* medals and took the form of a cross with a wreath of oakleaves extending between the arms and a large black enamel static swastika in the centre. It came in three classes, Silver for twenty-five years' work in the public sector (civil servants, Post Office staff, railway personnel and so on), Gold for forty years' public service and a Special Grade bearing the numeral '50' for that number of years' employment with a private company. An oakleaf cluster for fifty years' public service was created on 12 August 1944, but was never manufactured or conferred. The *Treudienst Ehrenzeichen* was suspended from a plain ribbon in cornflower blue, the colour of Germany's national flower and traditionally symbolic of loyalty. Hundreds of thousands of Faithful Service Decorations were ultimately bestowed. An award of a higher grade replaced one of a lower.

153. *Faithful Service Decorations.*
From left to right:
Cross for 25 years' public service, in presentation case;
Cross for 40 years' public service;
Special Grade for 50 years' service in the private sector.

154. *Left: The Police 18-Year Service Cross, with* Polizei *eagle embroidered into the ribbon;*
Right: The Police 8-Year Service Medal.

POLICE LONG-SERVICE AWARDS

On 30 January 1938, Police officers and men were given their own series of long-service decorations, again designed by Klein, comprising a Silver Medal for eight years, a Silver Cross for eighteen years and a Gold Cross for twenty-five years. An oakleaf cluster for forty years' service was instituted on 12 August 1944, but was never produced. Each award bore a representation of the Police wreathed eagle and swastika, and the two crosses also had Police emblems embroidered into their cornflower blue ribbons. Only one grade could be worn at a time.

RAD LONG-SERVICE AWARDS

Permanent staff members of the *RAD*, the National Labour Service, were also singled out for special recognition on 30 January 1938. New *RAD* medals featured a swastika and spade for male members, or a swastika above barley ears for females, and were bestowed in four grades, Bronze for four years' service, Silver for twelve years, Silver with an eagle on the ribbon for eighteen years, and Gold with an eagle for twenty-five years. *RAD* conscripts were not eligible for the awards. Once again, the ribbon was plain cornflower blue and only one medal could be worn at any one time.

155. *Service decorations.*
From left to right:
The RAD *Long-Service Award for 18 Years (males);*
The RAD *Long-Service Award for 18 Years (females);*
Air-Raid Defence Decoration 1st Class.

THE AIR-RAID DEFENCE DECORATION

The *Luftschutz Ehrenzeichen*, or Air-Raid Defence Decoration, was instituted in two grades on 30 January, 1938. The 2nd Class, a grey medal, was presented for general merit in the air-raid defence field, and was open not only to members of the *Luftschutz* organisation but also to factory guards,

Fire Brigade personnel, the Police etc. The 1st Class, a gold cross awarded less than 200 times, was reserved for those who performed exceptional services in the cause of Germany's civil defence. Both grades were designed by Egon Jantke of Berlin and hung from very distinctive ribbons in the *Luftschutz* colour of lilac, with narrow red, white and black edges.

THE MOTOR SPORTS BADGE

Germans who achieved continuous success in national and international driving competitions were recognised by an award of the *Deutsches Motorsportabzeichen*, or Motor Sports Badge,

156. *The Air-Raid Defence Decoration, 2nd Class.*

157. *The Motor Sports Badge.*

created on 18 February 1938. Sometimes erroneously referred to as the *NSKK* Sports Badge, it replaced the older Champion's Badge of the Central National Motor Sports Authority, and comprised a flying eagle grasping a car wheel in its talons, superimposed upon a large wreathed swastika. The *Motorsportabzeichen* was produced in '800' silver by Lauer of Nuremberg, and was conferred in three classes on a points basis:

> 3rd Class in Iron (blackened silver) – 50 points
> 2nd Class in Silver (polished silver) – 100 points
> 1st Class in Gold (gilded silver) – 150 points

Points were accumulated based on competition placings, with first positions in international and national events earning the winner twelve and eight points respectively. Fewer than 500 awards were made.

NSFK Awards

On 10 March 1938 General Friedrich Christiansen, the chief of the National Socialist Flying Corps (*NSFK*), which existed primarily to train boys and youths in all aspects of aviation, created a qualification badge for his licensed hot-air balloon pilots. It featured a balloon, oakleaf wreath and winged swastika embroidered in silver bullion on a blue-grey background. A later version in silvered metal replaced the winged swastika with the definitive Icarus emblem of the *NSFK*. Christiansen soon

introduced similar awards for his powered aircraft pilots, glider pilots, wireless operators and supporting members, and these were also subject to numerous design changes over the years. There was even an *NSFK* badge known as the *Modellflugleistungsabzeichen*, which was given in three grades for proficiency in building and flying model aeroplanes.

The *NSFK* was always a relatively small and low-profile organisation. At the last Nuremberg rally in 1938, for example, the *NSFK* contingent numbered only 2,400 men as opposed to 73,000 for the *SA* and 20,000 for the *SS*. None of the *NSFK* awards was viewed with high regard, even by their recipients, many of whom went on to win the much more prestigious *Luftwaffe* equivalents.

158. NSFK *awards.*
From left to right:
The Balloon Pilot's Badge;
The Powered Aircraft Pilot's Badge, 3rd pattern introduced on 26 January 1942;
The Large Glider Pilot's Badge.
The qualification criteria for such items varied, but were not onerous. The Large Glider Pilot's Badge, for example, was presented for completing an endurance flight lasting at least 5 hours, or for reaching an altitude of at least 3,300 feet three times in the course of a single flight. Around 2,000 examples were bestowed.

THE GOLDEN BOOK OF AIRMEN

On 20 April 1938, Hermann Göring introduced the *Goldene Buch der Flieger*, or 'Golden Book of Airmen', a roll of honour for those who achieved distinction in the field of civil aviation. The book eventually recorded thirty-five names, including test pilots and airship captains, and was permanently displayed in the Hall of Honour in the Air Ministry in Berlin. Most names were entered posthumously.

NATIONAL TRADE COMPETITION DECORATIONS

A new decoration to reward winners in the annual National Trade Competitions was also instituted on 20 April 1938. These events, which had been held since 1934, covered a wide variety of trades from forestry, mining and building to office practice, handicrafts and catering, and were organised jointly by the German Labour Front, or *DAF*, and the Hitler Youth. All Nazi-affiliated manual workers, commercial and technical apprentices and students, male or female, were eligible to enter provided they were under twenty-one years of age. The winners in each *Kreis*, or local district, competed against each other to become *Gau*, or regional, victors and they in turn competed to become the *Reichssieger*, or National Champions, in the various fields. All *Reichssieger* were automatically presented to Hitler in recognition of their success.

159. *The National Trade Competition Decoration for 1938* Kreissieger, *by Gustav Brehmer.*

The new National Trade Competition Victor's Badge, or *Siegerabzeichen im Reichsberufswettkampf*, was a heavy-quality piece comprising an eagle holding a *DAF* cogwheel and *HJ* diamond against a white enamel background featuring the appropriate title and date of award. It was produced principally by the Gustav Brehmer and Hermann Aurich firms, and was graded in Bronze for *Kreissieger*, Silver for *Gausieger* and Gold for *Reichssieger*. Thousands of awards were made on Labour Day, 1 May 1938. The largest ever competition finals were held in Cologne the following April, after which *DAF* chief Dr Robert Ley and *Reichsjugendführer* Baldur von Schirach between them bestowed 508 *Reichssieger* badges. A total of 6,600 *Gausieger* and 40,000 *Kreissieger* awards had already been conferred in the qualifying contests for 1939. Competitions continued to be held after the outbreak of war (then known as *Kriegsberufswettkampf*), but no further victors' badges were produced or presented until 1944, when much inferior versions of these awards in painted zinc were distributed for propaganda purposes by Reich Food Minister Herbert Backe and youth leader Artur Axmann. By that time, the qualification criteria had been considerably modified as most young people had volunteered or been conscripted for military service, and many of the 1944 recipients were well over fifty years of age. It is noteworthy that, apart from the *SA* Sports Badge, the *Siegerabzeichen* was the only Nazi decoration to be accorded the distinction of being featured on a postage stamp.

THE *HJ* LEADER'S SPORTS BADGE

On 15 May 1938 a heavy gilded brass version of the Hitler Youth Proficiency Badge, set against a black enamel backplate with gold laurel leaf border, was created as a fitness incentive for all adult *HJ* officers. This so-called *Goldene Führersportabzeichen* was bestowed on the highest scorers in a set decathlon comprising a 100 metre sprint, 1,000 metre run, high jump, long jump, shot put, weight put, 3,000 metre swim, supported shoot, unsupported shoot and route march. Two grades, A and B, existed, based on the age of, and number of points scored by, competitors. The relevant award serial number was stamped into the reverse of most badges.

Gustav Brehmer was again a principal manufacturer of this decoration, which was particularly convenient for the firm since the backplate of the new badge was interchangeable with that of the National Trade Competition Decoration. First bestowed at the Party Day celebrations in September 1938, an estimated 11,000 *Goldene Führersportabzeichen*

were ultimately distributed. Holders could wear the badge for a five-year period before they had to requalify for it.

DANZIG POLICE LONG-SERVICE AWARDS

On 20 June 1938 the Free City of Danzig Police received their own version of the *Polizei Dienstauszeichnungen*, with a Gilt Cross for twenty-five years' service, a Silver Cross for eighteen years and a Silver Medal for eight years. Each bore the Danzig coat of arms in place of the Nazi Police insignia. The reverse of the crosses was plain, while that of the medal featured the legend *Für treue dienste in der Polizei*. Very few awards were

160. *Awards of the Free City of Danzig.*
(a) The Police Long-Service Cross;
(b) The Police Long-Service Medal;
(c) The Faithful Service Decoration;
(d) The Fire Brigade Decoration.

a

b

c

d

made, as the whole series was superseded by the Reich Police Long-Service Decorations in the autumn of 1939.

THE DANZIG FAITHFUL SERVICE DECORATION

A *Treudienst Ehrenzeichen* for loyal civilian service in the Danzig public and private sectors was created on 28 June, 1938. It again came in three classes, a Silver Cross for twenty-five years' public service, a Gilt Cross for forty years' public service, and a Special Grade for fifty years with a private firm. The obverse bore the Danzig coat of arms and the reverses were plain in all cases. The decoration was replaced by the Reich equivalent in 1939.

THE DEFENCE ECONOMY LEADER'S DECORATION

On 1 September 1938 a small gold badge, in the form of a factory building and smoking chimneys surmounted by an eagle and swastika and the legend *Wehrwirtschaftführer*, was instituted for members of the Defence Economy Council which Göring had set up to mobilise the armaments industry. It was also conferred sparingly upon senior business managers who contributed significantly to the war effort. A stickpin version was authorised for daily wear, and bore the Nazi eagle above a banner with the abbreviated title *W.Wi.Fü.* One of the first recipients was Fritz Hase, Director of the Eisenach Aero Engine Works, who was awarded the decoration by *Luftwaffe* General Erhard Milch on the date of its inauguration.

161. *The Defence Economy Leader's Decoration.*

162. The Mother's Cross by Wilhelm Deumer, with presentation case. A few early examples of this finely produced decoration bore the Hitler quotation Das Kind adelt die Mutter *('The child enobles the mother') on the reverse. Hitler adored his own mother, who died when he was 18, and after coming to power he commemorated the date of her death by declaring it 'National Mother's Day'.*

THE MOTHER'S CROSS

The First World War decimated the male population of the Reich, and Hitler always placed great importance on the promotion of large families with a view to making up the horrendous manpower losses of 1914–18. To that end, the *Ehrenkreuz der Deutschen Mutter*, or Cross of Honour of the German Mother, was instituted on 16 December 1938. It came in three grades, Bronze for mothers of four or five children, Silver for mothers of six or seven children, and Gold for mothers of eight or more. It was therefore something akin to a female version of the Wound Badge! All the children had to be born alive and both parents were required to be of German blood, although there was no marriage stipulation.

Even from the date of institution, over 3 million women already qualified for one of these awards. *NSDAP Ortsgruppenleiter* were made responsible for submitting lists of nominees for the decoration, and for presenting the crosses when approved.

Designed by architect Franz Berberich of Munich, the delicate crosses were extremely well made in fine blue and white enamels, and were suspended around the neck from a narrow ribbon in the same colours. Each bore a facsimile of Hitler's signature stamped on the reverse, denoting the personal nature of the award which was considered a *Führergeschenk*, or 'gift of the *Führer*'. At least two examples of a gold Mother's Cross with diamonds set into the central swastika have also been reported. They were reputedly reserved for mothers of sixteen or more children, but that assertion has yet to be confirmed from original sources. Holders of the *Mutterkreuz* were entitled to various welfare benefits payable by the state, and also to the free services of a childminder.

THE CUSTOMS SERVICE DECORATION

Officials of the Customs Service received their own decoration, the *Zollgrenzschutz Ehrenzeichen*, on 17 February 1939. The bronze cross featured an eagle surrounded by an acanthus wreath, not unlike the Police insignia, and a similar emblem was embroidered in yellow thread on the cornflower blue ribbon. The award was presented in a single grade for general meritorious duty in the *Zollgrenzschutz*, with a minimum service qualification of four years for uniformed staff and eight years for civilian employees.

THE SOCIAL WELFARE DECORATION

On 1 May 1939, the traditional decorations of the German Red Cross, only semi-official since their inception, were at last superseded by a new award, the *Ehrenzeichen für Deutsche Volkspflege*, or German Social Welfare Decoration. It followed the general pattern of its predecessors, with similar grades still encompassing a large black stylised eagle and swastika set upon a white enamel cross, and the

163.   The Customs Service Decoration.

red ribbon with white edges remained unchanged. However, the Red Cross badge was now omitted from the design.

The Social Welfare Decoration was used to recognise meritorious achievement in all manner of services tending to the general and specific needs of the German population, including the fields of medicine, nursing, social work, charity, housing, education and recreation. Recipients included individuals from every walk of civil, political and military life. Many award recommendations were submitted through the *Nationalsozialistische Volkswohlfahrt* (*NSV*), the National Socialist People's Welfare Organisation, which ultimately included over 20 per cent of the entire German population in its membership. In 1942, Swords were added to the Social Welfare ribbon to denote military-related service, primarily on the part of doctors and nurses engaged in caring for war wounded on the eastern front. Social Welfare Decorations with Swords were accorded a far higher status than those without.

THE DANZIG FIRE BRIGADE DECORATION

The Danzig Fire Brigade Decoration was also created on 1 May 1939, with the same award criteria as its national counterpart. Almost

165. *The Social Welfare Medal.*

164. *The Social Welfare Decoration.*
Top: 1st Class;
Middle: 2nd Class;
Bottom: 3rd Class.

166. *The Pioneer of Labour Award.*

a

b

c

167. *Miscellaneous civil awards.*
(a) The Hitler Youth Decoration for Distinguished Foreigners;
(b) The Dr Fritz Todt Prize, with variant inscription;
(c) The Badge for Female Railway Staff.

identical in appearance, but with the Danzig coat of arms replacing the central swastika, this short-lived cross was superseded by the *Reich Feuerwehr Ehrenzeichen* after only four months.

THE PIONEER OF LABOUR AWARD

On 7 August 1940, shortly before the introduction of the War Merit Medal for lowly civilian workers, a decoration known as the Pioneer of Labour Award, or *Auszeichnung 'Pionier der Arbeit'*, was instituted to recognise efforts at the highest levels in the industrial and economic spheres. Its bestowal reflected the gathering momentum of Germany's war footing, with recipients including Gustav Krupp of munitions fame, Robert Bosch of the electrical conglomerate, aircraft designer Willy Messerschmitt and motor engineer Ferdinand Porsche. The simple but striking design of the badge incorporated a gold eagle holding a *DAF* cogwheel enclosing a black swastika. Fewer than twenty awards are known to have been made.

THE HITLER YOUTH DECORATION FOR DISTINGUISHED FOREIGNERS

A special badge was approved by the Hitler Youth leadership on 20 April 1941 for award to non-Germans in recognition of services to the Hitler Youth and pro-Nazi youth movements in other European countries. Given the somewhat grandiose title of Hitler Youth High Command Decoration for Distinguished Foreigners, it was manufactured by Hermann Aurich of Dresden and comprised an eagle clutching the *HJ* diamond over the legend *Hitler Jugend*. The badge was distributed in very limited numbers, and the high regard in which it was held is demonstrated by the fact that presentations tended to take place in Berlin, with Hitler in attendance.

THE POLICE EXPERT SKIER BADGE

The *Polizei Schiführerabzeichen* was introduced on 18 November 1942. This badge, featuring skis surmounting the Police eagle insignia, was given to a very small number of expert skiers in the Police. Recipients of the award were required to have passed the Police Ski Instructor's Advanced Examination, or to have successfully completed the annual Police expert skier tests five years in succession. The *Schiführerabzeichen* took precedence over all other Police alpine badges.

168. *The Police Expert Skier Badge was one of the rarest of all sports awards. Recipients probably numbered fewer than 100.*

THE GERMANIC PROFICIENCY RUNE

Himmler created a new *SS* award on 1 August 1943. Known as the *Germanische Leistungsrune*, or Germanic Proficiency Rune, it was open to native members of the so-called Germanic-SS, who fulfilled a Police support role in Flanders, Holland, Norway and Denmark, and was their equivalent of the *DRL* and *SA* Sports Badges worn by their German *SS* colleagues. The striking decoration comprised two black enamel Sig-runes, symbolic of victory and

169. *The Germanic Proficiency Rune, fewer than 10 examples of which are known to survive.*

long the emblem of the German *SS*, superimposed over a sunwheel swastika, which was associated with the various pro-Nazi political parties and paramilitary groups in occupied Western Europe. The design was therefore meant to reflect the close union between the German *SS* and the Germanic-SS.

The *Germanische Leistungsrune* came in two classes, Bronze and Silver, which were conferred according to the level of scoring in the prescribed qualifying tests. The latter included running, jumping, swimming, rope-climbing, throwing the hammer, shooting, completing an assault course, map-reading, distance-judging, observation, camouflage, first aid, signalling, verbal reporting, report-writing and Nazi theory. Training programmes meant that at least 120 hours' practice had to be completed every six months, and tests had to be passed annually in order to retain the badge. Undoubtedly, this was the hardest to win of all the Third Reich's many sports badges.

The first tests and examinations took place in January 1944 at the training school of the Dutch *SS* at Avegoor near Arnhem. Over 2,000 members of the Germanic-SS presented themselves, but only ninety-five passed. They were decorated with the *Leistungsrune* (eighteen Silver and seventy-seven Bronze) by Himmler on 1 February. The following June, twenty Danes received the badge at a ceremony at their training centre at Hovelte, and in August twenty-five members of the Norwegian *SS* were similarly decorated. The Allied invasion of Europe prevented more widespread distribution, and it is believed that total awards made numbered fewer than 200. Many badges were destroyed by their recipients at the end of the war, for obvious reasons.

THE *SA* SPORTS BADGE FOR WAR WOUNDED

On 15 December 1943, a special and entirely distinct version of the *SA* Sports Badge was instituted to encourage badly wounded servicemen and civilians to regain their physical fitness. Known as the *SA Wehrabzeichen für Kriegsversehrte*, this decoration generally resembled the basic *SA* Sports Badge, but was more stylised in appearance and had the addition of an Opfer-rune, symbolic of victims and self-sacrifice, at the base. It came in one class

170. The SA *Sports Badge for War Wounded.*

only, bronzed zinc, and could be worn at the same time as the ordinary *SA* Sports Badge if that was also held. Candidates had to meet a set of fitness standards commensurate with their particular disabilities. The sole manufacturer of the new award was Werner Redo of Saarlautern, and the first 100 presentations took place on 12 July 1944. Once again, widespread distribution was prevented by the deteriorating circumstances of the war.

171. The proposed Eastern Workers' Proficiency Badge, as illustrated in the 20 April 1944 edition of the periodical Deutschland im Kampf.

THE DR FRITZ TODT PRIZE

A major new national distinction was created on 8 February 1944, to reward those whose inventions or initiatives significantly furthered the war effort. Known as the Dr Fritz Todt Prize, it came in three levels which carried cash sums of 50,000 Reichsmarks, 30,000 Reichsmarks and 10,000 Reichsmarks respectively. It was therefore only the second award after the National Prize for Art and Science to constitute a substantial monetary payment, and that fact immediately ranked it as one of Germany's highest honours. Winners of the Dr Fritz Todt Prize were given a badge in gold, silver or iron as an outward sign of their achievement. It comprised an eagle clutching a cogwheel and swastika, similar to the centrepiece of the Pioneer of Labour Award, and bore the inscription *Dr.-Ing. Fritz Todt Preis*. No more than a handful of awards were made.

THE EASTERN WORKERS' PROFICIENCY BADGE

By early 1944, almost 2 million Russians and others from the conquered eastern territories, about half of them women, were working in Germany engaged in agriculture, mining, armaments and construction, and on the railways. On 20 April 1944, the German periodical *Deutschland im Kampf* announced the introduction of an Eastern Workers' Proficiency Badge comprising hands holding a sword and hammer within an oakleaf wreath, to be presented at the discretion of German managers to any Russians or Ukrainians in their employ. However, it is unlikely that the award was ever made or bestowed since on 1 July 1944 eastern workers became eligible for German decorations such as the War Merit Cross and Medal, as a better incentive to increase war production.

THE BADGE FOR FEMALE RAILWAY STAFF

A small badge comprising a winged wheel within a laurel wreath surmounted by a swastika was authorised during the autumn of 1944 for female members of the German railway system, the majority of whom had been recruited to fill the considerable gap left by railwaymen called up for active duty with the *Wehrmacht* and foreign travel directorates in the occupied territories. The badge was produced in Bronze for three years' service and Silver for six years. The first, and probably last, presentations of this rare award were made to thirty women on 13 October.

THE NAVAL DOCKYARD WORKERS' BADGE
The Naval Dockyard Workers' Badge, or *Werftarbeiterabzeichen*, instituted on 19 November 1944, comprised a stickpin featuring an eagle and swastika on top of a cogwheel enclosing a submarine. It was bestowed in very limited numbers to the most efficient U-boat construction staff, with a view to boosting their flagging morale.

It is remarkable that, even with total defeat staring them in the face, the leadership of the Third Reich continued to recognise the considerable incentive value of medals and decorations, and used them to great effect until the bitter end.

Order of Precedence of Political and Civil Awards

The general order of precedence of the main groups of Third Reich political and civil awards is shown below. It should be noted that a great deal of flexibility was often exercised in this regard, depending on dates of presentation, the various grades of an Order or decoration, and the status of recipients. Old Guard party members, for example, regarded their *NSDAP* veterans' decorations extremely highly, while non-Nazis looked upon them with disdain. This situation was complicated still further by the fact that, as the Third Reich progressed, political awards like the German Order and Golden Party Badge were increasingly rendered for services to the State, rather than to the *NSDAP*. Even two adjacent grades of a single decoration could have widely differing levels of prestige, a prime example being the Fire Brigade Decoration, with its 1st Class (a bravery award bestowed fewer than 200 times) ranking much higher in the general order of things than its

2nd Class (a long-service award with tens of thousands of recipients). Moreover, certain awards had very restrictive qualification criteria. The Order of the German Eagle, for instance, was almost exclusively reserved for non-Germans. In short, this listing can serve only as a loose guide to the precedence of the awards concerned.

POLITICAL

1. German Order
2. Golden Party Badge (for outstanding service)
3. Coburg Badge
4. Blood Order
5. Golden Hitler Youth Badge with Oakleaves
6. Golden Party Badge (for veteran membership)
7. 1929 Nuremberg Party Day Badge
8. Brunswick Rally Badge
9. *Gau* decorations, including Danzig Cross
10. *NSDAP* long-service decorations
11. Golden Hitler Youth Badge

CIVIL

1. National Prize for Art and Science
2. Dr Fritz Todt Prize
3. Pioneer of Labour Award
4. Order of the German Eagle
5. Eagle Shield of Germany
6. Goethe Medal for Art and Science
7. Bravery awards
8. Meritorious service decorations
9. Life-Saving Medal
10. Rescue awards
11. Long-service awards
12. Social welfare decorations
13. Olympic Games Decoration
14. Mother's Cross
15. Qualification badges
16. Sports badges
17. Commemorative awards
18. Youth awards
19. Red Cross decorations
20. Foreign decorations

3. Medal Miscellanea

Ribbons and Miniatures

The manner of wearing Third Reich orders, medals and decorations was governed by statutes which were periodically updated to take account of newly introduced awards. In addition, the *Wehrmacht*, *Waffen-SS*, Police, *SA*, Hitler Youth and other uniformed organisations had their own specific dress codes which had to be followed. These defined the combined general precedence of military, political and civil decorations as follows:

- **Neck orders.**
  The highest war decorations to be worn above peacetime decorations, arranged by free choice.
- **Decorations without ribbons**
  1. War decorations (i.e. the *DK*, *EK1*, *KVK1*, combat clasps etc.)
  2. Wound badges
  3. Silesian Eagle
  4. Baltic Cross
  5. *NSDAP* awards
  6. Peacetime decorations
  7. Sports awards

So far as pin-back decorations and badges worn on the left breast pocket were concerned, awards for valour took precedence over all others except the Golden Party Badge. No more than six pin-back awards could be displayed simultaneously, and no more than two sports badges could be worn together.

- **Decorations and medals with ribbons**
  1. Iron Cross 2nd Class
  2. War Merit Cross 2nd Class
  3. *Ostvolk* Decoration
  4. Social welfare decorations with Swords
  5. Eastern Front Medal

  6. War Merit Medal
  7. Imperial orders and medals
  8. Cross of Honour 1914–18
  9. Silesian Eagle
  10. Baltic Cross
  11. Life-saving Medal
  12. Long-service decorations
  13. Social Welfare decorations without Swords
  14. Olympic Games Decoration
  15. Anschluss/Sudetenland/Memel Medals
  16. West Wall Medal
  17. Olympic Games Medal
  18. Red Cross decorations
  19. Foreign awards

Members of the *Wehrmacht* who were recipients of the public service, Police, *RAD*, *SS*, *Luftschutz*, Fire Brigade or Mine Rescue Service decorations could wear only one armed forces long-service award in conjunction with any one grade of each of the others. The *Wehrmacht* long-service award always took precedence in such cases, with *NSDAP* long-service awards coming last.

Hitler continued imperial German tradition by utilising medal ribbons in several widths. Decorations were issued with a 30 mm or 35 mm ribbon, but were 'court mounted' for ceremonial wear using a 25 mm ribbon doubled over and draped behind the award. The 25 mm size was also used when looped through the second buttonhole of the tunic, for example with the *EK2*. Neck decorations were supposed to be suspended from 45 mm ribbons, but 8 mm, 10 mm or 15 mm widths were frequently used instead for the sake of comfort and convenience. Holders of the Knight's Cross of the Iron Cross often employed leather straps, thin chains, wide elastic bands and the like when wearing it in the field. Ribbons without medals were displayed on 17 mm high convex steel or zinc pin-back bars, which were worn above the left breast pocket and had holes to accommodate a selection of approved miniatures. Ribbons used on these bars were generally 15 mm or 25 mm, although some common pairings, particularly the *EK2/Ostmedaille*, *EK2/KVK2* and *KVK2/Ostmedaille* sets, featured a single 30 mm ribbon woven to resemble two 15 mm ribbons side by side. The principal manufacturers of Third Reich medal ribbons were the Munich firm of Karl Loy and the Berlin company of Carl Knoblauch.

The full-sized court-mounted group was to be worn only with parade uniform or formal evening dress. This so-called *Grosse Ordensspange*, or large medal clasp, came in two main varieties: with the decorations stitched firmly in place, or simply slipped over hooks protruding from the bar. Many medals had noticeably small suspension rings, which were made to fit over these hooks and could not properly accommodate lengths of ribbon in the usual way. Since only one row of awards was permitted to be worn at a time, mounted medals had to be overlapped to conserve space. Women usually wore full-size decorations from a bow on the left breast.

The small ribbon bar, or *Feldschnalle*, was intended for field or undress use. As well as the standard curved metal type, there were also

172. *Court-mounted group, or* Grosse Ordensspange, *comprising the following decorations and medals:*
The Iron Cross 2nd Class;
The War Merit Cross 2nd Class with Swords;

The Eastern Front Medal;
The Sudetenland Medal with Prague Castle Bar.
The ribbons are folded in the style known as Krause mit Rüsche, *or 'curly with ruffles'.*

Feldordensbleche

A) Fertige Einzelstücke.

in natürlicher Größe

Ausführungen:
*) **Rückseite voll:**   12000   12001   12002   12003
*) **Rückseite hohl:**   12000¹/₂   12001¹/₂   12002¹/₂   —
        ℛℳ 0.40   ℛℳ 0.60   ℛℳ 0.80   ℛℳ 0.80

*) **Rückseite voll:**   12004   12005   12006   12007
*) **Rückseite hohl:**   12004¹/₂   12005¹/₂   12006¹/₂   —
        ℛℳ 0.40   ℛℳ 0.60   ℛℳ 0.80   ℛℳ 0.80

*) **voll:**   12008   12009   12010   12012   12063
*) **hohl:**   12008¹/₂   12009¹/₂   —   12012¹/₂   12063¹/₂
     ℛℳ 0.60   ℛℳ 0.60   ℛℳ 0.80   ℛℳ 0.60   ℛℳ 0.40

10563   **12014**
*) Rückseite voll   *) Rückseite voll
ℛℳ 0.60   ℛℳ 0.60

*) **Ausführungen der Rückseiten:**

voll   hohl

Bandröllchen

10414 ℛℳ 0.40
10408 ist ohne Schwertchen ℛℳ 0.30
10580 ist EK u. Ehrenkreuzbd. ℛℳ 0.40

B) Beliebige Zusamenstellungen:

12013
18 mm hoch, Bandbreite 30 mm, volle Rückseite

10567
18 mm hoch, Bandbreite 25 mm, volle Rückseite

9848
18 mm hoch, Bandbreite 15 mm,
volle Rückseite

10176
12 mm hoch, Bandbreite 15 mm,
volle Rückseite

10571
*) Rückseite voll
kraus dekoriert ℛℳ 1.20

Preise für Ordensbleche, lose, ohne Band.

No.	für	1	2	3	4	5	6 Orden
		ℛℳ	ℛℳ	ℛℳ	ℛℳ	ℛℳ	ℛℳ
9848 10176 10571	Unterteil mit Bandplättchen	0.13	0.17	0.22	0.29	0.41	0.54
	Unterteil allein	0.10	0.11	0.13	0.17	0.26	0.36
	Bandplättchen allein ℛℳ 0.03						
10567 12013	Unterteil mit Bandplättchen	0.14	0.21	0.30	0.42	0.53	0.72
	Unterteil allein	0.11	0.14	0.20	0.28	0.36	0.54
	Bandplättchen allein ℛℳ 0.04						

Ordensbleche montiert mit Band.

No.	Bandbreite	ohne Schwertchen			
		für 1	2	3	4 Orden
		ℛℳ	ℛℳ	ℛℳ	ℛℳ
9848 10176	15 mm	0.32	0.40	0.60	0.90
10567	25 mm	0.40	0.60	0.80	1.10
10571	15 mm	0.70	1.—	1.30	1.60
12013	30 mm	0.60	0.80	1.10	1.40
Mehrpreis für Schwertchen-Auflage . . . ℛℳ 0.20					

173. A page from a typical Third Reich decoration producer's sales catalogue, advertising a range of assorted medal ribbons and bars with their prices.

cardboard-backed versions designed to be sewn to the tunic. War ribbons worn from the second buttonhole were not to be displayed simultaneously on the ribbon bar.

Ordensanstecknadeln, or stickpin miniatures, were authorised for wear on the left lapel of the civilian jacket, and were strictly regulated. The standard size was 9 mm, and miniatures were allowed only for the following:

- German war decorations
- German peacetime decorations without ribbons
- the Life-Saving Medal

No more than three decorations could be combined on a single stickpin. The only exceptions were the 'Doppel-EK' (the *EK1* and *EK2* pairing) and the Life-Saving Medal. Where these were concerned, a total

of four miniatures was allowed on one pin. War decorations could not be combined with peacetime decorations, other than the Life-Saving Medal, on a stickpin. Similarly, war badges and sports badges were not allowed to be worn on the same pin. The following Nazi awards were permitted as single stickpins:

- the Knight's Cross of the Iron Cross with Oakleaves and above
- the German Cross
- the Spanish Cross
- the War Merit Cross 1st Class
- the Wound Badge
- campaign shields
- war badges
- sports badges

174. *A selection of ribbon bars and buttonhole ribbons, showing the wide variety of styles, combinations and miniatures available.*

Examples of common stickpin combinations in-cluded:

- *EK1/EK2*/Wound Badge
- *EK2/KVK2*
- *EK1* and Bar/*EK2* and Bar/Spanish Cross/Wound Badge

There were eventually well over eighty authorised stickpin combinations, which could be purchased from military outfitters. Their principal producer was Wilhelm Deumer of Lüdenscheid.

The *Ordenskette*, or decorations chain, was usually worn with informal evening dress. It com-prised a number of miniatures, often of very high quality with plating and enamel work, suspended from a thin chain with pins at either end for attach-ing to the jacket. The miniatures were arranged in reverse order of importance, as they were hung at an angle on the lapel, with the highest award on the wearer's left.

For everyday civilian wear, an *Ordensknopf*, or buttonhole ribbon, could be fitted to the left lapel. This generally took the form of a ribbon bow, 8 mm in width and not more than 25 mm long, which was affixed to a button. During the Third Reich, the bow was restricted to a single ribbon. Alternatively, up to three ribbons, or four if the Life-Saving Medal was included, could be worn in the form of a buttonhole ribbon bar.

175. *Stickpin miniatures came in a range of sizes. They were normally retailed attached to cards bearing the 'LDO' logo of the* Leistungsgemeinschaft der Deutschen Ordenhersteller, *or Quality Control Board of German Orders Manufacturers, on the obverse and a statement of guaranteed quality on the reverse. The card illustrated has also been stamped with the 'L/59' mark of the maker, Alois Rettenmaier.*

The Knight's Cross of the Iron Cross and the Knight's Cross of the War Merit Cross could be worn as pendant miniatures, hanging from the ribbon bow. No other Nazi decorations were allowed to be worn in this form.

The following miniatures were required to be pinned to ribbon bars and bows as appropriate:

- Bar to the 1914 *EK2*
- Crossed swords – for the *KVK2* with Swords, the Cross of Honour 1914–18 with Swords and other combat awards 'with Swords'
- Oakleaves for the *Wehrmacht* Forty-Year Long-Service Award
- *Wehrmacht* eagle – for Army and Navy long-service awards
- *Luftwaffe* eagle – for Air Force long-service awards
- State eagle – for *RAD* awards and the Olympic Games Decoration 2nd Class
- Police eagle – for the two highest Police long-service awards

- Customs eagle – for the Customs Service Decoration
- Eagle in circular wreath – for *NSDAP* long-service decorations
- *SS* runes – for the two highest *SS* long-service awards
- Faithful Service Decoration
- Prague Castle bar – for the Sudetenland Medal with Bar
- rosettes, crowns or wreaths – as appropriate for imperial and foreign awards

The following were expressly forbidden to be worn in miniature form on ribbon bars and bows:

- *EK2*
- *KVK2*
- War Merit Medal
- *SS* four- and eight-year service medals
- *Anschluss* Medal
- Sudetenland Medal

176. *A typical decorations chain, above a selection of pendant and pin-back miniatures.*

- Memel Medal
- West Wall Medal

In accordance with Bulgarian, Hungarian, Romanian and other non-German regulations, higher foreign orders including Grand Crosses, stars and neck decorations could be represented on the small ribbon bar. The grade of Grand Cross was distinguished by a rosette on the ribbon with gold braid on either side. The ribbon for the neck decoration with star (Knight Commander or equivalent) had gold braid to the right of the rosette and silver braid to the left, while the ribbon for the neck decoration alone (Commander) had silver braid below the rosette. Italian ribbons featured three crowns for the Grand Cross, two crowns for the neck decoration with star and one crown for the neck decoration alone.

The rules and regulations governing the wearing of orders, decorations, medals, ribbons, stickpins and miniatures were therefore fairly complex, and it is not surprising that mistakes were made from time to time. Mountings and medal bars were occasionally constructed with the decorations fitted in the wrong order, or with unauthorised miniatures attached, while stickpin and pin-back miniatures frequently appeared in non-regulation sizes and combinations. Moreover, soldiers sometimes wore their *Feldschnallen* and even combat clasps upside down, or sported breast badges in the wrong order of precedence. In cases such as these, where the regulations were breached without malicious intent by men who were, after all, 'heroes of the Reich', no penalties were usually enforced even although non-compliance with a military service order was punishable under discipline.

The unauthorised wearing of medals and decorations by persons not entitled to them was, however, strictly and severely dealt with. One year's imprisonment, with a fine, was the mandatory sentence. Anyone who made, sold, traded in or otherwise brought into circulation fraudulent awards committed a serious offence, and it was also illegal to buy or sell an authorised replacement decoration without the purchaser producing valid identification and the appropriate award citation. Serious criminal conviction or loss of German citizenship automatically resulted in the forfeiture of all orders and decorations held. The *Wehrmacht* officers found guilty of treason after the July 1944 bomb plot, for example, including *Generalfeldmarschall* von Witzleben, were stripped of all their honours and awards before being executed.

177. *The ribbon bar worn by this Army* Oberfeldwebel *has been incorrectly mounted, since the Eastern Front Medal should be second in precedence rather than fourth.*

Cases and Citations

Most Third Reich awards were allocated protective cases or packets which varied according to the type of decoration involved. The *EK1* case, for instance, was a hinged thick cardboard box with a black paper covering pebbled to simulate leather. The lid exterior bore a silver outline of the Iron Cross, in a thin configuration for the 1914 *EK1* and a heavier design for the 1939 version. The inside of the lid was lined with white artificial silk and the base was in white velvet or flocking. More lowly awards were issued in unhinged two-part boxes with appropriate logos, or in beige or blue paper packets. The title of the decoration concerned was generally printed on the front of the packet, with the maker's name on the back. Where awards were privately purchased, the packaging was obliged to carry guarantee details, indicating the seller's legal responsibility to replace faulty goods free of charge.

178. *Presentation cases and packets for the Iron Cross 1st Class, the War Merit Cross 1st Class and the War Merit Medal.*

Citations and documents accompanying Nazi decorations also varied quite considerably. Some, like the Knight's Cross citation, were hand-finished on expensive parchment for display at home, while others were volume printed, typewritten or even stencilled, and were intended to be folded and carried in the *Soldbuch*. A small preliminary authorisation, or *Vorläufiges Besitzzeugnis*, often preceded the larger award document, or *Urkunde*. A few important citations were signed by Hitler, Göring and the like, but most were endorsed by junior officials, or even issued unsigned with only a franked stamp to authenticate a printed facsimile signature. Few included details of the specific action or achievement for which the decoration in question was bestowed.

For security reasons military citations completed in the field never bore the precise location of the issuing unit, but featured generalised locations such as *Afrika* or *Russland*, or one of the following abbreviations instead:

Abt.Gef.St. -	Battalion Field HQ
An Bord -	At sea (navy)
Div.Gef.Stand -	Divisional Field HQ
Div.Stabs-Qu. -	Divisional Staff HQ
Einsatzort -	Operational Zone
Gefechtsstand -	Battle HQ

179. *The citation for the Oakleaves and Swords to the Knight's Cross, presented to SS-Obergruppenführer Sepp Dietrich on 14 March 1943, after the victory at Kharkov. The document is signed personally by Hitler.*

180. *The citation for a National Trade Competition* Kreissieger *Decoration, awarded in 1938 for success in the building category. It bears the facsimile signatures of Dr Robert Ley, Head of the German Labour Front, and Reich Youth Leader Baldur von Schirach.*

H.Qu. -	HQ
Im Felde -	In the field
K.Gef.St. -	Company Field HQ
O.U. -	Temporary Base
Ortsunterkunft -	Temporary Base
Rgt.Gef.St. -	Regimental Field HQ
St.Qu. -	Staff HQ.

A sizeable minority of citations were completed in the problematic Sütterlin Script, an archaic handwriting style promoted by Berlin graphics teacher

Ludwig Sütterlin (1865–1917) and widely taught in German schools until September 1941. This renders even recipients' names difficult to decipher in some cases. It is interesting to note that the use of both Sütterlin and Gothic scripts was discontinued virtually overnight following general discussions at a routine publishing meeting held on 1 March 1941 attended by *Reichsleiter* Max Amann (director of Eher Verlag, the Nazi publishing house) and Hitler. During the talks, Hitler learned that Sütterlin and Gothic were in fact derived from so-called

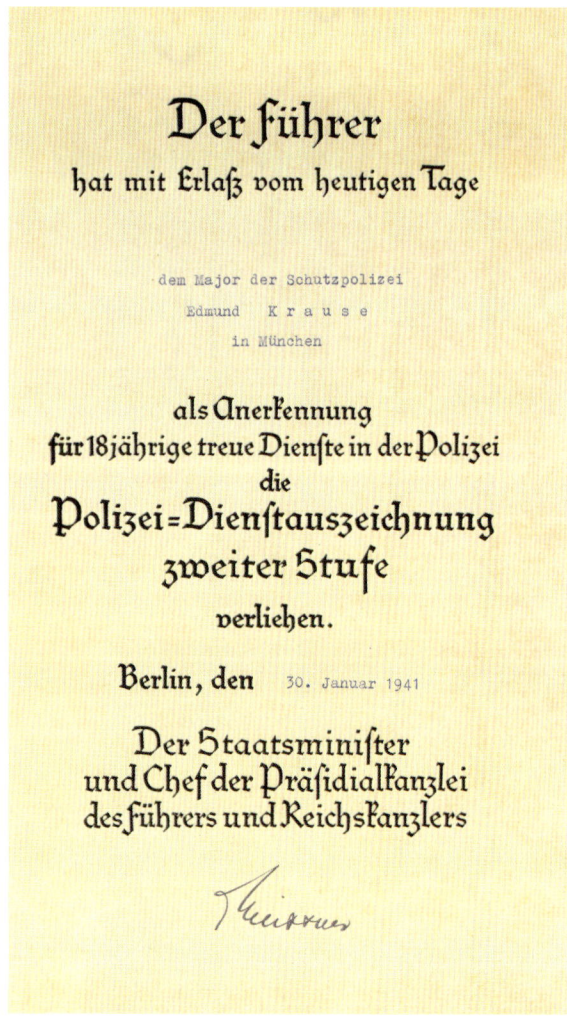

181. *The citation for the Police 18-Year Long-Service Award, bearing the facsimile signature of Otto Meissner, Head of Hitler's Presidential Chancellery.*

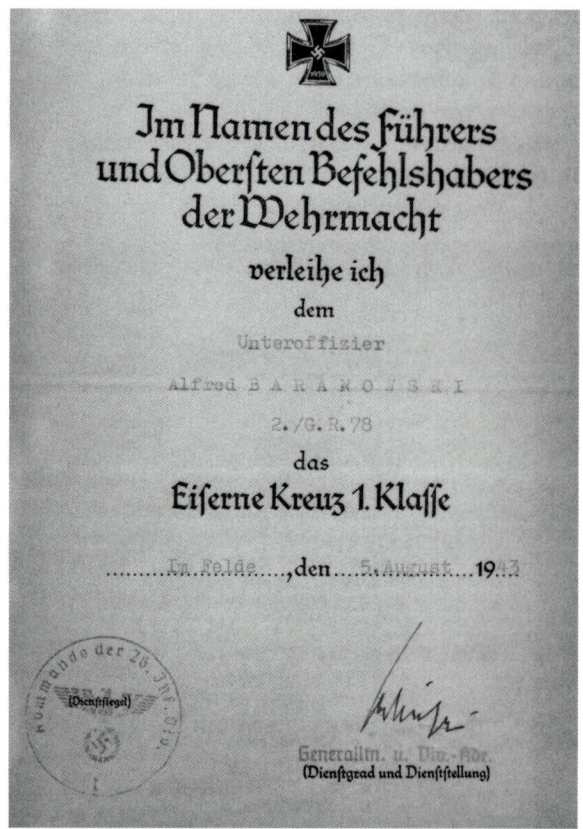

182. *The Citation for the Iron Cross 1st Class, signed personally by the commander of the 26th Infantry Division. This document, dated 5 August 1943, was doubtless printed prior to the dissemination of Hitler's order of 1 March 1941 which instructed that Gothic lettering should no longer feature on official paperwork. Old locally held stocks of Gothic citations like this one continued to be used by unit commanders well into 1944. Note also the* Im Felde *designation, denoting an award rendered in the field.*

Schwabacher Jew Lettering, which had been developed by early Jewish printers in Germany. That same day, Martin Bormann issued an instruction at Hitler's behest designating standard Latin script as the official typeface for *NSDAP* and all other national documents in future. Consequently, award citations printed after mid-1941 tended to feature Latin lettering and were much plainer than their ornate predecessors.

183. *Right: The Citation for the Close Combat Clasp in Bronze, illustrating the Latin lettering prescribed for general use on official documents from 1 March 1941. This award was conferred at the Field HQ of the 78th Grenadier Regiment on 19 May 1944, and the citation is signed personally by the regimental commander.*

184. *Below: Certified records of military decorations awarded were maintained in each holder's identity book. This example relates to a policeman who served with various combat units on the eastern front, and indicates at the bottom of the page that he received the Iron Cross 2nd Class on 6 April 1944.*

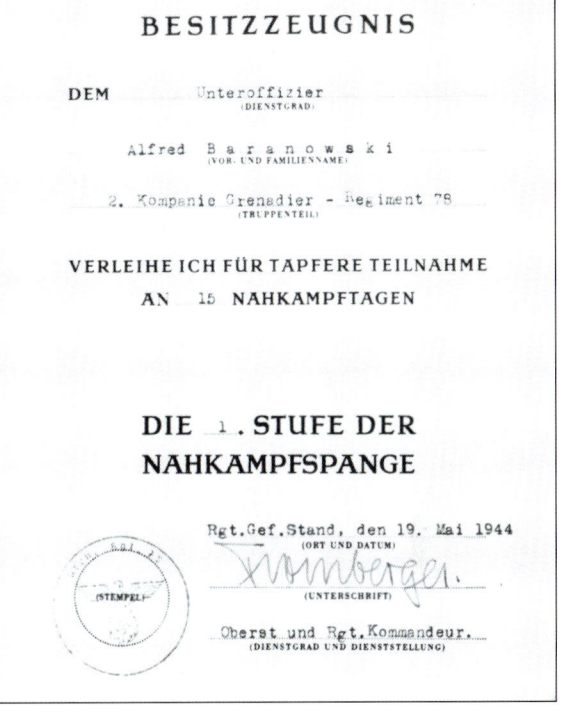

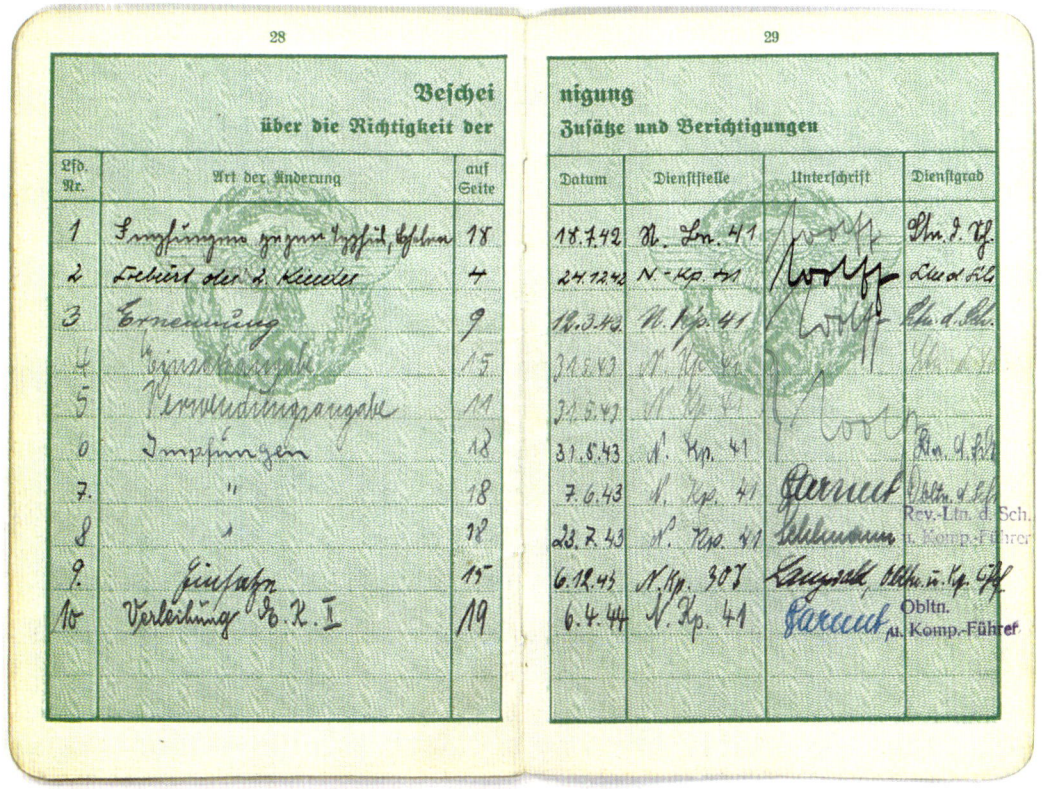

Appendix I

Makers', Designers' and Other Marks

Manufacturers' Marks and Code Numbers

Each German metalware firm authorised to produce State awards was registered with the *Präsidialkanzlei des Führers* and allocated one of a series of manufacturers' registration numbers, running from 1 to 142. Only the larger and more prestigious companies were licensed to sell decorations via their own retail outlets, and they received additional *Lieferant*, or 'supplier'

numbers, for use on goods produced for private sale. Some early Nazi badges, such as the cap insignia of the *DAF*, bore full supplier code designations, for example *Lieferant Nr. 10*. A much abbreviated form of supplier mark known as the 'L' number, in this case 'L/10', was used on awards. From March 1941, registration and 'L' numbers were required to be stamped on all state decorations in place of the maker's name or trademark. However, this requirement was not rigidly enforced

185. *The reverse of a standard-issue German Cross in Silver, showing the manufacturer's registration number '1' (Deschler & Sohn) stamped into the pin bar.*

186. *The reverse of a convex Iron Cross 1st Class, produced for private sale, showing the manufacturer's supplier mark 'L/57' (Boerger & Co.) stamped into the bottom of the lower arm.*

and many war badges, for example, retained standard markings, while around 20 per cent of all awards were completely devoid of any sort of maker's mark. Campaign shields, tank destruction badges and similar sleeve insignia were never marked.

The following table lists all the registration and 'L' numbers which were allocated, and the firms to which they referred. The designation (F) after the company's 'L' number on this list indicates that it was fully licensed to sell all decorations and awards via its own retail outlets, while (P) shows that it was part licensed and could offer only a restricted range of awards for sale. Known company trademarks are also shown, together with relevant numbers from the independent series of *RZM* makers' codes which had to be used on specified Nazi party political badges and decorations after 1935. Unfortunately, the destruction of Third Reich records means that this list cannot be totally exhaustive.

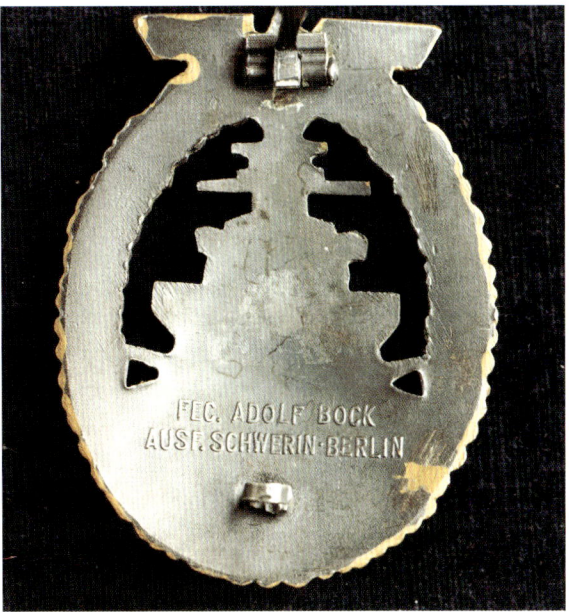

188. *The trademark on the reverse of a High Seas Fleet War Badge, with abbreviations showing that it was designed by Adolf Bock and manufactured by Schwerin & Sohn.*

187. *The reverse of an HJ Proficiency Badge, showing the maker's RZM code 'M1/63' (Steinhauer & Lück) cast into the design. The letter 'B' indicates that this particular example was produced as a duplicate for private purchase. Officially issued pieces were stamped with the award serial number in place of the 'B'.*

189. *The '800' silver hallmark stamped into the centre reverse of a 1914 Iron Cross 1st Class.*

Reg.No.	'L' No.	(F) or (P)	*RZM* Code	Trademark	Firm
1	L/10	(F)	M1/52		Deschler & Sohn, Munich
2	L/12	(F)	M1/182	CEJ	C.E. Juncker, Berlin
3	L/11	(F)	M1/120	W.D.	Wilhelm Deumer, Lüdenscheid
4	L/16	(F)	M1/63	SIh	Steinhauer & Lück, Lüdenscheid
5	L/17	(F)	M1/116	Jena W	Hermann Wernstein, Jena-Löbstadt
6	L/24	(F)	M1/72	FZS	Fritz Zimmermann, Stuttgart
7	L/13	(F)	M1/21	P.M.	Paul Meybauer, Berlin
8	L/19	(F)	M1/15		Ferdinand Hoffstätter, Bonn
9					*Liefergemeinschaft Pforzheimer Schmuckhandwerker* (consortium of small jewellery firms)
10	L/21	(F)	M1/77		Foerster & Barth, Pforzheim
11			M/130		Grossmann & Co., Vienna
12	L/20	(P)	M1/102		Frank & Reif, Stuttgart
13	L/60	(P)	M1/101	G.B.	Gustav Brehmer, Markneukirchen
14			M1/13	IN 1790	L. Christian Lauer, Nuremberg
15	L/14	(F)	M1/153	f.o.	Friedrich Orth, Vienna
16	L/59	(P)	M1/85		Alois Rettenmaier, Schwäbisch-Gmünd
17				C.S.u.S.	C. Schwerin & Sohn, Berlin
18			M1/34	KWM	Karl Wurster, Markneukirchen
19	L/51	(P)	M1/65		E. Ferdinand Wiedmann, Frankfurt
20	L/52	(F)			C.F. Zimmermann, Pforzheim
21	L/50	(P)			Gebrüder Godet & Co., Berlin
22	L/57	(F)	M1/74	B.B. & Co.	B. Boerger & Co., Berlin
23					*Arbeitsgemeinschaft für Heeresbedarf*, Berlin (consortium of military suppliers)
24					*Arbeitsgemeinschaft der Hanauer Plaketten Hersteller* (consortium of plaque-making firms)
25					*Arbeitsgemeinschaft der Hanauer Silberschmiede* (consortium of silversmiths)
26	L/18	(F)	M1/170		B.H. Mayer, Künstprägeanstalt Pforzheim
27			M1/146		Anton Schenkl, Vienna
28			M1/128	ESP	Eugen Schmidthaussler, Pforzheim
29				PR.ST.M.B.	Hauptmünzamt, Berlin
30					Hauptmünzamt, Vienna
31					Hans Gnad, Vienna
32				W.H.	Wilhelm Hobacher, Vienna
33	L/61	(P)	M1/45	F L L	Friedrich Linden, Lüdenscheid
34			M1/83	W A	Wilhelm Annetsberger, Munich
35	L/64	(P)	M1/17	A	F.W. Assmann & Söhne, Lüdenscheid
36					Bury & Leonhard, Hanau
37			M1/49	Ad.B. L.	Adolf Baumeister, Lüdenscheid
38				AGMuK	*Arbeitsgemeinschaft Metall- und Kunststoff*, Gablonz (consortium of metal and cloth goods manufacturers)
39					Rudolf Berge, Gablonz
40			M1/36	B & NL	Berg & Nolte, Lüdenscheid
41					Gebrüder Bender, Oberstein

Reg.No.	'L' No.	(F) or (P)	*RZM* Code	Trademark	Firm
42					Bindermann & Co., Oberkassel
43			M1/37		Julius Bauer & Söhne, Zella-Mehlis
44				J.B.& Co.	Jakob Bengel, Idar-Oberstein
45			M1/152		Franz Jungwirth, Vienna
46			M1/159		Hans Doppler, Oberdonau
47					Erhard & Söhne, Schwäbisch-Gmünd
48					Richard Feix, Gablonz
49			M1/141	JFS	Josef Feix & Söhne, Gablonz
50					Karl Gschiermeister, Vienna
51					Eduard Gorlach & Söhne, Gablonz
52					Gottlieb & Wagner, Idar-Oberstein
53	L/58	(P)	M1/109		Glaser & Söhn, Dresden
54			M1/53	(GWL)	Gebrüder Wegerhoff, Lüdenscheid
55					J.E. Hammer & Söhne, Geringswalde
56			M1/9		Robert Hauschild, Pforzheim
57			M1/6		Karl Hensler, Pforzheim
58					Artur Jökel & Co., Gablonz
59					Louis Keller, Oberstein
60					Katz & Deyhle, Pforzheim
61				R.K.	Rudolf Karneth & Söhne, Gablonz
62				K.O.	Kerbach & Österhelt, Dresden
63			M1/177		Franz Klast & Söhne, Gablonz
64			M1/93		Gottlieb Friederich Keck & Söhne, Pforzheim
65	L/26	(P)		K. & Q.	Klein & Quenzer, Idar-Oberstein
66					Friedrich Keller, Oberstein
67				(RK)	Robert Kreisel, Gablonz
68					Alfred Knobloch, Gablonz
69					Alois Klammer, Innsbruck
70					Lind & Meyrer, Oberstein
71					Rudolf Leukert, Gablonz
72					Franz Lipp, Pforzheim
73					Franz Möhnert, Gablonz
74					Carl Maurer & Sohn, Oberstein
75	L/65	(P)	M1/16		Franke & Co., Lüdenscheid
76			M1/27		Ernst Müller, Pforzheim
77					Hauptmünzamt, Munich
78					Gustav Miksch, Gablonz
79			M1/58	(MK)	Matthias Kutsch, Attendorn
80	L/63	(P)			G.H. Osang, Dresden
81			M1/24	⬦o|c O & C	Overhoff & Co., Lüdenscheid
82					Augustin Prager, Gablonz
83					Emil Peukert, Gablonz
84			M1/103		Carl Poellath, Schrobenhausen
85					Julius Pietsch, Gablonz
86			M1/78	P & CL	Paulmann & Crone, Lüdenscheid
87					Roman Palme, Gablonz
88	L/62	(P)	M1/100	W.R.	Werner Redo, Saarlautern
89			M1/139	R.R.S.	Rudolf Richter, Schlag
90					August Richter, Hamburg

Reg.No.	'L' No.	(F) or (P)	*RZM* Code	Trademark	Firm
91					Josef Rössler & Co., Gablonz
92					Josef Rückert & Sohn, Gablonz
93			M1/137	R.S. & S.	Richard Simm & Söhne, Gablonz
94			M1/61	Œ	Ossenberg-Engels, Iserlohn
95					Adolf Scholze, Grünwald
96				(R_K)	Robert Klein, Vienna
97	L/25	(F)			A.E. Köchert, Vienna
98	L/22	(F)		R.Z.	Rudolf Souval, Vienna
99			M1/155		Schwertner & Co., Graz-Eggenberg
100	L/55	(F)	M1/35		Rudolf Wächtler & Lange, Mittweida
101			M1/165		Rudolf Tam, Gablonz
102			M1/157		Philipp Türka, Vienna
103			M1/164		August Tam, Gablonz
104			M1/148		Heinrich Ulbricht, Kaufing
105					Heinrich Vogt, Pforzheim
106			M1/149	(B·S·W)	Gebrüder Schneider, Vienna
107			M1/92	C/W	Carl Wild, Hamburg
108					Arno Wallpach, Salzburg
109			M1/172	WH	Walter & Henlein, Gablonz
110					Otto Zappe, Gablonz
111					Ziemer & Söhne, Oberstein
112			M1/156		Argentorwerke Rust & Hetzel, Vienna
113			M1/105	开	Hermann Aurich, Dresden
114					Ludwig Bertsch, Karlsruhe
115			M1/50	R.S.S.	Richard Sieper & Söhne, Lüdenscheid
116	L/56	(P)	M1/106	F & BL	Funke & Brüninghaus, Lüdenscheid
117					Hugo Lang, Wiesenthal
118					August Menze & Sohn, Vienna
119			M1/127	(S)	Alfred Stübbe, Berlin
120					Franz Petzl, Vienna
121				JMME	Imme & Sohn, Berlin
122					J.J. Stahl, Strasbourg
123					Beck, Hassinger & Co., Strasbourg
124			M1/151		Rudolf Schanes, Vienna
125					Eugen Gauss, Pforzheim
126				EH	Eduard Hahn, Oberstein
127					Moritz Hausch, Pforzheim
128			M1/180		S. Jablonski & Co., Posen
129					Fritz Kohm, Pforzheim
130					Wilhelm Schröder & Co., Lüdenscheid
131				W	Heinrich Wander, Gablonz
132					Franz Reischauer, Idar-Oberstein
133	L/15	(F)	M1/75		Otto Schickle, Pforzheim
134					Otto Klein, Hanau
135					Julius Möser, Oberstein
136					J. Wagner & Sohn, Berlin
137					J.H. Werner, Berlin
138	L/23	(F)	M1/43	JM O	Julius Maurer, Oberstein
139	L/53	(P)		H&CL	Hymmen & Co., Lüdenscheid

Reg.No.	'L' No.	(F) or (P)	*RZM* Code	Trademark	Firm
140	L/54	(P)			Schauerte & Höhfeld, Lüdenscheid
141				SHuCo	Sohni, Heubach & Co., Oberstein
142	L/66	(P)			A.D. Schwerdt, Stuttgart
			M1/1		Meyer & Franke, Lüdenscheid
			M1/2		Richard Conrad, Weimar
			M1/3		Max Kremhelmer, Munich
			M1/4		Karl Gutenkunst, Oranienburg
			M1/5		Walter Simon, Dresden
			M1/7		Hermann Schanzlin, Pforzheim
			M1/8		Ferdinand Wagner, Pforzheim
			M1/10		Robert Schenkel, Pforzheim
			M1/11		Christian Balmberger, Nuremberg
			M1/12		Gebrüder Hahne, Lüdenscheid
			M1/14		Matthias Oeschsler & Sohn, Ansbach
			M1/18		Gold- und Silberwerk, Oberstein
			M1/20		Gustav Emil Ficker, Beierfeld
			M1/22		Johann Dittrich, Chemnitz
			M1/23		Wilhelm Borgas, Eutingen
			M1/25		Rudolf Reiling, Pforzheim
			M1/28		Gebrüder Trautz, Pforzheim
			M1/29		Otto Riedel, Zwickau
			M1/30		Robert Metzger, Pforzheim
			M1/31		Karl Pfohl, Pforzheim
			M1/32		Gustav Ramminger, Pforzheim
			M1/38		Carl Wächtler, Weimar
			M1/39		Robert Beck, Pforzheim
			M1/40		Meinel & Scholer, Klingenthal
			M1/41		H.A. Köhlers & Söhne, Altenburg
			M1/42		Kerbach & Israel, Dresden
			M1/44		C. Dinsel, Berlin
			M1/46		Herbert Tegge, Berlin
			M1/47	C.Th.D.	Christian Theodor Dicke, Lüdenscheid
			M1/48		Alexander Wollram, Dessau
			M1/51		Noelle & Hueck, Lüdenscheid
			M1/54		Fries, Beuster & Schild, Berlin
			M1/55		August Enders, Oberrahmede
			M1/56		Erfurter Knopffabrik, Erfurt
			M1/57		M. Winter, Munich
			M1/59		Paul Cramer, Lüdenscheid
			M1/60		Gebrüder Cosack, Neheim
			M1/62		Gustav Hähl, Pforzheim
			M1/64		Albert Winges, Trusen
			M1/66		Fritz Kohm, Pforzheim
			M1/67		Karl Schenker, Schwäbisch-Gmünd
			M1/68		Gustav Maier, Pforzheim
			M1/70		Franz Otto, Wuppertal
			M1/71		Gesell & Co., Pforzheim
			M1/73		Karl Erbacher, Pforzheim
			M1/76		Hillenbrand & Bröer, Lüdenscheid
			M1/79		Walter Amlauf, Leipzig
			M1/80		Dürr & Seiter, Pforzheim
			M1/81		Rütting & Mertz, Lüdenscheid
			M1/82		Leistner & Co., Leipzig
			M1/84		Ernst Schneider, Lüdenscheid

Reg.No.	'L' No.	(F) or (P)	RZM Code	Trademark	Firm
			M1/86		Ernst Conze, Lüdenscheid
			M1/87		Karolina Gahr, Munich
			M1/88		Josef Schulte-Ufer, Sundern
			M1/89		Gustav Bühnert, Döbeln
			M1/90		Apreck & Vrage, Leipzig
			M1/94		Friedrich Keck, Pforzheim
			M1/95		Josef Fuess, Munich
			M1/96		F.O. Naupert, Rosswein
			M1/97		M. Nett, Fürth
			M1/98		G. Danner, Mühlhausen
			M1/99		Peter Wilhelm Heb, Lüdenscheid
			M1/104		Otto Fechler, Bernsbach
			M1/107	(EJJ)	Emil Jüttner, Lüdenscheid
			M1/108		Schröder & Co., Lüdenscheid
			M1/110		Tweer & Turck, Lüdenscheid
			M1/111		Gebrüder Gloerfeld, Lüdenscheid
			M1/112		Robert Deitenbeck, Lüdenscheid
			M1/113		Gebrüder Dornbach, Lüdenscheid
			M1/114		Paul Cramer & Co., Lüdenscheid
			M1/117		K.F. Vogelsang, Lüdenscheid
			M1/118		Erich Gutenkunst, Berlin
			M1/119		Georg Bonitz, Schwarzenberg
			M1/121		Walter Demmer, Lüdenscheid
			M1/122		I. Deutschbein, Euskirchen
			M1/124		Gebrüder Lange, Lüdenscheid
			M1/125		Cramer & Dornbach, Lüdenscheid
			M1/126		Karl Friedrich Schenkel, Pforzheim
			M1/129		Seiler & Co., Geldern
			M1/136		Salcher & Söhne, Wagstadt
			M1/138		M. Oechsler & Sohn, Bodenbach
			M1/140		Bruno Czerch, Gablonz
			M1/142		Josef Hillebrand, Gablonz
			M1/143		Gebrüder Jäger, Gablonz
			M1/147		Eduard Gösel, Vienna
			M1/150		Franke & Sohn, Heidenreichstein
			M1/158		Karl Pichl, Innsbruck
			M1/160		E. Reihl, Linz
			M1/161		Anton Markovsky & Söhne, Gablonz
			M1/162		Konrad Seiboth, Gablonz
			M1/163		Franz Schmidt, Gablonz
			M1/166		Camill Bergmann & Co., Gablonz
			M1/167		Augustin Hicke, Tyssa bei Bodenbach
			M1/168		Wilhelm Fühner, Pforzheim
			M1/169		Paul Garthe, Milspe
			M1/173		Adam Donner, Wuppertal
			M1/174		Petz & Lorenz, Unterreichenbach
			M1/175		Walgo & Co., Kierspe
			M1/176		Heinrich Vogt, Pforzheim
			M1/178		Gustav Körtel, Peterswald
			M1/181		Wilhelm Müller, Posen
			M1/183	S. & S.	Schmal & Schulz, Wuppertal
			M1/184		W. Aurich, Leipe

Designers

In addition to makers' details, the names or marks of the designers of Third Reich medals and decorations occasionally appeared on their products. Principal designers, and their logos where known, are listed below.

Logo	Designer	Logo	Designer
B. v A.	Benno von Arent		Herbert Knötel
	Franz Berberich		Ernst Krause
	Adolf Bock		Elmar Lange
♂	Paul Casberg		Franz Moser
	Karl Diebitsch		Ottfried Neubecker
	Walter Eberbach		Wilhelm Ernst
	Josef Fuess		Peekhaus
	Otto Gahr	O P	Otto Placzek
	Karolina Gahr		
	Waldemar Raemisch		
	Eugen Godet		Robert Schlimmer
	Karl Goetz		Robert von Weech
	Walter Heck	J W	Josef Wegener
	Wilhelm Heitinger		Max Zankl
	Adolf Hitler		Otto Zappe
	Egon Jantke		Hans Zöberlein
⏚	Richard Klein		

Other Marks

The following marks can also be encountered from time to time on certain Nazi awards and/or their presentation cases.

Mark	Explanation
ALPAKA	Silver plated
AUSF.	*Ausführung:* Produced by
DRGM	*Deutsches Reichsgebrauchsmuster:* State-registered design
DRP	*Deutsches Reichspatent:* Patented
ENTWURF	Designed by
FEC.	*Fecit* (Latin): Designed by
GES.GESCH.	*Gesetzlich Geschützt:* Patent pending
SILBER	Silver
800	80 per cent silver content
835	83.5 per cent silver content
900	90 per cent silver content
935	93.5 per cent silver content
990	99 per cent silver content
LDO	*Leistungsgemeinschaft der Deutschen Ordenhersteller:* the Quality Control Board of German Orders Manufacturers
⚓	Logo of the *LDO*, used until March 1941 then replaced by the version above
RZM	Logo of the *RZM*, which always preceded the relevant *RZM* code number
⚡⚡	Logo introduced by Himmler to indicate that a design had been commissioned and approved by the *SS*

The presence of a maker's or other mark should never be viewed as a guarantee of authenticity, since most marks have been faked time and time again since 1945. The silver hallmark '925' is a British mark which equates to the Sterling Silver standard and has been stamped since 1904 on imported continental silverware. It was never used on Nazi awards.

Appendix II

Chronology of Third Reich Awards

This table charts the institution and revision dates of German decorations between 30 January 1933, when Hitler came to power, and 23 May 1945, when the Third Reich officially ended. For ease of reference, significant historical events are included and shown in parenthesis. It is clear that the creation of political and civil awards mirrored the fortunes of the Nazi regime, with ornate designs becoming ever grander and more baroque in character from 1937, when the imperial nature of the Reich was firmly established. The institution of new civilian honours tailed off dramatically after 1939, while that of military decorations accelerated considerably. The perceived incentive value of the latter, particularly during difficult periods of the Second World War, is also very evident. For example, the Close Combat Clasp was created at the height of the Battle of Stalingrad, and no fewer than twenty-eight new military awards (counting all grades) were instituted in November 1944 alone, when the heartland of Germany itself was threatened on all sides.

It is important to note that several months usually elapsed between the date of inauguration of an award and the first examples of it being presented. A good illustration of this is the Demjansk Shield, which commemorated participation in a battle which took place at the beginning of 1942 but which was not instituted until a year later, and not distributed until January 1944. Consequently, it is not surprising that many decorations created after July 1944 were never actually bestowed, or even manufactured. Unless otherwise indicated, all dates shown are institution dates.

1933

30 Jan.	(HITLER BECOMES CHANCELLOR)
16 Mar.	Baltic Cross and Silesian Eagle recognised as official awards
21 Mar.	(THIRD REICH DECLARED AT POTSDAM)
24 Mar.	(HITLER GIVEN DICTATORIAL POWERS)
7 Apr.	Hitler declares his intention to create and issue new German orders and decorations
19 May	Unauthorised manufacture of swastika insignia prohibited
26 May	Schlageter Memorial Badge
June	1923/25 *Gau* Badge
	Munich *Gau* Badge
	Thüringia *Gau* Badge
	Baden *Gau* Badge
	Commemorative Badge of the *Jungsturm Hitler*
22 Jun.	Life-Saving Medal
14 Jul.	(*NSDAP* BECOMES ONLY LEGAL POLITICAL PARTY IN GERMANY)
31 Jul.	Osthannover *Gau* Badge
25 Sep.	*DLRG* Water Life-Saving Badge
30 Sep.	*RAD* Anhalt Badge
13 Oct.	Golden Party Badge
9 Nov.	Blood Order
11 Nov.	Steel Helmet Veterans' Decoration
28 Nov.	*SA* Sports Badge
21 Dec.	Prussian Fire Service Award

1934

30 Jan.	German Federal Eagle added to design of Red Cross Decoration
	Individual German states again permitted to issue medals and awards
	General production of 'replacement' First World War decorations authorised
3 Feb.	Honour Chevron of the Old Guard
10 Apr.	*SS* Death's Head Ring

28 Apr.	*BDM* Proficiency Clasp
	JM Proficiency Clasp
30 Apr.	Baden Fire Service Award
	Hanover Fire Service Award
	Hesse Fire Service Award
	North Rhineland Fire Service Award
	Thüringia Fire Service Award
1 May	(EAGLE AND SWASTIKA EMBLEM OF THE *NSDAP* INCORPORATED INTO GERMAN ARMY UNIFORM)
3 May	*RZM* given control over the production of *NSDAP* awards
15 May	Restoration Statute declares the intention of the Nazi government to greatly extend its range of orders and decorations. The rights of individual German States to institute their own new medals and awards is rescinded
23 Jun.	Golden Hitler Youth Badge
	HJ Proficiency Badge
	HJ Expert Skier Badge
30 Jun.	('NIGHT OF THE LONG KNIVES' PURGE ELIMINATES THE *SA* CHALLENGE TO HITLER'S AUTHORITY)
13 Jul.	Cross of Honour 1914–18
2 Aug.	(HITLER BECOMES HEAD OF STATE AND CHIEF OF THE ARMED FORCES)
1 Oct.	(HITLER ORDERS CREATION OF A NEW *LUFTWAFFE* AND EXPANSION OF THE ARMY AND NAVY)
13 Dec.	Danzig Red Cross Decoration
20 Dec.	*RZM* proofmark becomes obligatory on all *NSDAP* insignia
	Unauthorised manufacture or wearing of *NSDAP* insignia and awards becomes punishable by imprisonment

---

1935

19 Jan.	*Luftwaffe* Aircrew Badge
15 Feb.	*SA* Sports Badge upgraded and opened to the public at large
1 Mar.	(GERMANY RECOVERS THE *SAAR* TERRITORY FROM FRANCE)
16 Mar.	(CONSCRIPTION REINTRODUCED IN GERMANY)
	System of *RZM* codes formalised
20 Apr.	Golden Hitler Youth Badge with Oakleaves
	Teno Decoration
30 Jun.	Essen *Gau* Badge
15 Sep.	(SWASTIKA BECOMES THE OFFICIAL NATIONAL EMBLEM OF THE GERMAN STATE)
	Swastika added to Eagle Shield of Germany
	Swastika added to Goethe Medal for Art and Science

26 Sep.	*DJ* Proficiency Badge
1 Oct.	*Luftwaffe* 'von Richthofen' and 'Boelcke' Cuff Titles
14 Nov.	*DRL* Championship Badges
	Unauthorised trade in orders and decorations prohibited
	Unofficial 1914–18 and *Freikorps* awards prohibited
16 Nov.	Further wear of the Order of St. John prohibited

1936

10 Jan.	(*LUFTWAFFE* EQUIPPED WITH FIRST NEW MULTI-CREW BOMBERS)
30 Jan.	1914–18 Wound Badge reissued
4 Feb.	Olympic Games Decoration
7 Mar.	(GERMANY REOCCUPIES THE RHINELAND)
16 Mar.	*Wehrmacht* Long-Service Awards
26 Mar.	*Luftwaffe* Pilot/Observer Badge supersedes Aircrew Badge
	Luftwaffe Pilot Badge
	Luftwaffe Observer Badge
	Luftwaffe Radio Operator/Air Gunner Badge
	Luftwaffe Retired Aircrew Badge
20 Apr.	(FIRST THIRD REICH FIELD MARSHAL APPOINTED)
21 Jun.	*Teno* Long-Service Cuff Titles supersede *Teno* Decoration
29 Jun.	*Wehrmacht* Marksmanship Lanyards
18 Jul.	(SPANISH CIVIL WAR BREAKS OUT)
31 Jul.	Olympic Games Medal
10 Aug.	Army Mountain Leader's Badge
	Police Expert Mountaineer Badges
20 Aug.	*HJ* Marksmanship Badge
	DJ Marksmanship Badge
12 Sep.	Wear of the Olympic Games Decoration with *NSDAP* uniform during parades prohibited
10 Oct.	(GÖRING HEADS FOUR-YEAR ECONOMIC PLAN TO PREPARE GERMANY FOR WAR)
31 Oct.	Berlin *Gau* Badge
5 Nov.	*Luftwaffe* Paratroop Badge
6 Nov.	Coburg Badge, 1929 Nuremberg Party Day Badge and Brunswick Rally Badge elevated to national award status
13 Nov.	Mine Rescue Decoration
28 Nov.	National Senate of Culture Badge
30 Nov.	1914–18 Wound Badge regulations revised to acknowledge long-term effects of more serious injuries
1 Dec.	National Food Estate Awards
22 Dec.	National Fire Brigade Decoration supersedes earlier state awards

1937

26 Jan.	*SS* Marksmanship Badge
30 Jan.	National Prize for Art and Science Decoration
23 Feb.	German Expert Horseman's Badge
	Badge for the Care of Horses
28 Feb.	Heavy Athletics Badge
6 Apr.	Swastika added to the design of Red Cross Decoration
20 Apr.	Long-Service Award for *Wehrmacht* Civilian Employees
	Badge for Civilian Workers in the Aircraft Industry
28 Apr.	Order of precedence prescribed for the wearing of Third Reich decorations on medal bars
1 May	Order of the German Eagle
15 Jun.	Army Paratroop Badge
1 Jul.	Titles and Orders Statute regulates the issue and wear of Nazi decorations and abolishes all awards of the individual German states
	Red Cross Nursing Sisters' and Matrons' Long-Service Awards
10 Jul.	Swastika added to design of Life-Saving Medal
1 Sep.	Swastika added to design of German National Sports Badge and National Youth Sports Badge
25 Sep.	(STATE VISIT OF MUSSOLINI TO BERLIN) Eagle Order Grand Cross in Gold with Diamonds

1938

21 Jan.	German Academy for Aeronautical Research Decoration
30 Jan.	Golden Party Badge award criteria extended to cover outstanding service to the Party or State
	Faithful Service Decoration
	SS Long-Service Decorations
	Police Long-Service Awards
	RAD Long-Service Awards
	Air-Raid Defence Decoration
	Fire Brigade Decoration revised
	Mine Rescue Decoration revised
18 Feb.	Motor Sports Badge
10 Mar.	*NSFK* Balloon Pilot's Badge
12 Mar.	(GERMANY OCCUPIES AUSTRIA)
20 Apr.	Golden Book of Airmen
	National Trade Competition Decorations
1 May	Austrian *Anschluss* Medal
15 May	*HJ* Leader's Sports Badge
30 May	Blood Order award criteria extended

20 Jun.	Danzig Police Long-Service Awards
28 Jun.	Danzig Faithful Service Decoration
1 Jul.	Increased punishments set for unauthorised trading in orders and decorations
12 Jul.	*NSFK* Powered Aircraft Pilot's Badge
12 Aug.	East Prussia *Gau* Badge
1 Sep.	Defence Economy Leader's Decoration
1 Oct.	(GERMANY OCCUPIES THE SUDETENLAND)
18 Oct.	Sudetenland Medal
21 Oct.	Design of *SS* 4-Year Long-Service Medal revised
30 Oct.	1914–18 Cross of Honour eligibility extended to residents of Austria and the Sudetenland
3 Dec.	*HJ* Sharpshooter/Champion Shot Badges
5 Dec.	*NSDAP* decorations and the basic party membership badge permitted to be worn on uniforms of civilian state authorities such as the Police, Railway and Customs Services
16 Dec.	Mother's Cross
19 Dec.	*Wehrmacht* Marksmanship Lanyards revised

1939

1 Jan.	Army Paratroop Badge discontinued as all paratroop formations come under *Luftwaffe* control
27 Jan.	(FASCISTS VICTORIOUS IN SPANISH CIVIL WAR)
30 Jan.	*SA* Sports Badge revised to reflect military emphasis
17 Feb.	Customs Service Decoration
10 Mar.	40 Years' Cluster for *Wehrmacht* Long-Service Awards
15 Mar.	(GERMANY OCCUPIES CZECHOSLOVAKIA)
22 Mar.	(GERMANY ANNEXES MEMEL)
14 Apr.	Spanish Cross
20 Apr.	Eagle Order Grand Cross in Gold
	Swords authorised for Eagle Order
	NSDAP Long Service Decorations
	1914–18 Wound Badge eligibility extended to residents of Austria, the Sudetenland and Memel
1 May	Social Welfare Decoration
	Prague Castle Bar to Sudetenland Medal
	Memel Medal
	Danzig-West Prussia *Gau* Badge
	Danzig Fire Brigade Decoration
22 May	(GERMAN-ITALIAN PACT)
	'Spanish' Wound Badge
21 Jun.	'Spanien 1936–1939' Cuff Title
10 Jul.	Condor Legion Tank Badge

2 Aug.	West Wall Medal
23 Aug.	(NAZI-SOVIET PACT)
31 Aug.	Danzig Cross
1 Sep.	(GERMANY INVADES POLAND, CAUSING GREAT BRITAIN AND FRANCE TO DECLARE WAR)
	Iron Cross reinstituted, with Bars
	Wound Badge
	SS Long-Service Decorations superseded by Wehrmacht Long-Service Awards for the duration of the war
27 Sep.	(POLAND SURRENDERS)
13 Oct.	U-Boat War Badge
18 Oct.	War Merit Cross
8 Nov.	(FAILED ATTEMPT TO ASSASSINATE HITLER IN MUNICH)
20 Dec.	Infantry Assault Badge in Silver
	Tank Battle Badge in Silver

1940

30 Jan.	Wartheland Gau Badge
9 Feb.	Strict quality controls imposed on manufacturers of orders and decorations with reinforced prohibition of unapproved production
27 Feb.	Luftwaffe Honour Goblet
9 Apr.	(GERMANY INVADES DENMARK AND NORWAY)
1 May	National Trade Competition Decorations suspended
10 May	(GERMANY INVADES LOW COUNTRIES)
1 Jun.	Infantry Assault Badge in Bronze
	Tank Battle Badge in Bronze
	General Assault Badge
	Iron Cross 2nd Class to be automatically awarded to those receiving the Wound Badge in Silver or Gold
3 Jun.	Oakleaves to Knight's Cross of the Iron Cross
4 Jun.	Destroyer War Badge
22 Jun.	(GERMANY VICTORIOUS IN THE WEST)
1 Jul.	Medallion for Outstanding Achievement in the Technical Branch of the Luftwaffe
19 Jul.	(BERLIN VICTORY PARADE MARKS HEIGHT OF HITLER'S POPULARITY)
22 Jul.	237 Knight's Crosses of the Iron Cross awarded to this date
7 Aug.	Pioneer of Labour Award
19 Aug.	Knight's Cross of the War Merit Cross
	War Merit Medal
	Narvik Shield
25 Aug.	(FIRST RAF RAID ON BERLIN)
31 Aug.	Minesweeper War Badge

14 Sep.	Posthumous presentations of the Iron Cross authorised for the first time
17 Sep.	(HITLER POSTPONES INVASION OF GREAT BRITAIN)
27 Sep.	(GERMAN-JAPANESE PACT)
16 Dec.	Luftwaffe Glider Pilot Badge
31 Dec.	Proposed 1939–40 Campaign Medal shelved

1941

10 Jan.	Luftwaffe Flak Battle Badge
30 Jan.	Luftwaffe Operational Flying Clasps for Fighters, Bombers and Reconnaissance Aircraft
14 Feb.	Awards of Wehrmacht Marksmanship Lanyards suspended for the duration of the war
1 Mar.	System of makers' code numbers formalised by the LDO
	LDO regulates the wear of miniature decorations on ribbon bars
	Hitler orders Latin script to replace Sütterlin and Gothic on all official documents including award citations
5 Mar.	Further production of convex Iron Crosses and convex War Merit Crosses forbidden by the LDO
7 Mar.	First award of the Knight's Cross of the Iron Cross to an enlisted man
16 Mar.	(HITLER DECLARES THAT GERMANY WILL WIN THE WAR BEFORE THE END OF 1941)
31 Mar.	(GERMAN OFFENSIVE OPENS IN NORTH AFRICA)
1 Apr.	Blockade-Breaker Badge
6 Apr.	(GERMANY INVADES THE BALKANS)
20 Apr.	HJ Decoration for Distinguished Foreigners
24 Apr.	Auxiliary Cruiser War Badge
30 Apr.	High Seas Fleet War Badge
30 May	E-Boat War Badge
	Addition of Golden Oakleaves to the Knight's Cross of the Iron Cross considered but rejected by Hitler
21 Jun.	Swords to the Knight's Cross of the Iron Cross
22 Jun.	(GERMANY INVADES THE SOVIET UNION)
24 Jun.	Coastal Artillery War Badge
1 Jul.	Roll of Honour of the German Army
	Army High Command Commendation Certificate
15 Jul.	Diamonds to the Knight's Cross of the Iron Cross
16 Jul.	(GERMANS TAKE SMOLENSK)
18 Jul.	Army Anti-Aircraft Badge

11 Aug.	763 Knight's Crosses of the Iron Cross awarded to this date
19 Sep.	(GERMANS TAKE KIEV)
20 Sep.	(GERMAN ASSAULT ON MOSCOW BEGINS)
28 Sep.	German Cross
	Iron Cross and War Merit Cross permitted to be worn together
3 Oct.	(HITLER ANNOUNCES VICTORY OVER THE SOVIET UNION AND THE BEGINNING OF A NEW ORDER IN EUROPE)
22 Oct.	Private sale by commercial firms of 'duplicate' German Crosses, Knight's Crosses, Oakleaves and Swords strictly forbidden
19 Nov.	*Luftwaffe* Operational Flying Clasp for Transport/Glider aircraft
5 Dec.	(GERMANS ABANDON ASSAULT ON MOSCOW)
11 Dec.	(GERMANY DECLARES WAR ON THE USA)
19 Dec.	(HITLER ASSUMES PERSONAL COMMAND OF THE ARMY)
20 Dec.	*Führer* Commendation Certificate
31 Dec.	Proposed 1939–41 Campaign Medal shelved

1942

26 Jan.	*NSFK* Large Glider Pilot Badge
30 Jan.	Swords added to Social Welfare Decoration
5 Feb.	(*WEHRMACHT* LOSSES REACH 1 MILLION)
11 Feb.	German Order
1 Mar.	Lacquered zinc begins to be used universally in the manufacture of lower-grade decorations and badges, replacing enamelled or plated bronze, brass, tombak, nickel silver and aluminium
9 Mar.	Tank Destruction Badge in Silver
31 Mar.	*Luftwaffe* Ground Assault Badge
1 Apr.	*Wehrmacht* demand for Iron Crosses exceeds stocks available
15 Apr.	(HEAVY BOMBING OF GERMAN CITIES BEGINS)
3 May	War badges protected by regulations prohibiting their unauthorised manufacture and wear
8 May	Unofficial manufacture of cloth war badges prohibited
13 May	*Luftwaffe* Operational Flying Clasp for Long-Range Fighter Aircraft
26 May	Eastern Front Medal
27 May	(ASSASSINATION OF REINHARD HEYDRICH DEMONSTRATES VULNERABILITY OF NAZI HIERARCHY)
30 May	(1,000 BOMBER RAID ON COLOGNE)

1 Jun.	New automatic manufacturing process devised to speed up the production of Iron Crosses
5 Jun.	Active-service version of German Cross in Gold
15 Jun.	*Luftwaffe* Salver of Honour
21 Jun.	(ROMMEL CAPTURES TOBRUK)
22 Jun.	*Luftwaffe* Air Gunner/Flight Engineer Badge
26 Jun.	Star Pendant for *Luftwaffe* Operational Flying Clasps
1 Jul.	Cholm Shield
	National Youth Sports Badge discontinued
14 Jul.	*Ostvolk* Decoration
25 Jul.	Krim Shield
14 Aug.	*Luftwaffe* Operational Flying Clasp for Night-Fighter Aircraft
16 Oct.	Kreta Cuff Title
23 Oct.	Front-Line Driver Badge
31 Oct	(HIGH POINT OF GERMAN EXPANSION IN THE EAST)
2 Nov.	(BRITISH OFFENSIVE OPENS IN NORTH AFRICA)
18 Nov.	National Sports Badge for War Wounded
	Police Expert Skier Badge
19 Nov.	(BATTLE OF STALINGRAD COMMENCES)
25 Nov.	Close Combat Clasp
26 Nov.	*Ostvolk* Decoration in Silver with Swords extended to German personnel

---

1943

8 Jan.	Regulations published governing the forfeiture and revocation of orders and decorations for those found guilty of treason or cowardice
15 Jan.	Afrika Cuff Title
20 Jan.	Eastern Front Medal extended to include foreign volunteers and civilian auxiliaries
27 Jan.	(GERMAN WOMEN FORMALLY CONSCRIPTED FOR WAR WORK)
30 Jan.	Design of E-Boat War Badge revised
31 Jan.	Proposed Stalingrad Shield shelved
1 Feb.	Navy Honour Table
2 Feb.	(GERMANS SURRENDER AT STALINGRAD)
18 Feb.	(GOEBBELS MOBILISES THE GERMAN CIVILIAN POPULATION FOR 'TOTAL WAR')
23 Feb.	Order of precedence for the wearing of two or more campaign shields published
12 Mar.	1914–18 Honour Cross eligibility extended to residents of Bohemia and Moravia
15 Mar.	(GERMAN VICTORY AT KHARKOV)
31 Mar.	Wound Badge extended to uniformed civilians

1 Apr.	In the most publicised medal ceremony of the war, intended to be an incentive to other *Wehrmacht* forces, thirty Knight's Crosses and hundreds of other decorations are presented to *Waffen-SS* men for their part in the recapture of Kharkov	1 May	National Trade Competition Decoration reinstated
			Teno Decoration reinstated
		13 May	Navy Honour Roll Clasp
		15 May	U-Boat Combat Clasp in Bronze
12 Apr.	*Luftwaffe* Honour List	16 May	(PEAK OF GERMAN ARMAMENTS PRODUCTION)
25 Apr.	Demjansk Shield		
13 May	(GERMAN FORCES IN NORTH AFRICA CAPITULATE)	6 Jun.	(D-DAY LANDINGS IN NORMANDY)
		1 Jul.	Eligibility for German decorations generally extended to Russian volunteers and Eastern workers
24 May	(GERMANS DEFEATED IN THE BATTLE OF THE ATLANTIC)		
30 May	(WARSAW GHETTO DESTROYED)	5 Jul.	*Luftwaffe* Honour Roll Clasp
1 Jun.	Army Paratroop Badge resurrected for paratroopers of the 'Brandenburg' Regiment	8 Jul.	Balloon Observer Badge
		17 Jul.	(RUSSIANS ADVANCE INTO POLAND)
22 Jun.	Numbered Tank Battle Badges	20 Jul.	(FAILED ATTEMPT TO ASSASSINATE HITLER IN EAST PRUSSIA)
	Numbered General Assault Badges		
5 Jul	(BATTLE OF KURSK COMMENCES)		Wound Badge of 20 July 1944
10 Jul.	Front Cross proposed	1 Aug.	(WARSAW UPRISING BEGINS)
22 Jul.	Decoration for Ethnic Germans proposed		Low-grade zinc, or *Kriegsmetall*, now commonly used in its bare slate-grey form in the manufacture of awards
28 Jul.	Clasp for Female *SS* Auxiliaries		
1 Aug.	Germanic Proficiency Rune		
26 Aug.	(LONG GERMAN RETREAT ON THE EASTERN FRONT BEGINS)	12 Aug.	Faithful Service Decoration Cluster for 50 Years in the public sector
			Fire Service Decoration Cluster for 40 Years
8 Sep.	(ITALY CAPITULATES)		Police Long-Service Cluster for 40 Years
20 Sep.	Kuban Shield	20 Aug.	Sniper Badge
13 Oct.	(ITALY DECLARES WAR ON GERMANY)	7 Sep.	1914–18 Honour Cross eligibility extended to *Volksdeutsche* in south-east Europe
2 Dec.	(HITLER ORDERS GERMAN YOUTHS BELOW CONSCRIPTION AGE TO VOLUNTEER FOR FRONT LINE SERVICE)		
		12 Sep.	(US ARMY REACHES GERMAN BORDER BUT STOPS TO REGROUP)
15 Dec.	*SA* Sports Badge for War Wounded		
18 Dec.	Tank Destruction Badge in Gold	25 Sep.	(*VOLKSSTURM* HOME GUARD FORMED)
27 Dec.	Order of the German Eagle regraded	8 Oct.	Prohibition on award of the Iron Cross to persons of Jewish or part-Jewish descent
		10 Oct.	West Wall Medal reissued
			Bar to West Wall Medal

1944

1 Jan.	Sudetenland *Gau* Badge	13 Oct.	Badge for Female Railway Staff
3 Jan.	Blue Division Medal	19 Oct.	Golden Knight's Cross of the War Merit Cross
30 Jan.	Army Honour Roll Clasp	24 Oct.	Metz 1944 Cuff Title
	Guerrilla Warfare Badge	25 Oct.	Selected army unit cuff titles permitted to be conferred upon individual soldiers for bravery or merit
8 Feb.	Dr Fritz Todt Prize		
14 Feb.	*Ostvolk* Decoration in Silver without Swords extended to German personnel		
4 Mar.	(US AIR FORCE BOMBS BERLIN, HERALDING CONTINUAL DAY AND NIGHT BOMBING CAMPAIGN OVER GERMANY)	31 Oct.	Himmler and Goebbels participate in a series of well-publicised and orchestrated award ceremonies, decorating the defenders of Germany
		3 Nov.	*Luftwaffe* Tank Battle Badge
			Luftwaffe Close Combat Clasp
29 Mar.	Prohibition on wearing of Italian decorations by Germans	10 Nov.	Numbered *Luftwaffe* Ground Assault Badges
12 Apr.	*Luftwaffe* Operational Flying Clasp for Air-to-Ground Support Aircraft		Numbered *Luftwaffe* Tank Battle Badges
		15 Nov.	Prohibition on wearing of Finnish, Bulgarian and Romanian decorations by Germans
20 Apr.	Eastern Workers' Proficiency Badge		
29 Apr.	Numbered Pendants for *Luftwaffe* Operational Flying Clasps	18 Nov.	Newly manufactured cuff titles to be shortened to conserve material
		19 Nov.	Naval Combat Clasp
			Naval Dockyard Workers' Badge

165

24 Nov.	U-Boat Combat Clasp in Silver
27 Nov.	*Luftwaffe* Sea Battle Badge
30 Nov.	Frogman Combat Badges
10 Dec.	Warsaw Shield
16 Dec.	(HITLER OPENS OFFENSIVE IN THE ARDENNES)
29 Dec.	Golden Oakleaves, Swords and Diamonds to the Knight's Cross of the Iron Cross

1945

1 Jan.	Front-line decorations now consistently awarded 'on paper' only, in the form of crude typewritten citations, or entries in the paybook, without accompanying medals or badges
2 Jan.	(LAST DITCH GERMAN OFFENSIVE COMMENCES IN HUNGARY)
12 Jan.	Aircraft Destruction Badge Balkan Shield
14 Jan.	(SOVIET FORCES SWEEP THROUGH EAST PRUSSIA)
3 Mar.	(US ARMY CROSSES THE RHINE)
12 Mar.	Kurland Cuff Title
19 Mar.	(HITLER ORDERS 'SCORCHED EARTH' POLICY ACROSS GERMANY)
20 Apr.	(NUREMBERG FALLS TO THE AMERICANS) Hitler's last public appearance, presenting Iron Crosses to Hitler Youths in the Reich Chancellery gardens
22 Apr.	Hitler delegates authority to Army group commanders and equivalents to bestow the Knight's Cross, German Cross and Honour Roll Clasp without reference to the *Wehrmacht* High Command
23 Apr.	(RUSSIANS ENTER BERLIN)
25 Apr.	(US AND RUSSIAN FORCES LINK UP AT TORGAU)
30 Apr.	(HITLER COMMITS SUICIDE)
7 May	(GENERAL JODL SIGNS GERMAN SURRENDER)
22 May	Last official presentation of Nazi awards in the name of *Grossadmiral* Dönitz
23 May	(DÖNITZ GOVERNMENT DISBANDED. THIRD REICH OFFICIALLY ENDS)

Appendix III

How Awards Were Won

The criteria for the bestowal of Nazi medals and decorations could vary quite considerably. While some awards such as the Infantry Assault Badge and the *Ostmedaille* had well-defined qualifying conditions, many others like the Iron Cross and the German Cross did not, and their conferment might depend on a number of variables. The general war conditions at a specific moment in time, the ferocity or ease of a particular campaign and the balancing of the actions of one individual against those of his colleagues were usually taken into account. However, perhaps the most decisive factor of all was the willingness, or otherwise, of both junior and senior officers to submit recommendations for awards on behalf of the men and women under their command. As well as the basic personality clashes which, of course, came into the equation, the standards of higher ranks differed widely. While one officer might happily support a submission for a decoration for one of his soldiers, another could just as easily reject a similar submission made under almost identical circumstances. There is no doubt that many soldiers never received the combat awards to which they were entitled simply because their officers, lacking definitive guidance on the subject, were reluctant to put pen to paper on their behalf. While there was no 'sure way' of winning an award, the following selection of short case studies describes how both higher- and lower-grade decorations were achieved by specific individuals. They give a good general idea of what these decorations represented in practical terms.

HAUPTMANN HANS-JOACHIM MARSEILLE: KNIGHT'S CROSS WITH OAKLEAVES, SWORDS AND DIAMONDS

Hans-Joachim Marseille was born in Berlin on 13 December 1919 and enlisted in the *Luftwaffe* at the age of eighteen. In 1940, flying a Messerschmitt 109, he scored his first aerial victory against a British Spitfire. He was shot down four times during the Battle of Britain, but ended the campaign with the Iron Cross 2nd and 1st Classes and seven enemy aircraft to his credit. In April 1941, Marseille transferred to North Africa and it was in this theatre of operations that he gained rapid recognition and fame. His impressive flying skills took their toll on the opposing fighter pilots, and he downed another seven planes in quick succession. By 22 February

190.   Hauptmann *Hans-Joachim Marseille wearing the Knight's Cross with Oakleaves and Swords conferred upon him by Hitler on 18 June 1942. He never lived to receive his Diamonds.*

191. Oakleaves, Swords and Diamonds to the Knight's Cross, as presented posthumously to Marseille's next-of-kin.

1942 his kill tally had reached fifty, resulting in the award of the Knight's Cross of the Iron Cross. On 3 June 1942, Marseille was able to shoot down six aircraft in eleven minutes, using only ten 20 mm cannon shells and 180 rounds of machine-gun ammunition fired in short bursts. This accuracy of shooting was unheard of and earned him the Oakleaves on 6 June, as well as the nickname 'Star of Africa' and the reputation for being far and away the best aerial gunner in the *Luftwaffe*.

Marseille continued to astound his superiors with his flying abilities, and on 18 June he was awarded the Swords to the Knight's Cross after destroying a total of 101 enemy planes. His greatest achievement came on 1 September when he downed seventeen British aircraft in a few hours during the course of three operational sorties. The following day, he became the fourth recipient of the Oakleaves, Swords and Diamonds. The 22-year-old Marseille was killed on 30 September 1942 when his Messerschmitt developed engine trouble and crashed. He had flown a total of 382 missions and shot down 158 aircraft, and all of his victories were against skilled pilots flying excellent planes, unlike those of some of his comrades who fought on the eastern front. It is noteworthy that Marseille died before he was actually presented with his Diamonds device, which was later displayed for many years in the *Luftwaffe* Museum in Uetersen. It was stolen in 1989 and has never been recovered.

FREGATTENKAPITÄN OTTO KRETSCHMER: KNIGHT'S CROSS WITH OAKLEAVES AND SWORDS

Otto Kretschmer, the highest-scoring ship-killer in the *Kriegsmarine*, was born in Heidau on 1 May 1912 and embarked upon a career in the U-boat arm during the late 1930s. As commanding officer of the U-99, he sank eight British ships totalling 50,000 tons on a single patrol early in 1940, and on 4 August that year he was presented with the Knight's Cross by *Grossadmiral* Raeder at the Lorient naval base in recognition of his submarine having accounted for 117,000 tons of enemy shipping. Exactly three months later, Kretschmer's total reached 200,000 tons, for which he received the Oakleaves from Hitler personally. A further 100,000 tons were added to this tally before the U-99 was sunk in the Atlantic on 17 March 1941 and Kretschmer was taken prisoner. By that time he had become something of a national celebrity and had even had a naval song, the 'Kretschmer March', composed in his honour. On 26 December, over nine months after his capture, Kretschmer was advised rather belatedly by Major Veitch, the commandant of the Bowmanville prisoner-of-war camp in Canada, where he was then incarcerated, that he had been promoted and awarded the Swords to the Knight's Cross with effect from 1 March 1941. Kretschmer returned home in 1947 and later rose to become a *Konteradmiral* in the West German Navy and Chief of Staff to NATO Forces, Baltic Approaches.

MAJOR PETER FRANTZ: KNIGHT'S CROSS WITH OAKLEAVES

Born on 25 July 1917, Peter Frantz served as commanding officer of the 16th Assault Gun Company, 'Grossdeutschland' Regiment. His unit achieved a great defensive victory in the Tula area of Russia on 13 December 1941 when its self-propelled artillery destroyed fifteen enemy tanks and prevented a Soviet breakthrough. On 4 June 1942, Frantz received the Knight's Cross in recognition of the fact that his company had scored over fifty victories against Russian armour. In tank battles east of Borisovka near Kharkov on 14 March 1943, Frantz's men destroyed a further forty-three enemy tanks in the space of a few hours, and for this resounding success he was presented with the Oakleaves by

Hitler at the Reich Chancellery on 14 April that year. While Frantz doubtless exhibited considerable personal bravery, his senior awards were attributable in no small part to the courage, determination, skill and resourcefulness of the many ordinary soldiers and gunners under his command.

SS-*STURMMANN* FRITZ CHRISTEN: KNIGHT'S CROSS OF THE IRON CROSS

Fritz Christen was born in Wredenhagen on 29 June 1921 and served in the anti-tank detachment of the *SS-Totenkopf* Division, receiving the Iron Cross 2nd Class on 20 July 1941. At noon on 24 September 1941, he was manning his 50 mm anti-tank gun during a strong Russian assault on German positions near Lushno and was exposed to heavy artillery and infantry fire. The neighbouring anti-tank guns had been knocked out, and the Soviets had already penetrated *SS* dugouts in the immediate vicinity. In a demonstration of the highest personal initiative, Christen remained alone at his post, the only surviving member of his battery, and coolly destroyed one enemy tank after another until six lay ablaze and the remainder turned back. That night, cut off from the rest of his unit and subjected to a continual hail of mortar and machine-gun fire, he carried new stocks of shells to his gun from the disabled batteries around him. At dawn the following day, ten Russian tanks and supporting infantry attempted to break through once again. Christen proceeded to destroy a further seven enemy armoured vehicles, single-handedly repelling the attack and bringing his personal tally to thirteen tanks within a twenty-four-hour period.

On 27 September the Russians were finally driven out of the Lushno area and his astounded comrades found Christen still crouched behind his anti-tank gun. During the preceding three days, he had killed over 100 enemy soldiers. He was immediately awarded the Iron Cross 1st Class by Theodor Eicke, the *Totenkopf* divisional commander, and on 20 October 1941 he received the Knight's Cross in recognition of his bravery during these engagements. Christen was the first and youngest enlisted man from the ranks of the *Waffen-SS* to win this coveted decoration, which he achieved through sheer personal courage. He was doubtless spurred

192. SS-Sturmmann *Fritz Christen.*

on by the knowledge that, so far as Eicke's men who wore the death's head collar patch were concerned, the Russians took no prisoners.

OBERST ALFRED BORCHERT: GERMAN CROSS IN GOLD

Alfred Borchert was born at Barmstedt on 5 December 1891 and served with the German Army between 1914 and 1918, winning the Iron Cross 1st and 2nd Classes and the Hamburg Hanseatic Cross. In 1920, he embarked upon a civil Police career and after the outbreak of the Second World War saw action with security units in Poland and France, receiving the Bars to the 1914 *EK2* and *EK1* on 25 September 1939 and 23 June 1940 respectively. During the invasion of the Soviet Union Borchert commanded the 3rd Police Rifle Regiment and repeatedly demonstrated outstanding bravery, particularly in the battle around Leningrad. On 21–22

December 1941 the Russians succeeded in opening a gap 400 yards wide through the German positions at Novo Ssusi, south of Tschudowo, and they attempted to expand this local success by bringing forward strong infantry forces and heavy artillery. After gathering all available Army and Police troops, including those from rear areas, Borchert personally led a surprise counter-attack and pushed back the intruding forces, which suffered heavy casualties. The Russians lost over 200 dead in this action, as well as large amounts of weapons, ammunition and other equipment.

Upon closing the Novo Ssusi gap, Borchert then led a five-day advance through hip-deep snow and broke the local enemy supply lines. He had transformed a defensive battle into an offensive one and played a significant part in the failure of the Soviet attempts to break through the encirclement of Leningrad.

On 22 March 1942, Borchert's regiment was relieved by the 58th Infantry Division. However, when the Russians again broke through and penetrated deeply into the German positions three days later, Borchert immediately counter-attacked once more and regained the lost ground. For his continuous military achievements between December 1941 and March 1942, he was decorated with the German Cross in Gold.

VARIOUS SOLDIERS: ROLL OF HONOUR OF THE GERMAN ARMY

The following translation of an Army order of the day illustrates how a small group of soldiers from the Motorcycle Battalion of *SS*-Division 'Reich' came to be recommended for inclusion in the Roll of Honour of the German Army:

Corps Headquarters   10 August 1941
XXXXVI *Panzer* Corps
Order of the Day

After heavy defensive fighting to the north-east of Yelnia, near Smolensk, Förster's section of the 2nd *SS*-Motorcycle Battalion, which had been given the task of protecting the unit's left flank, was discovered. *SS-Unterscharführer* Förster, with his hand on the release cord of his last grenade, had been shot in the head. *Rottenführer* Klaiber, his machine-gun still

at his shoulder with a bullet in the chamber ready to fire, had also been shot through the skull. *Sturmmann* Buschner and *Sturmmann* Schyma lay dead in their trench, with rifles in the shooting position. The dispatch rider, *Sturmmann* Oldeboerhuis, was dead on his knees by his motorcycle. The driver, *Sturmmann* Schwenk, lay dead in his trench. Of the enemy, there were only dead men to be seen who lay in a semicircle around the group's position, a hand grenade's throwing distance away. This is an example of what 'defence' means. We stand in awe and respect before such heroism. I have applied for these names to be published in the Roll of Honour of the German Army.

von Vietinghoff-Scheel, General of *Panzer* Troops.

JÄGER HEINRICH BAUER: *LUFTWAFFE* GROUND ASSAULT BADGE

Early in 1943, 18-year-old Heinrich Bauer was serving as a paratrooper with 1st Battalion, 5th *Fallschirmjäger* Regiment deployed in the vicinity of Bou-Arada, Tunisia. His company was decimated during repeated assaults on Ridge 331, which was in the hands of the British. The scenario was always the same. Organised into groups of a dozen men, the German paratroops would storm the ridge with limited means, usually rifles, sub-machine-guns and hand grenades, only to be forced back by tanks and artillery a few hours later. Of the twelve men who took part in the initial assault, only two survived. Among the dead were the Schneider twins, aged seventeen, one of whom was killed while coming to the assistance of his mortally wounded brother. After several such attacks, all of which proved unsuccessful, the strength of Bauer's company was reduced from 180 to thirty men. It was subsequently removed from the front line to be bolstered by the addition of fresh new recruits from Germany. For his participation in these actions, *Jäger* Bauer received the *Luftwaffe* Ground Assault Badge.

PROF. DR WERNHER FREIHERR VON BRAUN: KNIGHT'S CROSS OF THE WAR MERIT CROSS WITH SWORDS

Wernher von Braun was born at Wirsitz in 1912 and as early as 1930 confided in a friend at Zurich University that his ambition was to put a man on the moon. He graduated in engineering at Berlin in 1932 and later the same year, still aged only 20, became head of the German Army's embryonic rocket research programme. In 1936, Hitler inaugurated a secret weapons facility at Peenemünde on the Baltic, where von Braun and his colleagues began work on missile experimentation. This resulted in a number of new and terrifying vehicles of destruction, most notably the V-1 'flying bombs' and V-2 rockets which showered London in large numbers from 12 June 1944. Von Braun's efforts in pioneering these 'reprisal weapons' were rewarded on 28 October that year when Hitler conferred upon him the Knight's Cross of the War Merit Cross with Swords.

After the war, von Braun was encouraged to emigrate to the United States, whose government turned a conveniently blind eye to the fact that he had been an ardent Nazi who had held the rank of *Sturmbannführer* in the *Allgemeine-SS*. His great technical knowledge was now put to good use in winning the space race for the West, and developing the Saturn V rocket which ultimately landed an American expedition on the surface of the moon. Von Braun's youthful but visionary ambition had at last been realised.

DRK-HILFSSCHWESTER EMILIE HACHENTHAL: WAR MERIT MEDAL

Emilie Hachenthal served as a nurse with the German Red Cross in Mainz between 1941 and 1945. From April 1942 the city, as part of a designated transport attack zone, was subjected to area bombing by the RAF. This caused widespread destruction and heavy civilian casualties, with many cases of horrendous injury and mutilation having to be dealt with by hard-pressed hospital staff operating under desperate conditions. In recognition of her work in this connection, and as an incentive to carry on with it, Emilie Hachenthal was presented with the War Merit Medal by her local *NSDAP Kreisleiter* on 1 September 1943.

SS-ROTTENFÜHRER WILHELM LEHSAU: GOLDEN PARTY BADGE

Born on 10 February 1905 at Osterwieck, Wilhelm Lehsau served his apprenticeship as a dairy farmer and moved to Hilserberg in 1924 to pursue a career in animal husbandry. However, unemployment followed and on 15 March 1926 a disillusioned Lehsau joined the infant Nazi party with *NSDAP* membership number 32084, also enrolling in the *SA* the same day. He eventually secured work in 1929 at a farm in Ranstadt, but on moving to that town found he was the sole Nazi resident. As a result, he suffered regular verbal abuse, physical attacks and general persecution from his fellow workers, the majority of whom were confirmed Socialists and Communists. A less determined individual might have resigned from the *NSDAP*, but the situation he endured served only to strengthen Lehsau's ardent political views and he remained loyal to the Nazi party.

Lehsau quit the north German *SA* in disgust after it revolted against Hitler in 1931, and he was soon welcomed into the more reliable *SS*, with *SS* membership number 19571. At the end of 1933, still aged only twenty-eight, his loyalty to Hitler was recognised when he received the Golden Party Badge as an Old Guard member of the *NSDAP*. On 30 September 1937 Himmler decreed that every *SS* member, regardless of rank, who held the Golden Party Badge would henceforth automatically qualify for the *SS* Death's Head Ring. Consequently, a year later, Lehsau became one of only fifty *SS* enlisted men to receive the coveted *Totenkopfring*, which was usually reserved for long-serving officers.

Lehsau joined the *Waffen-SS* at the outbreak of the Second World War, but he was never promoted to officer rank. He was still a *Rottenführer* when last recorded as serving at the veterinary station of the *SS* Cavalry Brigade at Radom in Poland in May 1941. It is possible that Lehsau perished during the anti-partisan sweeps which were conducted by the *SS* cavalry in support of *Einsatzgruppen* extermination squads operating in western Russia during the autumn of that year. However, he may have survived these actions: his well-worn *SS* ring was found on the banks of the River Isar in Munich in 1995.

REICHSLEITER KARL FIEHLER: BLOOD ORDER

Karl Fiehler was born on 31 August 1895 at Brunswick and served in the German Army during the First World War, being severely wounded. After

193. Reichsleiter *Karl Fiehler wore his Blood Order displayed prominently for this official portrait.*

a minor political career in Munich, he joined the Nazi party with *NSDAP* membership number 37 and marched alongside Hitler as a member of his elite *Stosstrupp* during the Beer Hall *Putsch* of 8–9 November 1923, for which he received a fifteen-month prison sentence. By 1933 Fiehler had become head of the Nazi Office for Municipal Policy and from 20 March that year he was the high-profile *Oberbürgermeister* of Munich, which had been designated 'Capital City of the Nazi Movement'. In 1934, Fiehler received the Blood Order in recognition of his participation in the Munich *Putsch*.

SA-STABSCHEF VIKTOR LUTZE: GERMAN ORDER

Born in Bevergern on 28 December 1890, Viktor Lutze fought in the German Army between 1914 and 1918, losing an eye in action and winning the Iron Cross 1st Class and several other gallantry decorations. In 1922 this petty Post Office official joined the *NSDAP* and rose rapidly through the ranks of the *SA*, becoming an *Obergruppenführer* in 1933. Later that year he was appointed Police President of Hanover. Lutze's lack of personality was surpassed only by his obsequious loyalty to Hitler, and his outright fear of Himmler, and after the murder of Ernst Röhm in the 'Night of the Long Knives' purge of 30 June 1934 he was considered a 'safe' choice for the vacant post of *SA-Stabschef*. Happy to oversee a virtually powerless organisation, Lutze thereafter enjoyed a comfortable and stress-free life on his large estate outside Berlin, complete with horse racing track and swimming pool, which had been confiscated from a wealthy Jewish family.

When war came in 1939, the *SA* regained some of its lost prestige, for it was again very much needed. New *SA-Wehrmannschaften* formations directed pre-military training, strengthened civilian security forces such as the *Stadtwacht* and rehabilitated wounded servicemen, while personnel from the *SA* Guard *Standarte 'Feldherrnhalle'* were incorporated into *Luftwaffe Fallschirmjäger* units and the 271st Infantry Regiment. Lutze visited the front line on several occasions and his presence in areas of danger did much to bolster the morale of combat soldiers, particularly those who were also members of the *SA*. On 2 May 1943, Lutze was killed in a car accident. The following week, he became the third recipient of the German Order, conferred upon him at his state funeral in recognition of his services to the *SA* and the Nazi war effort.

LENI RIEFENSTAHL: OLYMPIC GAMES DECORATION

Leni Riefenstahl was born in 1902 and achieved considerable popular acclaim during the 1920s as home-grown star of the so-called 'mountain movies', German feature films set in the Alps. She successfully underwent the transition from actress to director and was duly commissioned by Hitler to produce a documentary about the 1933 Nuremberg Party Day rally. The film met with the *Führer*'s approval and Riefenstahl subsequently became the semi-official camerawoman of the Third Reich. Her most influential films were *Triumph of the Will*, which portrayed the 1934 *NSDAP* rally, and *Olympia*, covering the 1936 Berlin Olympic Games. Both of these movies won international film awards,

194. SA-Stabschef *Viktor Lutze sporting his Golden Party Badge above the left breast pocket, which was, strictly speaking, contrary to regulations. Also of interest is his unique* SA Honour Dagger, *presented by his staff. Such edged weapons were, in their own right, awards of sorts.*

members specialised in anti-Communist and anti-Semitic philosophy. In 1920 he enrolled in the Nazi party with membership number 18 and immediately won Hitler's attention with the publication of the first of his many books attacking Judaism. In 1922 he took part in the 'Battle of Coburg' and also participated in the Munich Putsch the following year.

Rosenberg was nominated by the *Führer* as editor of the *NSDAP* newspaper, the *Völkischer Beobachter*, which thereafter vigorously denounced Communists, Jews, Freemasons and Christians. He ultimately proposed a new religion which would counter the 'weak doctrine of Christian love' with a strong ideal of racial superiority. In 1930 Rosenberg produced his major work, *The Myth of the Twentieth Century*, a massive tome which concluded that culture would always decay when humanitarian ideals obstructed the right of the dominant race to rule those whom it had subjugated. The latter were degraded in the book to the level of *Untermenschen*, or sub-humans. According to Rosenberg the mixture of blood, and the sinking of the racial standard contingent upon it, was the primary cause of the demise of all cultures. Although over 20 million copies of *The Myth of the Twentieth Century* were eventually sold, few people could be found who actually had the stamina to wade through it from cover to cover. Even Hitler himself had to admit to giving up halfway through the book. Nevertheless, Rosenberg's writings became the cornerstones of *NSDAP* theory and were used to justify the Nazis' racial programmes.

In 1934, Hitler appointed Rosenberg 'head of the entire spiritual and ideological training of the party' and on 7 September 1937 awarded him the National Prize for Art and Science in recognition of his work. On 17 July 1941, Rosenberg was nominated Minister for the Occupied Eastern Territories, and returned to the land of his youth with the idealistic aim of 'uniting the Aryan White Russian people against the Jewish-Slavic Red tide'. However, the real ruler in the east was Himmler, and extermination and subjugation became the orders of the day. Rosenberg was ultimately held accountable for this reign of terror, and was hanged at Nuremberg on 16 October 1946.

despite the fact that their slant was overtly political. For her ground-breaking work in directing *Olympia*, which was a cinematic as well as a propaganda masterpiece, Leni Riefenstahl received the Olympic Games Decoration.

REICHSLEITER ALFRED ROSENBERG: NATIONAL PRIZE FOR ART AND SCIENCE

Born the son of an Estonian shoemaker in 1893, Alfred Rosenberg studied in Russia and received a degree in architecture from the University of Moscow. Having fled to Germany after the Bolshevik Revolution, he settled in Munich and joined the Thule Society, whose intellectual

GENERALLEUTNANT EMILIO ESTEBAN-INFANTES:
ORDER OF THE GERMAN EAGLE

Emilio Esteban-Infantes assumed command of the German Army's 'Blue Division' on 12 December 1942. Under his direction, this Spanish volunteer formation acquitted itself with distinction in a number of heavily fought engagements on the Eastern front, most notably those at Poselok and Krasny Bor. The division suffered 75 per cent casualties in the latter battle, with 3,645 Spaniards killed or wounded. However, the fighting cost the Russians 11,000 men. The survivors of the emaciated Blue Division were finally repatriated to Spain at the end of 1943. Esteban-Infantes' leadership was recognised by the award of the Knight's Cross of the Iron Cross, and as a foreign national he also received the Order of the German Eagle 1st Class.

CHRISTIAN MEYER: FAITHFUL SERVICE DECORATION, SPECIAL GRADE

Christian Meyer left school in 1883 at the age of fourteen and went to work in the Howaldtswerke engineering factory in Stuttgart. Breaking only to serve with the Army reserves during the First World War, he remained with the factory until his retirement. On 15 July, 1938, as a *DAF* member, he became the first recipient of the Special Grade of the Faithful Service Decoration, marking fifty years' employment with the Howaldtswerke.

PROF. DR ERNST HEINKEL: PIONEER OF LABOUR AWARD

Born the son of a plumber in January 1888 at Grunbach, Ernst Heinkel studied mechanical engineering, and after witnessing the burning of a Zeppelin which had been struck by lightning decided that the future of aviation lay with aeroplanes. In the summer of 1911 he built his first aircraft, a fragile machine driven by a 50-horsepower engine, and made ten successful flights in it before crashing. By 1913, Heinkel was designing planes without the typical wires and struts of that era, and he subsequently built a number of seaplanes for the Hansa-Brandenburg company. During the 1920s and 1930s, he established his own factories and became progressively ever more obsessed with speed, constructing record-breaking aircraft, including the

Heinkel 176 which was rocket-driven. His He 178 monoplane of August 1939 was the first aircraft propelled by a turbojet engine, while the Heinkel 111 became the workhorse of the German bomber fleet during the Second World War. The recipient of many decorations for his aviation prowess, Heinkel was presented with the Pioneer of Labour Award by Hitler on 1 May 1942.

While it is interesting to note how certain awards were won, perhaps more fascinating is the fact that a number of prominent individuals who undoubtedly qualified for high decorations never received them. The uniforms of Martin Bormann, Josef Goebbels, Rudolf Hess and Albert Speer, for instance, were conspicuous by their lack of medals and awards.

One of the prime examples was that of Heinrich Himmler, who at the height of his influence was *Reichsführer-SS*, Chief of Police, Minister of the Interior, an *NSDAP Reichsleiter*, a member of the *Reichstag*, Commissioner for the Consolidation of Germanism, Commander-in-Chief of the Home Army, Chief of Military Armaments and commander of army groups on the Rhine and Vistula. In effect, he controlled all military, paramilitary and police forces on the German home front during the Second World War and by the end of 1944 was considered to be Hitler's natural successor. Yet, discounting low-grade long-service and commemorative awards, he received no significant national decorations after the Golden Party Badge and Blood Order which he was given in 1934. The Finnish, Italian and other friendly governments showered Himmler with honours, but he did not receive the War Merit Cross, the German Cross in Silver or any comparable Third Reich decoration, while many of his closest subordinates did.

Perhaps Bormann, Goebbels, Hess, Himmler and Speer shared Hitler's dislike of an ostentatious show of medals and awards. However, it is more probable that they came to be regarded as the 'fountains of honours', that is to say the givers of national awards rather than their recipients. So far as the most senior members of the Nazi political hierarchy were concerned, with the obvious exception of the flamboyant Göring, it seems that death was the prerequisite for bestowal of the highest decorations.

Appendix IV

Where to Obtain Third Reich Decorations

Third Reich medals and decorations have been popular with militaria collectors since 1945. They can be bought from specialist dealers, at auction, or by attending the arms fairs regularly held at weekends throughout the country. Some relevant contact addresses are shown below. However, it must be borne in mind that there are many fake Nazi awards around and caution must always be exercised.

Dealers

A. Beadle
P.O. Box 1658
Dorchester
DT2 9YD
Tel. 01308 897904

Blunderbuss Antiques
29 Thayer Street
London
W1M 5LT
Tel. 020 7486 2444

Chelsea Military Antiques
Unit N13/14, Antiquarius
131–141 King's Road
London
SW3 4PW
Tel. 020 7352 0308

M. Coverdale
Glenwood
210 Darlington Lane
Stockton-on-Tees
TS19 8AD
Tel. 01642 603627

J. Cross
P.O. Box 73
Newmarket
Suffolk
CB8 8RY
Tel. 01638 750132

A. Forman
P.O. Box 163
Braunton
EX33 2YF
Tel. 01271 816177

C. James
Medals & Militaria
Warwick Antiques Centre
22–24 High Street
Warwick
CV34 4AP
Tel. 01926 495704

Just Military
701 Abbeydale Road
Sheffield
S7 2BE
Tel. 0114 255 0536

M. & T. Militaria
The Banks
Bank Lane
Victoria Road
Carlisle
CA1 2UA
Tel. 01228 531988

Military Antiques
11 The Mall Antiques Arcade
359 Upper Street
Islington
London
N1 OPD
Tel. 020 7359 2224

Mons Military Antiques
221 Rainham Road
Rainham
Essex
RM13 7SD
Tel. 01277 810558

The Old Brigade
10a Harborough Road
Kingsthorpe
Northampton
NN2 7AZ
Tel. 01604 719389

Platoon
77-79 Chapel Street
Salford
Manchester
M3 5BZ
Tel. 0161 839 5185

Regimentals
P.O. Box 130
Hitchin
Herts.
SG5 4AP
Tel. 01462 713294

The Treasure Bunker
21 King Street
Glasgow
G1 5QZ
Tel. 0141 552 4651

Ulric of England
P.O. Box 285
Epsom
Surrey
KT17 2YJ
Tel. 020 8393 1434

Auction Houses

Bosleys Military Auctioneers
42 West Street
Marlow
Buckinghamshire
SL7 2NB
Tel. 01628 488188

Kent Sales
The Street
Horton Kirby
Dartford
DA4 9BY
Tel. 01322 864919

Wallis & Wallis
West Street Auction Galleries
Lewes
Sussex
BN7 2NJ
Tel. 01273 480208

Warwick & Warwick
Chalon House
Scar Bank
Millers Road
Warwick
CV34 5DB
Tel. 01926 499031

Arms Fair Organisers

A.J.W. Militaria
P.O. Box HP96
Leeds
L56 3XU
Tel. 0113 275 8060

Antique Militaria Exhibitions
P.O. Box 104
Warwick
CV34 5ZG
Tel. 01926 497340

Arms & Armour UK
58 Harpur Street
Bedford
MK40 2QT
Tel. 01234 344831

H & S Militaria Fairs
P.O. Box 254
Tonbridge
Kent
TN12 7ZQ
Tel. 01892 730233

Appendix V

Price Guide

The market values of Third Reich decorations can vary quite significantly depending upon a number of factors, primarily whether pieces are being bought or sold and whether dealers or auction houses are involved. In general terms dealers seek to make at least 30 per cent profit on any transaction, while auctioneers charge customers a range of commissions to allow for their percentage and overheads. Items can normally be obtained more cheaply at auction, but two determined bidders may easily raise the final hammer price to one which is well above the lot's catalogue estimate. Condition, quality and the presence or otherwise of an accompanying citation or presentation case also have dramatic effects on desirability and cost. Consequently, as in every field of collecting, there can be no such thing as a 'set value' for any given Nazi medal or award.

This section is intended to provide a general guide to the average prices which collectors might expect to pay if purchasing original pieces in good condition from reputable dealers, based on the market at the time of publication. Scarce and highly sought-after Third Reich decorations have consistently risen in value over the decades, a typical example being the Knight's Cross of the Iron Cross which has shown the following price increases:

1970 – £50
1980 – £600
1990 – £1900
2000 – £3500

However, more common medals and badges like the *Ostmedaille* and the Wound Badge in Black have had far more moderate rises. In short, the normal rules of 'supply and demand' hold good.

For ease of reference, decorations are grouped and listed in the same order as they appear in the main text. Where awards were subdivided into a range of different grades, only a representative selection of the most readily available of these have been priced for comparison purposes. Unique and exceptionally rare pieces very seldom come onto the open market and, when they do, change hands for astronomical sums, beyond the reach of most collectors. Interest in the cost of such items is therefore purely academic, and they are shown in the table as having 'speculative' value. Pre-1933 decorations, foreign medals and projected awards are not included.

SENIOR MILITARY AWARDS	£
Knight's Cross of the Iron Cross with Oakleaves and Swords and above	Speculative
Knight's Cross of the Iron Cross with Oakleaves	6,000
Knight's Cross of the Iron Cross	3,500
Iron Cross 1st Class	80
Iron Cross 2nd Class	30
1939 Bar to 1914 Iron Cross 1st Class	120
1939 Bar to 1914 Iron Cross 2nd Class	80
Army Honour Roll Clasp	900
Navy Honour Roll Clasp	1,200
Luftwaffe Honour Roll Clasp	1,000
German Cross in Gold	950
German Cross in Gold: active-service version in cloth	200
German Cross in Silver	1,300

MILITARY MERITORIOUS SERVICE DECORATIONS	£
Golden Knight's Cross of the War Merit Cross	Speculative
Knight's Cross of the War Merit Cross with Swords	2,000
Knight's Cross of the War Merit Cross without Swords	2,300
War Merit Cross 1st Class with Swords	60
War Merit Cross 1st Class without Swords	70
War Merit Cross 2nd Class with Swords	20
War Merit Cross 2nd Class without Swords	25
War Merit Medal	15
Spanish Cross in Gold with Swords and Diamonds	Speculative
Spanish Cross in Gold with Swords	600
Spanish Cross in Silver with Swords	450
Spanish Cross in Silver without Swords	550
Spanish Cross in Bronze with Swords	350
Spanish Cross in Bronze without Swords	400
Spanish Cross for Next-of-Kin	1,000
Wehrmacht 40-Year Long-Service Award	200
Wehrmacht 25-Year Long-Service Award	90
Wehrmacht 18-Year Long-Service Award	60
Wehrmacht 12-Year Long-Service Award	40
Wehrmacht 4-Year Long-Service Award	20
Wehrmacht Marksmanship Lanyards (various grades)	50–200
SS 25-Year Long Service Decoration	Speculative
SS 12-Year Long Service Decoration	1,200
SS 8-Year Long Service Decoration	200
SS 4-Year Long Service Decoration	190
Cross of Honour 1914–18 for Combatants	10
Cross of Honour 1914–18 for Non-Combatants	15
Cross of Honour 1914–18 for Next-of-Kin	20
Anschluss Medal	25
Sudetenland Medal	20
Prague Castle Bar	40
Memel Medal	90
West Wall Medal	15
Ostvolk Decoration 1st Class in Gold	70
Ostvolk Decoration 1st Class in Silver	60
Ostvolk Decoration 2nd Class in Gold	50
Ostvolk Decoration 2nd Class in Silver	40
Ostvolk Decoration 2nd Class in Bronze	30

CAMPAIGN HONOURS AND WOUND BADGES	£
Narvik Shield in Gold	140
Narvik Shield in Silver	130
Cholm Shield	450
Krim Shield	80
Demjansk Shield	150
Kuban Shield	120
Lappland Shield	Speculative
Kreta Cuff Title	180
Afrika Cuff Title	160
Kurland Cuff Title	500
Eastern Front Medal	20
Blue Division Medal	60
Spanish Wound Badge in Gold	200
Spanish Wound Badge in Silver	140
Spanish Wound Badge in Black	90
1939 Wound Badge in Gold	50
1939 Wound Badge in Silver	30
1939 Wound Badge in Black	10
Wound Badge of 20 July 1944	Speculative

WAR BADGES	£
Condor Legion Tank Badge	1,500
Army Paratroop Badge	450
Infantry Assault Badge in Silver	50
Infantry Assault Badge in Bronze	60
Numbered Tank Battle Badges (various grades)	400–1,500
Tank Battle Badge in Silver	65
Tank Battle Badge in Bronze	80
Numbered General Assault Badges (various grades)	350–1,500
General Assault Badge	50
Army Anti-Aircraft Badge	200
Tank Destruction Badge in Gold	300
Tank Destruction Badge in Silver	180
Front-Line Driver Badge in Gold	40
Front-Line Driver Badge in Silver	30
Front-Line Driver Badge in Bronze	20
Close Combat Clasp in Gold	400
Close Combat Clasp in Silver	180
Close Combat Clasp in Bronze	130
Guerrilla Warfare Badge in Gold	800
Guerrilla Warfare Badge in Silver	500
Guerrilla Warfare Badge in Bronze	450
Balloon Observer Badge	Speculative
Sniper Badge	Speculative
Naval war badges with diamonds	Speculative
U-Boat War Badge	90
Destroyer War Badge	80
Minesweeper War Badge	60
Blockade-Breaker Badge	160
Auxiliary Cruiser War Badge	180
High Seas Fleet War Badge	150
E-Boat War Badge 1st Pattern	350
E-Boat War Badge 2nd Pattern	180
Coastal Artillery War Badge	70
U-Boat Combat Clasp in Silver	500
U-Boat Combat Clasp in Bronze	350
Aircrew Badge	Speculative
Pilot Badge	250

Observer Badge	270
Combined Pilot/Observer Badge with Diamonds	Speculative
Combined Pilot/Observer Badge	450
Glider Pilot Badge	350
Radio Operator Badge	260
Air Gunner Badge	280
Retired Aircrew Badge	350
Luftwaffe Paratroop Badge	180
Flak Battle Badge	150
Ground Assault Badge	120
Operational Flying Clasps with Diamonds	Speculative
Operational Flying Clasps with Numbered Pendants	400–1,500
Operational Flying Clasps with Star Pendants	300–900
Operational Flying Clasps in Gold	200–800
Operational Flying Clasps in Silver	180–700
Operational Flying Clasps in Bronze	130–500

NON-PORTABLE MILITARY AWARDS	£
Luftwaffe Honour Goblet	2,000
Luftwaffe Salver of Honour	Speculative
Army High Command Commendation Certificate	800
Führer Commendation Certificate	2,000
Reichsmarschall Commendation Certificate	Speculative
Reichsführer-SS Commendation Certificate	Speculative
Gauleiter Commendation Certificate	300
Flak Auxiliary Commendation Certificate	200
Luftwaffe wall plaques	150–500
Army and *Luftwaffe* unit medallions	30–250
Unit cap badges	25–200

Political Awards	£
German Order (various grades)	Speculative
Blood Order 1st Pattern	2,500
Blood Order 2nd Pattern	2,000
Golden Party Badge for Outstanding Service	1,200
Golden Party Badge for Veteran Membership	350
Coburg Badge	Speculative
1929 Nuremberg Party Day Badge	120
Brunswick Rally Badge	100
Frontbann Badge	Speculative
Schlageter Memorial Badge	130
1923/25 *Gau* badges	750
Thuringia *Gau* Badge	1,500
Baden *Gau* Badge	1,000
Munich *Gau* Badge	130
Osthannover *Gau* Badge	500
Essen *Gau* Badge	1,200

Berlin *Gau* Badge	1,800
East Prussia *Gau* Badge	1,600
Danzig-West Prussia *Gau* Badge	1,600
Wartheland *Gau* Badge	Speculative
Sudetenland *Gau* Badge	2,000
Golden Hitler Youth Badge with Oakleaves	1,800
Golden Hitler Youth Badge	120
Nazi Party 25-Year Long-Service Decoration	800
Nazi Party 15-Year Long-Service Decoration	180
Nazi Party 10-Year Long-Service Decoration	60
Danzig Cross 1st Class	1,200
Danzig Cross 2nd Class	400

CIVIL AWARDS	£
National Prize for Art and Science	Speculative
Dr Fritz Todt Prize Badge (various grades)	300–900
Pioneer of Labour Award	Speculative
Order of the German Eagle 1st Class and above	Speculative
Order of the German Eagle 2nd Class	2,500
Order of the German Eagle 3rd Class	1,100
Order of the German Eagle 4th Class	750
Order of the German Eagle 5th Class	450
Medal of the Order of the German Eagle	170
Eagle Shield of Germany	Speculative
Goethe Medal for Art and Science	2,500
German Academy for Aeronautical Research Decoration (various grades)	Speculative
Defence Economy Leader's Decoration	750
Life-Saving Medal	350
DLRG Water Life-Saving Badge	90
Mine Rescue Decoration	120
Länder Fire Service awards (various)	60–150
Fire Brigade Decoration 1st Class, 1st Pattern	1,800
Fire Brigade Decoration 1st Class, 2nd Pattern	500
Fire Brigade Decoration 2nd Class	90
Danzig Fire Brigade Decorations	Speculative
Air-Raid Defence Decoration 1st Class	450
Air-Raid Defence Decoration 2nd Class	35
Customs Service Decoration	150
Faithful Service Decoration for 50 Years	180
Faithful Service Decoration for 40 Years	40
Faithful Service Decoration for 25 Years	20
Danzig Faithful Service Decorations	Speculative
Police 25-Year Long-Service Award	180
Police 18-Year Long-Service Award	120

Police 8-Year Long-Service Award	60
Danzig Police Long-Service Awards	Speculative
RAD 25-Year Long Service Awards (male/female)	600/900
RAD 18-Year Long Service Awards (male/female)	300/450
RAD 12-Year Long Service Awards (male/female)	100/150
RAD 4-Year Long Service Awards (male/female)	50/75
Badge for Female Railway Staff	300
Naval Dockyard Workers' Badge	250
Social Welfare Decoration 1st Class	950
Social Welfare Decoration 2nd Class	450
Social Welfare Decoration 3rd Class	200
Social Welfare Medal	40
Olympic Games Decoration 1st Class	1,500
Olympic Games Decoration 2nd Class	550
Olympic Games Medal	70
Mother's Cross in Gold	40
Mother's Cross in Silver	35
Mother's Cross in Bronze	30
National Trade Competition *Reichssieger* Decoration	500
National Trade Competition *Gausieger* Decoration	250
National Trade Competition *Kreissieger* Decoration	180
Police Expert Skier Badge	Speculative
Police Expert Mountaineer Badges	Speculative
NSFK Balloon Pilot's Badge	850
NSFK Powered Aircraft Pilot's Badge	1,000
NSFK Large Glider Pilot's Badge	1,200
DRL Sports Championship badges	70
German National Sports Badge in Gold	70
German National Sports Badge in Silver	40
German National Sports Badge in Bronze	30
German National Sports Badge for War Wounded	140
SA Sports Badge in Gold	150
SA Sports Badge in Silver	60
SA Sports Badge in Bronze	30
SA Sports Badge for War Wounded	180
Germanic Proficiency Rune in Silver	1,800
Germanic Proficiency Rune in Bronze	1,500
Motor Sports Badge	1,200
Heavy Athletics Badge	450

German Expert Horseman's Badge	1,000
German Horseman's Badge in Gold	130
German Horseman's Badge in Silver	100
German Horseman's Badge in Bronze	70
German Horse Driver's Badge	130
German Young Horseman's Badge	120
Badge for the Care of Horses	200
National Youth Sports Badge	30
Teno Decoration	250
Anhalt Badge	200
Steel Helmet Veterans' Decoration with date '1918'	1,500
Steel Helmet Veterans' Decoration with dates '1919'–'1932'	40
HJ Decoration for Distinguished Foreigners	400
HJ Leader's Sports Badge	300
HJ Expert Skier Badge	Speculative
HJ Marksmanship Badges	40
DJ Marksmanship Badges	50
HJ Proficiency Badge in Silver	40
HJ Proficiency Badge in Bronze	50
HJ Proficiency Badge in Black	60
DJ Proficiency Badge	70
BDM Proficiency Clasp	130
JM Proficiency Clasp	80
Red Cross Decorations (various grades)	30–450
Danzig Red Cross Decorations	Speculative
National Food Estate Awards	20–80
Rifle Association Awards	20–80

It may be noted that some very rarely awarded items such as the Dr Fritz Todt Prize Badge, the *HJ* Decoration for Distinguished Foreigners and the Badge for Female Railway Staff have been priced relatively low. This is because many more of these pieces were produced than were actually bestowed. Considerable quantities have survived, and they have never been the most popular items with collectors.

Appendix VI

Post-1945 Reproductions

Having discussed where to buy Third Reich decorations and what to pay for them, some consideration needs to be given to the thorny issue of faking, for almost every Nazi award has been copied in recent years to satisfy the growing and ever more lucrative collector's market.

At the end of the Second World War, the Nazi party and its affiliated organisations were immediately declared illegal and the swastika was outlawed. Moreover, on 21 September 1949 the Allied High Commission in Germany prohibited the further wearing of all *Wehrmacht* as well as *NSDAP* uniforms, badges and decorations. The manufacture of such items was duly made punishable by five years' imprisonment and a fine of 25,000 Deutschmarks, penalties which still hold good to this day. As a result, reproducing Third Reich militaria in Germany became, and remains, a potentially dangerous and costly trade.

The new governments in West and East Germany soon inaugurated their own independent ranges of medals to fill the considerable gap left by the abolition of Nazi decorations. In 1951 the Order of Merit of the German Federal Republic was created, and the German Democratic Republic (*DDR*) followed suit in 1953 with its Order of Karl Marx. West Germany subsequently approved many new awards for bestowal by its provincial authorities, which were often based both in appearance and qualifying criteria on their Third Reich equivalents. Federal Fire Service crosses, for example, generally featured flames in their designs and were clearly modelled on the Nazi Fire Brigade Decoration. The *DDR*, on the other hand, looked to Russia for inspiration when creating its own pseudo-Soviet series of 176 national awards.

While East Germany always aligned itself closely with the Communist regimes of the Warsaw Pact and so could never recognise the validity of honours conferred upon its citizens during the Third Reich, the newly raised West German armed forces of the 1950s included in their ranks many former *Wehrmacht* officers who made a strong case for the renewed recognition of their wartime actions, particularly those which had been performed on the Russian front. The Cold War environment made such claims generally acceptable, and on 26 July 1957 a decree was issued by the federal government allowing 'de-Nazified' replacement versions of selected Third Reich decorations to be manufactured and worn on *Bundeswehr* and civil uniforms. These new strikings followed the original designs as closely as possible, but the swastika, and in some cases the eagle, were omitted. War badges, campaign shields and other combat awards were also permitted to be sported in miniature form on blue-grey ribbon bars for the first time. While these were officially sanctioned 'reproductions', they were generally poor in quality when compared with even their latest Nazi counterparts and were viewed as having a token value only.

Third Reich decorations which had been overtly political in character, such as the *NSDAP* and *SS* long-service awards, were not reauthorised in 1957. However, less obviously 'Nazi' pieces like the Spanish Cross, the Mother's Cross, the Social Welfare Decoration and sports badges also remained prohibited. The table below lists all the medals and awards which are known to have been reproduced in de-Nazified form by virtue of the 1957 edict:

Military Decorations
Iron Cross
German Cross
Honour Roll clasps
War Merit Cross

Combat clasps
War badges
Wound badges
Campaign shields
Cuff titles
Ostvolk Decoration
Eastern Front Medal
Cross of Honour, 1914–18
Wehrmacht qualification badges
Wehrmacht Long-Service Award

Civil Awards
Life-Saving Medal
Mine Rescue Decoration
Fire Brigade Decoration
Air-Raid Defence Decoration
Customs Service Decoration
Police Long-Service Award
RAD Long-Service Award
Faithful Service Decoration
Olympic Games Decoration
Red Cross Decoration

Following the reunification of Germany in 1990, manufacture of the de-Nazified awards ceased and a wholly new series of national decorations began to be created to replace those of the Federal and Democratic Republics. The range was built up over a period of years with some items, especially Fire Service awards, again being based on Third Reich designs.

Official post-1945 German decorations such as those described have never been popular with collectors, who still prefer to seek eagerly for ever-scarcer original Third Reich medals and awards. This demand has spawned a thriving business in the manufacture and distribution of fake Nazi decorations, with copies of varying quality now emanating from the United States, Europe and the Far East.

The majority of the earliest fakes dating from the 1950s and 1960s tended to be crudely cast in soft lead-based compounds or cheap glittery alloys, using plaster moulds, and fooled no one. Others, restruck with original dies by Souval of Vienna, a firm authorised to manufacture decorations under the Third Reich and not subject to the West German prohibitions stemming from the Allied High Commission decree of 1949, were of much better quality. However, even these could still be readily

identified by their modern pin assemblies, particularly the distinctive Souval retaining clip comprising a circular piece of sheet metal with a central strip cut out and bent over to hold the pin in place.

As the years went by, collectors became accustomed to the usual reproductions and this resulted in the emergence of the 'super fake'. The days are now long gone when the best way to detect a spurious piece was by its shoddy appearance. Copies of badges like the U-Boat Combat Clasp and the *SA* Sports Badge for War Wounded, which were not instituted until after the 1942 watershed and so were always made in zinc, now circulate in nickel silver, bronze and other substantial metals. In these cases, the material quality of the fakes is actually better than that of the originals. For instance, there are at least eleven fake variations of the Guerrilla Warfare Badge currently in circulation. Original examples of this award were in hollow-backed zinc with narrow pins, and were unmarked. The fakes can be hollow or solid, in brass, tombak or aluminium. Some have broad flat pins, others needle pins, and they can feature a range of makers' marks, including 'C.E. Juncker, Berlin', '2' and 'L56'. The reason why so many good reproductions of the Guerrilla Warfare Badge and similar awards are about is simply the rarity of the genuine articles and the consequent high prices they command. It is worthy of note that copies of some war and qualification badges like the Army Paratroop Badge and the *Luftwaffe* Glider Pilot Badge have been manufactured in '800' silver, a material never used in the construction of such awards during the Third Reich. This grade of silver is actually a very low one, which would not qualify for hallmarking in Great Britain, and so these particular fakes are not expensive to produce.

The current height of super faking has been achieved by the reproduction of diamond-studded Nazi awards. Diamond- (or at least glass/cubic zircona-) encrusted fakes include those of: the Oakleaves, Swords and Diamonds to the Knight's Cross; the Spanish Cross in Gold with Diamonds; the German Cross in Gold with Diamonds; the U-Boat War Badge with Diamonds; and the Combined Pilot-Observer Badge in Gold with Diamonds. If the authenticity of these reproductions is questioned, they are invariably explained away by the story that they are wartime 'jeweller copies', made as replacements in case the original presentation pieces were lost or damaged on the battlefield. This is pure rubbish. Jewellers simply did not sit in their corner shops across Hitler's Germany churning out diamond-studded awards. Such a practice would have been illegal and carried extremely stiff penalties. These decorations were the highest honours which the very uniform-orientated Third Reich could bestow and every example was made under the most strictly controlled conditions by firms contracted to the Government. An officer could not just walk into his nearest jeweller's and place an order for a 'spare' Spanish Cross in Gold with Diamonds. During the 1980s, the Austrian jeweller Klein made very good reproductions of the Oakleaves, Swords and Diamonds to the Knight's Cross, bearing his distinctive marks of a K in a circle and three chevrons, and sold them legitimately on the collector's market

as copies priced at around £500 each. These fakes are now being passed on as originals and regularly change hands for the 'bargain price' of £5,000 or more. One badly damaged set was recently offered for sale at an exorbitant price, purporting to having been recovered from the body of Hans-Joachim Marseille after his fatal air crash in 1942, an assertion nullified by the fact that Marseille was killed before the Diamonds he had won could be presented to him by Hitler.

In a similar vein, much 'mumbo jumbo' has been written regarding varieties of the Knight's Cross, with odd markings and flawed frame beading patterns being attributed to a range of different makers. Again, the term 'jeweller copy' is often used to justify a fake *Ritterkreuz*. It is worth keeping in mind that while massive quantities of duplicate lower-grade Iron Crosses were readily available for private purchase throughout the war, the sale of replacements for lost or damaged Knight's Crosses

195. *A good-quality fake of the* Luftwaffe *Tank Battle Badge for 100 actions, manufactured during the early 1960s by the Viennese firm of Rudolf Souval.*

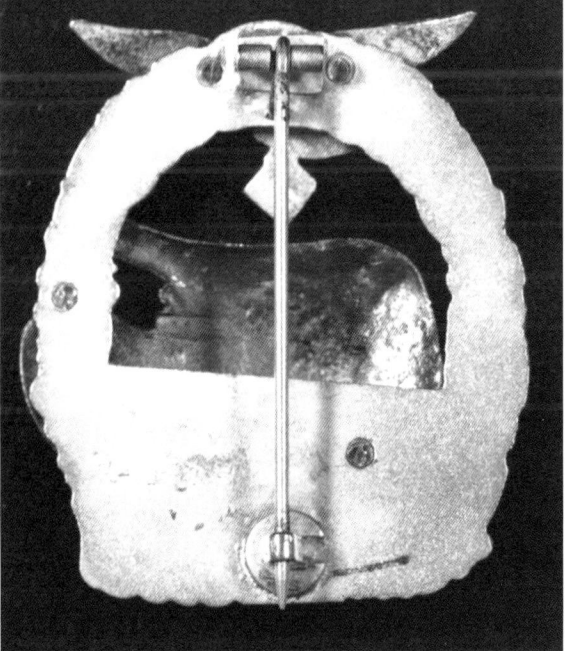

196. *Many postwar copies can be distinguished instantly by their characteristic pin-retaining clips of the type illustrated at the bottom of this badge. It comprises a circular piece of metal with a strip cut out and bent over to secure the pin in place. No such clips were used during the Third Reich period.*

was expressly forbidden as early as 22 October 1941, when only 800 or so out of a total of over 7,000 had been bestowed. After that date, duplicates produced by the sole government-contracted maker, Steinhauer & Lück of Lüdenscheid, were available only upon application through official channels. In short, there never was a great variety of authentic Knight's Crosses.

One mark which frequently appears on good-quality copies is 'L/12', originally used on its 'private sale' pieces by the C.E. Juncker firm of Berlin. When this company ceased trading in the late 1950s, its dies and stamps were purchased by a noted German medal researcher and author who subsequently used them to reproduce Grand Crosses and Knight's Crosses of the Iron Cross, all marked 'L/12'. In 1969, the twenty-fifth anniversary of the bomb plot against Hitler, fakes of the Wound Badge of 20 July 1944 were added to the 'L/12' range, whereas originals of this rare decoration had borne Juncker's official registration number '2'.

All types of makers' marks have been copied and used on reproduction pieces. It is impossible to be in any way definitive in this area, but the following list shows those marks most commonly encountered on recent fakes.

- Oakleaves & Swords to the Knight's Cross: '900 21'
- Knight's Cross of the Iron Cross: 'L/12'; '925'
- Iron Cross 1st Class: 'L/15'; 'L/21'; 'L/58'
- Iron Cross 2nd Class: '16'; '100'; '113'; '333' (the latter mark never existed during the Third Reich)

- 1939 Bar to the 1914 Iron Cross 1st Class: 'L/21'
- 1939 Bar to the 1914 Iron Cross 2nd Class: 'L/16'
- War Badges: '1'; 'L/10'; 'L/23'; 'Frank & Reif, Stuttgart' (sometimes rendered erroneously as 'Fank & Reif, Stuttgart'); 'C.E. Juncker, Berlin' (sometimes rendered erroneously as 'C.E. Junker, Berlin'); 'G.B.'; 'Imme'; 'Klaas'; 'O.M.'; 'G.H. Osang, Dresden'; 'W.H.'
- Frogman Clasps: 'L/12'
- Wound Badges: 'L/40' (this mark never existed during the Third Reich)

As well as stamps, spurious engraving is sometimes employed, even on original decorations, so as to make pieces more attractive to would-be buyers. One example which immediately springs to mind concerns a German Cross in Gold supposedly presented on 12 December 1941 as the first such award bestowed, and engraved accordingly. In fact, the first German Crosses were awarded in October 1941. Such engraving can triple the value (or at least the asking price – an entirely different thing) of an item.

Another ploy sometimes used by the less honest dealers is to place fake medals and badges in original cases which, due to their obvious age, help to convince the collector that the awards inside are genuine. Moreover, the fact that the fake decorations are protected in this way gives the seller the ideal excuse for their mint (i.e. new) condition. In a similar vein, original citations are often married up with reproduction medals, while

197.   A woven reproduction of the 'Metz 1944' Cuff Title.

genuine *Wehrpasses* have spurious entries added to them relating to the presentation of senior awards. Other items to be wary of are fake or altered award documents of varying qualities, some of which do not even coincide with the dates of introduction of the decorations concerned. One such doctored citation recently offered for sale bore the date 'September 1942', but related to the Close Combat Clasp which was not created until two months later. In cases such as these, the benefits of thorough research and comprehensive knowledge of the subject become all too apparent.

The lowest of the low so far as purists are concerned are the 'fantasy' pieces, the results of over-active post-1945 imaginations, which cannot be classed even as reproductions since they have no original counterparts. Crude in design, construction and quality, it is inconceivable that anything remotely like them would have seen the light of day in Hitler's Germany. Examples include a piece comprising the wreath from a fake *Luftwaffe* Air Gunner Badge surmounted by a reproduction of the British 17th/21st Lancers skull and crossbones insignia, and another featuring a copy War Merit Cross 1st Class glued to a large six-pointed star. One notable early 'fantasy' was the 'RSA Sports Badge', produced

in very small quantities as a prop for the 1942 British feature film *Silver Fleet*, which circulated after the war and appeared in various publications as an 'original but unidentified' Nazi award!

Contrary to popular belief, not all antique dealers are experts in their field. It is true to say that they, like collectors, do get caught out by fakes from time to time. However, most dealers are honest, and when asked if a piece is authentic or not they are obliged to make their position clear. There is a world of difference between a dealer who deliberately defrauds the public and one who merely errs in judgement concerning authenticity. Even if he is genuinely uncertain, the dealer can express an opinion. At this point, of course, the ultimate onus of satisfaction returns to the buyer, and even among the experts there will invariably be areas of disagreement or contention. In short, money-back guarantees mean little in these circumstances and '*Caveat emptor*' still holds good. If the would-be buyer has any 'gut feeling' reservations about the originality of a piece offered for sale he should leave it alone, for an honest collector will readily admit that the vast majority of his 'maybes' turned out to be fakes.

198. *A Klein fake of the Diamonds to the Knight's Cross (obverse), with its distinctive short swords and so-called 'hedgehog-back' shape.*

199. *A Klein fake of the Diamonds to the Knight's Cross (reverse). It bears the silver hallmark '925', never used on Nazi awards.*

Bibliography

The following books are recommended further reading on the subject of Nazi awards.

Angolia, J.R., *For Führer & Fatherland, Vols. 1 & 2.* (Bender, USA, 1976-8)

Bowen, V., *The Prussian and German Iron Cross* (Published privately, 1986)

Doehle, Dr H., *Die Auszeichnungen des Grossdeutschen Reichs* (Berlin, 1943)

Dombrowski, H., *Orden, Ehrenzeichen und Titel des Nationalsozialistischen Deutschlands* (Berlin, 1940)

Kahl, R., *Insignia, Decorations & Badges of the Third Reich and Occupied Countries* (Published privately, undated)

Klietmann, Dr K.G., *Deutsche Auszeichnungen* (Berlin, 1957)

Littlejohn, D. and Dodkins, C.M., *Orders, Decorations, Medals & Badges of the Third Reich, Vols. 1 & 2.* (Bender, USA, 1968-73)

Lumsden, R., *A Collector's Guide to Third Reich Militaria* (Ian Allan, Shepperton, 1987)

Lumsden, R., *Detecting the Fakes* (Ian Allan, Shepperton, 1989)

Niemann, D., *Orden und Ehrenzeichen Deutschland, 1871-1945* (Hamburg, 1999)

Nimmergut, J., *Das Eiserne Kreuz, 1813-1939* (Munich, 1990)

Index